Magnificent Prayer

Other Books by Nick Harrison

Promises to Keep:
    Daily Devotions for Men Seeking Integrity

365 WWJD:
    Daily Answers to "What Would Jesus Do?"

His Victorious Indwelling:
    Daily Devotions for a Deeper Christian Life

Magnificent Prayer

366 DEVOTIONS
to deepen your
PRAYER EXPERIENCE

NICK HARRISON

ZONDERVAN®

ZONDERVAN.com/
AUTHORTRACKER
follow your favorite authors

ZONDERVAN

Magnificent Prayer
Copyright © 2001 by Nick Harrison

Requests for information should be addressed to:
Zondervan, Grand Rapids, Michigan 49530

Library of Congress Cataloging-in-Publication Data

Magnificent prayer: 366 devotions to deepen your prayer experience/
    Nick Harrison.
       p. cm.
     ISBN 978-0-310-23844-7
     1. Devotional calendars.   2. Prayer—Christianity.
I. Harrison, Nick.
BV4810 .M35 2001
242'.2—dc21   2001026581

Interior design by Beth Shagene

Printed in the United States of America

Dedication

A few years ago a friend told me he was going to build what he called a "prayer cabin" in the woods behind his house. It seemed like an interesting idea, but I wondered if he would really follow through. Nobody else I know has ever gone to such lengths to establish a place to pray.

But sure enough, Paul Harris and his wife, Cynthia, built their prayer cabin. When it was finished they invited believers from the community to a small dedication ceremony. Paul announced that the cabin would be named "Listening" and that it would be open to anyone who wanted to pray, at any time.

A simple wooden cross was fashioned to hang on the door when "Listening" was in use. If the cross wasn't there, the cabin was free. Paul furnished the cabin simply — no comfortable lounge chairs or any other creature comforts. And no heat. When you come to "Listening," you come to pray.

For their commitment to prayer and because in so many ways they're a wonderful example to Christians everywhere, I'd like to dedicate *Magnificent Prayer* to Paul and Cynthia Harris.

A Note

In preparing *Magnificent Prayer* I researched many fine books by some truly excellent authors. But as I considered the importance of this book, I became determined to include only the very best words I could find on the subject of prayer. It should come as no surprise then that some writers' names will occur more frequently than others on the following pages. Certain men and women in the course of church history have given themselves to prayer in a way that few others have. E. M. Bounds, Andrew Murray, Charles Haddon Spurgeon, Oswald Chambers, Robert Murray McCheyne, Madame Guyon, and Amy Carmichael are just a few of the deep Christian pray-ers whose words I found to count a bit heavier as they wrote about prayer. Each of these men and women bore the unmistakable imprint of someone who knew firsthand what prayer really is. Their words ring true.

During the next twelve months, some readers may wish to supplement this devotional by reading additional books on prayer by these mighty warriors of the faith. For that reason, I've included a suggested list of the best books I've found on prayer. That list is located at the back of the book.

Some themes on prayer will be visited more than once during the next year's reading. Different authors offered diverse but nonetheless equally true perspectives on these themes.

Finally, because some of the best authors wrote in past centuries, I've taken the liberty, where appropriate, of updating the original language to make it more compatible to the contemporary ear.

Acknowledgments

Few books are a result of one person's effort. That's certainly true of *Magnificent Prayer*.

First, I must acknowledge the men and women whose words make up such a large portion of this devotional. They have carved a prayer path that, if we will follow, will result in a renewal of our lives, our families, our churches, our communities, and our nation.

Second, the support of a loving family is a tremendous asset for an author. So thank you to my wife, Beverly, my grown children, Rachel, Mike and Rebecca, and Bethany; and to my wonderful parents.

Finally, a big thank you is offered to the professionals at Zondervan who are the behind-the-scenes workers of wonders. Thanks to all but especially to Cindy Hays, Robert Hudson, and John Topliff. You were great.

Introduction

When, as a young man, I became a Christian, my mother gave me a plaque with the famous words of Alfred, Lord Tennyson inscribed in needlepoint:

> *More things are wrought by prayer*
> *Than this world dreams of,*
> *Wherefore, let thy voice*
> *Rise like a fountain for me day and night.*

That's a wonderful sentiment. And like most Christians, I've considered prayer an important part of my spiritual life. Through the years God has answered many of my requests in unexpected and wonderful ways. But a large number of my petitions to God have seemingly gone unanswered — so far. God, I've discovered, isn't on the same timetable I am. And so I wait.

While waiting, I've been thinking about why God sometimes delays His answers. I also wonder why occasionally the answer is a firm "No!" All my requests seem perfectly reasonable to me. Mostly, though, I think about the whole concept of prayer.

Let's see if I've got it right: There's this omnipotent, omnipresent God who created me, redeemed me, provides daily for my needs, and loves me infinitely more than any human possibly could. This God is so vitally interested in me personally that He knew me and chose me to belong to Him before time began. He's numbered the very hairs on my head, fashioned my body and personality, and has given me His own Spirit to live inside me. He has arranged it so that I will never die but will spend eternity with Him and His people in a home He's especially prepared for me. Further, He continually invites me to bask in His love and to come boldly to Him for all my needs, promising to answer my requests.

Amazing, isn't it? When I think about prayer in this way, something begins to happen. For one thing, I seem to pray less and less, "Oh, Lord, keep that light green until I get through the intersection." Instead, I begin to see prayer as something far greater, more powerful, more magnificent than I had previously thought. I get a glimpse of what God is really offering us in the practice of prayer: fellowship with Him. And as for those "unanswered prayers," I somehow feel more confident about trusting God's timetable rather than my own.

Prayer is truly, wonderfully, amazingly *magnificent*. Prayer is an invitation to us from God Himself, asking us to please communicate with Him. Through prayer we speak to Almighty God and Almighty God speaks to us. Through prayer we ask for and receive good things from our heavenly Father. Through prayer we are invited to ask of Him of whom an angel told Mary, "Nothing is impossible with God" (Luke 1:37). Miracles, yes — but certainly prayer itself is the greatest miracle. Think of it—personal access to the most powerful and most loving Being in the universe, the great Creator.

We, in our humanity, too often lose the sense of just how marvelous, how tremendous, how magnificent prayer really can be. Rather than a burdensome and often passive Christian *duty*, prayer should be an active Christian *pleasure* for every believer.

During the next year we'll rediscover the true greatness of prayer through the words of godly men and women of years past. They learned how to appreciate the magnificence of prayer, and so should we. Some of their names may be familiar, some may not. But these godly Christians—E. M. Bounds, Rees Howells, Madame Guyon, Andrew Murray, Oswald Chambers, Charles Haddon Spurgeon, and many others—gave themselves to prayer and to recording their observations in print so that Christians in succeeding generations might follow their example. From their writings I've harvested some of their richest words about prayer.

Through their experiences we'll discover the hindrances some of them faced and how they overcame obstacles to prayer. But not only will we read and think about prayer, we'll also *pray*. Far too many books on prayer offer great advice, but unless you put your knees to the floor and actually *pray*, all the advice in the world about prayer won't do a bit of good.

As we learn and put into practice the kind of prayer that God hears—magnificent prayer—I believe we'll see answers to our prayers as daily we turn our hearts boldly toward the God who is eager to hear from us—and anxious to answer. As Billy Graham has noted, heaven is full of answers to prayers that nobody has bothered to pray.

Church: let's bother to pray. It's time to return to persistent, prevailing, powerful praying.

January 1

Behold, I make all things new.

REVELATION 21:5 KJV

If your faith in Christ doesn't lead you to pray, then have nothing to do with it: get rid of it, and God help you to begin again.

CHARLES HADDON SPURGEON

Pray About It: The past year is over, the new year begins. As we think about the twelve months ahead, let's invite God to oversee *all* that crosses our path. Let's give Him charge over every aspect of our lives, including our prayer life.

Today, as we pray—perhaps feebly, perhaps with doubts and worries—let's begin again. If yesterday's faith didn't lead us to be effective pray-ers, let's be done with it, as Charles Haddon Spurgeon recommends. God is the God of today, not yesterday; God of the living, not the dead. His manna is always fresh and ready for the taking. His answers to our prayers are always right, always on His perfect timetable, and *always* for our good.

Lord Jesus, at the start of this new year, we ask for a fresh beginning. Wipe our sins away with Your precious blood. Cleanse our hearts of bitterness toward others. Help us to live each day in close communication with You, our true and faithful guide.

CORRIE TEN BOOM

January 2

In the morning, O Lord, you hear my voice;
   in the morning I lay my requests before you.

PSALM 5:3

Prayer prevails. It brings power. It brings life. It brings God. Let us dare to be definite with God; let us dare to lay hold of the promises and to wait in faith until the answer comes.

MRS. CHARLES E. COWMAN

Pray About It: Not many Christians know the story of Charles and Lettie Cowman. This godly man and woman were both pray-ers and missionaries. But like many Christians, the most lasting work to come from their lives was to be after much suffering.

Mrs. Cowman, like so many others, found the secret to a successful life of service: a life of prevailing prayer. Each morning at 5:30, Mrs. Cowman woke up to have her time with God.

When Charles took sick, Mrs. Cowman prayed and nursed him. But during that time of suffering and praying and considering God's will, she pieced together a book of her favorite sayings and quotations. With the book she hoped to gain some small funds to help support the missionary work. Although Charles died, leaving Lettie a widow at age fifty-four, this woman of God would live another thirty years and fulfill the worldwide ministry God had prepared for her. It was to be the book that Lettie compiled during Charles's sickness that would be the unlikely answer to the couple's prayers. That book, still in print and a best-seller after seventy-five years, is possibly the best-loved devotional book of all time: *Streams in the Desert.*

Dare to lay hold of the promises of God, as Mrs. Cowman did. She could never have guessed how God would do it—she only knew that He would.

Wait in faith until the answer comes.

> The voice of agonizing prayer breaks the stillness of the morning. I have but little fear of the noise of praying Christians. The prayers of some of these precious people are heaven-moving, heaven-opening. What wonderful and striking types of men [and women]. What glorious Christians.
>
> CHARLES E. COWMAN

January 3

Call a sacred assembly. Summon the elders and all who live in the land to the house of the LORD your God, and cry out to the LORD.

JOEL 1:14

[The following words are from George Mueller's journal entry for January 3, 1842.]

This evening we had a precious prayer meeting. When the usual time for closing the meeting came, some of us wanted to continue to wait upon the Lord. I suggested that those who had bodily strength, time, and a desire to wait longer upon the Lord, do so. At least thirty remained, and we continued in prayer until after ten. I never knew deeper prayer in the Spirit. I experienced an unusual nearness to the Lord and was able to pray in faith, without doubting.

GEORGE MUELLER

Pray About It: George Mueller was one of the most successful pray-ers in Christian history. Through faith in God alone, expressed through prayer, Mueller fed and clothed thousands of orphans in the five homes he opened in obedience to God.

It's no wonder that this man of God was partial to prayer meetings — he came to Christ in 1825 at such a meeting in a private home. Such prayer meetings among Christians were common then. Even up until recent years, many churches had weekly times set aside to gather for corporate prayer. Often this was Wednesday night. Though some churches still offer this midweek service, far too many have abandoned the practice or allowed it to turn into simply another powerless church gathering. But as Mueller noted, and as many others have found, God will show up for prayer meetings, if only the people will.

Does your church have the kind of prayer meeting where the people are reluctant to leave? Is it possible that you could host a prayer meeting in your home? It's not necessary for there to be many in number. God will meet with just a handful.

Today, pray for the spirit of prayer to return to the church of Christ. Pray for believers to be drawn back to prayer. Pray for ministers to catch a vision for their churches to be, above all else, *praying* churches.

Prayer meetings are dead affairs when they are merely asking sessions. There is adventure, hope, and life when they are *believing* sessions, and the faith is corporately, practically, and deliberately affirmed.

NORMAN GRUBB

January 4

Thou shalt love the LORD thy God with all thine heart.

DEUTERONOMY 6:5 KJV

We should make a private chapel of our heart where we can retire from time to time to commune with Him, peacefully, humbly, lovingly.

BROTHER LAWRENCE

Pray About It: It would greatly surprise Brother Lawrence to find that nearly five centuries after his death, his teachings on prayer are considered classic.

And what is this classic teaching?

Brother Lawrence worked for thirty years in the kitchen of the monastery to which he belonged. As he washed dishes and went about his other routine chores, he prayed.

Brother Lawrence believed that God wasn't too busy to hear us, even when we're busy with our necessary work. His short book, *The Practice of the Presence of God*, is still in print and widely read by Christians around the world.

Put Brother Lawrence's teaching to the test today. Set aside a place in your heart and retire there often throughout the day where you can practice God's presence, no matter your activity.

> Build yourself a cell in your heart and retire there to pray.
>
> CATHERINE OF SIENA

January 5

I will instruct you and teach you in the way you should go; I will guide you with My eye.

PSALM 32:8 NKJV

All practical power over sin . . . depends on maintaining closet communion. Those who abide in the secret place with God show themselves mighty to conquer evil, and strong to work and to war for God.

They are seers who read His secrets; they know His will; they are the meek whom He guides in judgment and teaches His way. They are His prophets who speak for Him to others, and even forecast things to come. They watch the signs of the times and discern His tokens and read His signals.

A. T. PIERSON

Pray About It: This definition of a pray-er finds many of us falling short. We possess little power because we pray so little. The power we possess as Christians will be in proportion to our communion with God. Weak Christians are often weak because they don't spend time with the source of strength.

Today, cast all your weakness on Him. Claim His strength as your own. He who lives in you can face anything on today's agenda. Watch, and He will guide you with His eye.

No Christ, no prayer. Little Christ, little prayer. Much Christ, much prayer.

RUTH PAXSON

January 6

We must help the weak, remembering the words the Lord Jesus himself said: "It is more blessed to give than to receive."

ACTS 20:35

What ministries are in our hands for working miracles in the wonderful realm of prayer! We can take sunshine into cold and sullen places. We can light the lamp of hope in the prison-house of despondency. We can loose the chains from the prisoner's limbs. We can take gleams and thoughts of home into the far country. We can carry heavenly cordials to the spiritually faint, even though they are laboring beyond the seas. Miracles in response to prayer!

JOHN HENRY JOWETT

Pray About It: The result of all serious prayer before God is that we sense God's heart toward others. He daily sends those who need a miracle across our path, but unless we've been with God, we don't recognize His divine appointments. Today pray that God will direct someone across your path, someone to whom you can minister in a practical way.

From your place of prayer, export sunshine to the cold and sullen places. Light the lamp of hope. Loose chains.

Prayers for people are far more important than prayers for things because people more deeply concern God's will and the work of Jesus Christ than things.

E. M. BOUNDS

January 7

"For my thoughts are not your thoughts, neither are your ways my ways," declares the LORD. "As the heavens are higher than the earth, so are my ways higher than your ways and my thoughts than your thoughts."

ISAIAH 55:8-9

Sometimes people speak of God having answered their prayer, but what they mean is that He has answered it according to their desire and done something about which they are glad. If He does something different they say sadly, "He has not answered." All this is a mistake.

Prayer is always heard if the one who prays comes to the Father in the Name of our Lord Jesus.

I know that sometimes we can't see how the thing granted is at all what we desire. And yet it is (I write for His lovers only). For, after all, what the deepest in us wanted was not our own will, but the will of our Father. So what is given is our heart's desire; He has not withheld our request. But God always answers us in the deeps, never in the shallows of our soul: in hours of confusion, it can help to remember this.

AMY CARMICHAEL

Pray About It: We must never dictate to God how He must answer our prayer. In fact, God delights in surprising us with unusual grantings of our requests in keeping with His will.

The best attitude is to pray and rest. Today, tell God your needs — leave it at that. God will answer, but it will be *His* answer, not necessarily yours.

Never make the blunder of trying to forecast the way God is going to answer your prayer.

OSWALD CHAMBERS

January 8

What wilt thou that I should do unto thee?

MARK 10:51 KJV

Do not pray without any desire in your heart. All prayers should be governed by heart desire. Look how our Lord pays attention to this. Bartimaeus, a blind beggar, cried out to the Lord: "Jesus, thou son of David, have mercy on me." The Lord Jesus answered him: "What wilt thou that I should do unto thee?"

Now the Lord will ask you precisely the same question: "What wilt thou that I should do unto thee?" Can you answer that question? Some brothers and sisters, after they have prayed for ten or twenty minutes, may not be able to tell you what they have asked God. Though many words are spoken in their prayer, nevertheless what is asked is even unknown to themselves. Such utterance is heartless and aimless and cannot be considered as prayer.

WATCHMAN NEE

Pray About It: Prayer begins with a desire in our heart. From there it works itself into our consciousness and we speak it in prayer to God. Such prayers are easily answerable because their genesis was in God Himself when He implanted the desire in our heart.

We can't pray lifeless prayers and expect the God who offers abundant life to grant our requests. We must know what we want. Open your heart as you pray. Hear Jesus ask, "What wilt thou that I should do unto thee?"

Tell Him what you want.

If you have no definite purpose in prayer, you can expect no definite results from it. Be sure you know what you want before you pray and that God knows what you want when you are through.

NORMAN B. HARRISON

January 9

I sought the LORD and He heard me.

PSALM 34:4 NKJV

The power of prayer rests in our faith that God hears us. It is this faith that gives a Christian courage to pray and to have power to prevail with God.

The moment I'm assured that God hears me, I feel drawn to pray and to persevere in prayer. I feel strong to claim and to take in faith the answer God gives.

One great reason for prayerlessness is the lack of the living, joyous assurance that God will hear us. But if God's servants get a vision of the living God waiting to grant their request, and to bestow all the heavenly gifts of the Spirit they are in need of, for themselves or those they are serving, how everything would be set aside to make time and room for this wonderful power that ensures heavenly blessing—the power of faith!

ANDREW MURRAY

Pray About It: Are you confident that God will hear you as you pray today? Or do you see Him as a passive but perhaps sympathetic bystander to your quiet times? If so, then you must change your theology today. Faith is active and powerful. Faith accesses all God's provision for our every need. Without faith, prayer is a colossal waste of time.

Get hold of faith in God, and prayer will get a greater hold on you.

When a Christian can, and does say, in living faith, "My God will hear me!" surely nothing can keep him from prayer.

ANDREW MURRAY

January 10

Lord, teach us to pray, as John also taught his disciples.

LUKE 11:1 KJV

Without doubt these disciples were praying men. Jesus had already talked to them a great deal about prayer. But as they noticed how large a place prayer had in His life, and what some of the marvelous results were, the fact came home to them with great force that there must be some fascination, some power, some secret in prayer, of which they were ignorant. This Man was a master in the fine art of prayer. They really did not know how to pray, they thought.

How their request must have delighted Him! At last they were being aroused concerning the great secret of power. May it be that this simple recital of His habit of prayer may move everyone of us to get alone with Him and make the same earnest request. For the first step in learning to pray is to pray, "Lord, teach me to pray." And who can teach like Him?

Prayer brings power. Prayer is power. The time of prayer is the time of power. The place of prayer is the place of power. Prayer is tightening the connections with the divine dynamo so that the power may flow freely without loss or interruption.

S. D. GORDON

Pray About It: God is still the great prayer teacher. Just as Jesus was delighted to instruct His disciples in prayer, so too God is eager to have men and women who are united in prayer with His will. A book on prayer is good, so are sermons, but both fall short of on-the-job training with God as your supervisor.

Today, ask God to be your personal prayer trainer in the weeks ahead. Ask Him to show you how to pray, where to pray, for what to pray, and for how long to pray. As the weeks pass, all of these questions will be settled. By God's grace, you *will* learn how to pray.

Teach me to pray. Pray thou thyself in me.

FRANÇOIS FÉNELON

January 11

In this manner, therefore, pray: Our Father in heaven, hallowed be Your name.

MATTHEW 6:9 NKJV

[Regarding prayers, when I hear] "Dear Lord," and "Blessed Lord," and "Sweet Lord," used over and over again as vain repetitions, [I cringe].

I must confess I would feel no revulsion to the words, "Dear Jesus," if they came from the lips of a true man or woman of God, but when I hear these expressions hackneyed by persons not at all remarkable for their spirituality, I'm inclined to wish that they could come to a better understanding of the true relations existing between man and God.

The word "dear" has come from daily use to be so common, and so small, and in some cases so silly and pretentious, that punctuating one's prayers with it isn't edifying.

My strongest objection exists to the constant repetition of the word, "Lord," which occurs in the early prayers of young converts . . . the words, "O Lord! O Lord!" grieve us when we hear them so perpetually repeated.

"Thou shalt not take the name of the LORD thy God in vain," is a great commandment, and although this law may be broken in all innocence, its breach is still a sin and a very solemn one.

God's name is not to be a stop-gap to make up for our want of words. Take care to use most reverently the name of the infinite Jehovah. The

Jews in their sacred writings either leave a space for the word "Jehovah," or else write the word, "Adonai," because they conceive that holy name to be too sacred for common use. We need not to be so superstitious, but it behooves us to be more reverent in our choice of words.

CHARLES HADDON SPURGEON

Pray About It: Is Spurgeon being too harsh? I don't think so. God's name was, is now, and always will be *holy*. And yet how often we invoke His name carelessly. When Jesus taught His disciples to pray, His prayer opened with a "hallowing" of God's name. And yet today the wonderful name of the Lord Jesus Christ has turned into a bumper-sticker slogan—and by those who love Him. This ought not to be.

In our prayers to our heavenly Father, let's be careful of His name. Treat Him with respect and awe. And *never* let a reference to God become an interjection in casual conversation.

As you pray today, spend time hallowing God's name.

We are directed to make the name of God our chief end. Let all our petitions center in this and be regulated by it.

MATTHEW HENRY

January 12

Jesus said, "Let the little children come to me, and do not hinder them, for the kingdom of heaven belongs to such as these."

MATTHEW 19:14

You say you do not know how to pray? . . . Follow the leading of simplicity in prayer, there can never be excess of it, for God loves to see us like little children in His presence.

JEAN-PIERRE DE CAUSSADE

Pray About It: God designed prayer to be simple, not hard. The kingdom of God is, in fact, for those who would become like little children before their Father.

Today, your prayers should be simple and direct, not lavish and vague.

In this respect, less is more. Better a few words from an overflowing heart than a verbal dictionary emanating from a cold, religious heart.

Live as a child of God, then you will be able to pray as a child, and as a child you will most assuredly be heard.

ANDREW MURRAY

January 13

My grace is sufficient for you, for My strength is made perfect in weakness.

2 CORINTHIANS 12:9 NKJV

Oh, do not pray for easy lives! Pray to be stronger men and women! Do not pray for tasks equal to your powers; pray for powers equal to your tasks! Then the doing of your work shall be no miracle. But you shall be a miracle. Every day you shall wonder at yourself, at the richness of life which has come in you by the grace of God.

PHILLIPS BROOKS

Pray About It: How often we pray for God to remove our problems when God has designed these problems to be vehicles for His strength.

Whereas in the past we've prayed for days equal to our strength, today we must pray for power equal to our days. Remember today His strength will be made perfect in your weakness.

Prayer imparts the power to walk and not faint.

OSWALD CHAMBERS

January 14

Nothing is impossible with God.

LUKE 1:37

Whatever God can do, faith can do; and whatever faith can do, prayer can do when it is offered in faith.

An invitation to prayer is, therefore, an invitation to omnipotence, for prayer engages the Omnipotent God and brings Him into our human affairs. Nothing is impossible to the Christian who prays in faith, just as nothing is impossible with God. This generation has yet to prove all that prayer can do for believing men and women.

A. W. TOZER

Pray About It: Is there a better reason for prayer than that it "engages the Omnipotent God and brings Him into our human affairs"?

When we pray, God is truly on our side. May ours be the generation that proves what prayer can do.

Today, boldly invite God into your affairs. And He will come boldly.

Prayer is releasing the energies of God. For prayer is asking God to do what we cannot do.

CHARLES TRUMBULL

January 15

But the days will come, when the bridegroom shall be taken away from them, and then shall they fast in those days.

LUKE 5:35 KJV

Give yourselves to fasting and prayer.

1 CORINTHIANS 7:5 KJV

When we fast, let our fasting be done unto the Lord, with our eye singly fixed on Him. Let our intention be this and this alone: to glorify our Father in heaven; to express our sorrow and shame for our many transgressions of His holy law; to wait for an increase of purifying grace, drawing our affections to things above; to add seriousness and earnestness to our prayers; to avert the wrath of God; and to obtain all the great and precious promises which He hath made to us in Jesus Christ. . . .

Let us beware of fancying we *merit* anything of God by our fasting. We cannot be too often warned of this; inasmuch as a desire to establish our own righteousness is so deeply rooted in all our hearts.

Fasting is only a way which God has ordained, wherein we wait for His undeserved mercy; and wherein, without any merit of ours, He has promised freely to give us His blessing.

JOHN WESLEY

Pray About It: Fasting is a legitimate part of the Christian's prayer life. After checking with your doctor, you can begin to fast as God leads. Many believers adhere to the fast as practiced among the Jews of Jesus' day; that is, they fast from evening to evening rather than from morning to morning.

Never fast to prove yourself to God or to gain His favor. All our righteousness is in Christ, not our works. God cannot love you more through your fasting than He does now. Still, we should fast as God directs because Christ admonished us to. During times of great trial or in making a hard decision, fasting can be of great value.

Although many fine books have been written on the subject of fasting, I've found *God's Chosen Fast* by Arthur Wallis to be among the best

If fasting is new to you, perhaps today you could fast for one meal. Instead of eating, get away by yourself and spend the time with God. Open with praise, read Psalm 119 in its entirety, and then spend a few silent moments before Him. And by the way, don't announce your plans to others. This is between you and God alone.

> Prayer is reaching out after the unseen. Fasting is letting go of all that is seen and temporal. Fasting helps express, deepen, confirm the resolution that we are ready to sacrifice anything, even ourselves to attain what we seek for the kingdom of God.
>
> ANDREW MURRAY

> When you fast, do not look somber as the hypocrites do, for they disfigure their faces to show men they are fasting. I tell you the truth, they have received their reward in full. But when you fast, put oil on your head and wash your face, so that it will not be obvious to men that you are fasting, but only to your Father, who is unseen; and your Father, who sees what is done in secret, will reward you.
>
> MATTHEW 6:16–18

January 16

Yet not my will, but yours be done.

Spread out your petition before God, and then say, "not my will but yours be done." The sweetest lesson I have learned in God's school is to let the Lord choose for me.

Pray About It: In the early stages of our Christian life, our prayers are often remarkably similar to a child's Christmas list for Santa Claus. We want this; we think we need that. But then as we grow in Christ and we see God answer prayers *His* way, our prayers change. Like Dwight L. Moody, we have learned to let God make our choices for us.

Today, let your will be set aside. Remove yourself from making the choice. The results will indeed be sweet when you allow the Lord to choose for you.

Being of one mind and spirit with Him in His giving up everything to God's will, living like Him in obedience and surrender to the Father; this is abiding in Him; this is the secret of power in prayer.

January 17

Let us therefore come boldly to the throne of grace, that we may obtain mercy and find grace to help in time of need.

HEBREWS 4:16 NKJV

How shall we deal with this matter of concentration in prayer? In the past, has your mind in any way become passive, and under the hold of the enemy? So much has been generally accepted as "natural" that could be traced back to some supernatural experience which has since been forgotten, but which left its mark on the mind.

Everything that comes from the Spirit of God *invigorates* every part of the being, and does not injure nor dull it; yet there are supernatural experiences which leave those who pass through them with no concentration of mind.

The reason is that there has been a complete "letting go" of the mind, instead of recognizing that God quickens and energizes it. If you see that this has happened, you can deal with it this moment, without going into the past, if you say, "If I ever in any way gave ground to evil spirits by passivity of mind, I now take back that ground, and claim the liberation of my mental faculties because of the victory of Christ at Calvary." But if you insist upon accepting that lack of concentration as purely "natural," you will not get deliverance from it.

JESSIE PENN-LEWIS

Pray About It: Many Christians mistakenly think that prayer is entirely passive. Their thinking is akin to that of New Age devotees who numbly sit cross-legged, their minds open to any spiritual influence that calls itself God.

But our God does not wish us to be passive in prayer. Silent sometimes — yes. Waiting sometimes — yes. Listening sometimes — yes. But even such quiet activities are in essence spiritually active, rather than passive.

We are instructed to come boldly to our loving Father, as a child who presents his earnest need to an attentive father.

As you pray today, be active — not passive.

> Prayer is made vigorous by asking, urgent by supplication, and pleasing and acceptable by thanksgiving.
>
> MARTIN LUTHER

January 18

You may ask me for anything in my name, and I will do it.

JOHN 14:14

To pray in Christ's name is not to use His name as a good luck charm or talisman, as though the repetition of it were all that's required to open the treasures of infinite grace. Let us not degrade this dearest promise of our Lord into such a superstition as that.

The Jewish cabalists believed that the pronunciation of certain magical words engraved on the seal of Solomon would perform miracles. That was incantation. And we in like manner make Christian incantation of this blessed privilege of the Gospel if we put such an interpretation as this upon Christ's words.

The name of Christ stands for Christ Himself. And to pray in the name of Christ is to pray in Christ, in the mind and spirit and will of Christ.

A. J. Gordon

Pray About It: Most of us have been guilty of simply tacking "in Jesus' name" at the end of our prayers, hoping that by so doing it gave our requests that extra bounce into heaven. But praying in Christ's name is more about the living Christ Himself than uttering syllables. We can pray in Christ's name without words. And we can pray the words "in Christ's name" and still be far from Him.

Today, truly pray in Christ's name by doing so in the mind, will, and spirit of our Lord.

To ask in His name means to be taken by the hand and led to prayer by Him. It means His kneeling by our side and His desires flowing through our heart.

Samuel Ridout

January 19

And when you pray, do not be like the hypocrites, for they love to pray standing in the synagogues and on the street corners to be seen by men. I tell you the truth, they have received their reward in full. But when you pray, go into your room, close the door and pray to your Father, who is unseen. Then your Father, who sees what is done in secret, will reward you.

MATTHEW 6:5–6

The prayer life is a lonely life. The hypocrite requires an audience when he prays. He wants to be heard when he prays. He must impress.

True prayer requires sincerity. True prayer requires purity. In heaven there will be no praying. All the faith we exercise must be exercised here. All the praying must be done here, for heaven will not be a place to make up a pitiable backlog of unfinished praying.

LEONARD RAVENHILL

Pray About It: Maybe part of our reluctance to head for our prayer closets is because it shuts us out from all our earthly social relations. And of course, from God's viewpoint, that's the distinct advantage to solitary prayer.

Today, as you get alone to pray, remember that you're never really alone when you're with God. You are, in fact, never less alone than when sitting at His feet.

Relish your time in His presence. It's the best time you'll ever have on this earth.

True prayer is a lonely business.

SAMUEL CHADWICK

January 20

Love the LORD, all his saints! The LORD preserves the faithful, but the proud he pays back in full. Be strong and take heart, all you who hope in the LORD.

PSALM 31:23–24

We must bear in mind that mere resolutions to take more time for prayer and to conquer reluctance to pray will not prove lastingly effective unless there is a wholehearted and absolute surrender to the Lord Jesus Christ.

A. E. RICHARDSON

Pray About It: Many times we begin the new year with resolutions to be more faithful in prayer. By January 20, we'll have a good idea if the resolution will be kept. If the promise was made as a legalistic gesture, it will ultimately fail. But if it was a result of "wholehearted and absolute surrender to the Lord Jesus Christ," it will succeed.

If your decision was the former, it can still be turned into the latter. Be honest with God. Ask Him to renew your passion for prayer. It will begin with a renewed passion for Him.

The place you give Jesus Christ in your life determines the place you give prayer.

RUTH PAXSON

January 21

Now to Him who is able to do exceedingly abundantly above all that we ask or think, according to the power that works in us.

EPHESIANS 3:20 NKJV

Beware in your prayer, above everything, of limiting God, not only by unbelief, but by trying to figure out what He will do.

Expect unexpected things, above all that we ask or think. Each time you intercede, be quiet first and worship God in His glory. Think of what He can do, of how He delights to hear the Christian pray, of your place in Christ; and expect great things.

ANDREW MURRAY

Pray About It: A test of true relinquishment in prayer is to so abandon our own plans that when God answers, it *exceeds* our expectations. Expect Him to do above all that you can ask or think. Give God room to create a miracle.

> Thou art coming to a King,
> Large petitions with thee bring
> For His grace and power are such
> None can ever ask too much.

JOHN NEWTON

January 22

Devote yourselves to prayer, being watchful and thankful. And pray for us, too, that God may open a door for our message, so that we may proclaim the mystery of Christ, for which I am in chains. Pray that I may proclaim it clearly, as I should.

COLOSSIANS 4:2–4

The more praying there is in the world the better the world will be, the mightier the forces against evil everywhere.

Prayer, in one phase of its operation, is a disinfectant and a preventive. It purifies the air; it destroys the contagion of evil. Prayer is no fitful, short-lived thing. It is no voice crying unheard and unheeded in the silence. It is a voice that goes into God's ear, and it lives as long as God's ear is open to holy pleas, as long as God's heart is alive to holy things.

God shapes the world by prayer. Prayers are deathless. The lips that uttered them may be closed in death, the heart that felt them may have ceased to beat, but the prayers live before God, and God's heart is set on them and prayers outlive the lives of those who uttered them; outlive a generation, outlive an age, outlive a world.

E. M. BOUNDS

Pray About It: Heaven has many surprises in store for us. One of the best will be to see all that our prayers accomplished in the advancement of God's kingdom. We can fashion future history through prayer. Revivals such as the Great Awakening and the Welsh Revival early in the last century began, as do all revivals, through prayer. Wars have been won through prayer, freedom has been secured through prayer, and peace has been maintained through prayer.

By praying for our leaders, world events, our brothers and sisters in Christ around the world, we help determine their destiny—and ours. We may not live to see all the answers to our prayers, but one day in heaven we'll see. There are many who prayed years ago for us and our generation. They are now in heaven and they know what their prayers wrought. Now it's our turn to pray for the generations to follow. In our prayers, we propel the church forward.

You must go forward on your knees.

J. HUDSON TAYLOR

January 23

He who dwells in the shelter of the Most High will rest in the shadow of the Almighty. I will say of the LORD, "He is my refuge and my fortress, my God, in whom I trust."

PSALM 91:1–2

Every pray-er should have a place, be it only a chair or a corner, where he or she is accustomed to meeting the Lord. . . . It is in such a spot the soul can best gird itself for prayer with the sense of truly succeeding.

Out from such a closet, from its habitual meeting in private, personal interview with the Father, one can go to face a world of sin, of difficulty and discouragement, undaunted and undismayed.

NORMAN B. HARRISON

Pray About It: Where do you pray? We can, of course, pray anywhere. We can pray as we drive, as we shower, as we do the dishes, or engage in a hobby. But each of us needs a special place, a private place, where we hold court with God. If you haven't already done so, search out such a place. Make sure it has no distractions and is entirely private. And then consider that God will be there waiting for you at the appointed time. Be sure you show up too.

O, let the place of secret prayer become to me the most beloved spot on earth.

ANDREW MURRAY

January 24

Then I heard a loud voice in heaven say: "Now have come the salvation and the power and the kingdom of our God, and the authority of his Christ. For the accuser of our brothers, who accuses them before our God day and night, has been hurled down. They overcame him by the blood of the Lamb and by the word of their testimony; they did not love their lives so much as to shrink from death."

REVELATION 12:10–11

[Samuel Brengle was one of the early leaders of the Salvation Army. In the following account of his morning prayers, he discloses an experience known by many pray-ers—the attempts of the enemy to accuse them of all sorts of evil. In so doing he aims to undermine our power in prayer.]

Once when I knelt for morning prayers I felt a sort of deadness in my soul, and just then the "accuser of the brethren" became busy reminding me of things that had long since been under the Blood.

I cried to God for help, and the blessed Comforter reminded me that my Great High Priest was pleading my case; that I must come boldly to the throne of grace. I did, and the enemy was routed!

What a blessed time of communion I had with my Lord! Had I given in to the enemy's accusations instead of *fighting* I could never have received what God had for me because had I not labored fervently in prayer; I could not have *reaped* because I had not *sown*.

SAMUEL LOGAN BRENGLE

Pray About It: Satan hates to see us pray. He has many tactics that he will use mercilessly to thwart our time with God. The most despicable are his constant accusations against us. He may suggest to our minds, "How can you expect God to hear your prayers—after all that you've done!" Or he might whisper, "You don't really believe that *all* your sins are forgiven, do you?"

Satan stands night and day accusing us of many things. But Jesus Christ is our advocate with the Father. By Him we stand. All is under the blood. Refuse to allow Satan's accusations to undermine your prayer power.

Do as Brengle did—rout the enemy!

Remember that Satanic accusation may cripple the most spiritual and useful person and reduce him to naught. A weakened conscience weakens the entire person.

WATCHMAN NEE

January 25

This is the one I esteem: he who is humble and contrite in spirit, and trembles at my word.

ISAIAH 66:2

God isn't looking for brilliant men and women, nor is He depending upon eloquent men and women, nor is He determined to use only talented Christians in sending His Gospel out into the world.

God is looking for broken people, for those who have judged themselves in the light of the cross of Christ. When He wants anything done, He takes up men and women who have come to an end of *themselves,* and whose trust and confidence is not in themselves but in *God.*

H. A. IRONSIDE

Pray About It: The beginning of answered prayer is at the end of man's natural abilities. God's strength is for the weak, for God is attracted to weakness like a divine magnet. As you pray today, put no trust in yourself. Let yourself be broken. Place all your confidence in Him. Trust. Abide. Rest.

Prayer doesn't consist of gifted speech and elegant phrases, but of brokenness of heart.

JOHN MASON

January 26

Elijah was a man just like us. He prayed earnestly that it would not rain, and it did not rain on the land for three and a half years. Again he prayed, and the heavens gave rain, and the earth produced its crops.

JAMES 5:17

When we read that Elijah was a man subject to the same passions as ourselves, we're apt to suppose that those passions were the driving force of his life. But Scripture shows that the results of his wonderful career were achieved, not by his passion, but by his prayer!

Elijah, though capable of the same vehement earnestness with which we're all endowed, refused to accomplish his life-work by using human passion, but instead determined to obtain the results he desired through prayer. He was a man of like passions with ourselves, but he prayed earnestly. He turned his passion into prayer.

F. B. MEYER

Pray About It: When we read the stories in the Bible, we seem amazed at the wonderful men and women God used. But then when we read that they were just like we are, we're even more amazed. Can it be true that Elijah was like us? If so, then God's message is that the wonders that Elijah and others like him in the Bible accomplished can also be accomplished by us—but only in prayer, not in the sweat of our natural energy or passion.

Never underestimate your prayers before God. Why? Because the secret isn't in the vessel praying, nor in his or her passion, but in the God to whom we pray. We don't need extraordinary faith. Ordinary faith in an extraordinary God will move mountains.

> How can the church pray small prayers when she comes before the God of such abundance? She cannot make little requests before such a great God. To come before the great God is to expect great things to happen.
>
> WATCHMAN NEE

January 27

With this in mind, we constantly pray for you, that our God may count you worthy of his calling, and that by his power he may fulfill every good purpose of yours and every act prompted by your faith.

2 THESSALONIANS 1:11

[The following words were taken from the journal of Edward Payson, one of the church's largely unheralded prayer warriors of the nineteenth century.]

I was favored with a spirit of prayer beyond all my former experience. I was in great agony and wrestled both for myself and others with great power.

God seemed to bow the heavens and come down and open all His treasures, bidding me, take what I would.

EDWARD PAYSON

Pray About It: So persistent in prayer was Payson that next to his bed where he prayed were deep grooves in the hardwood floor where his knees had left their indentations. And the effect of his prayers? He often experienced the reality of Christ that can only come through prayer. "I seemed carried out of myself into the presence of God," he once wrote.

Numerous revivals characterized by "a depth and power seldom seen" were birthed under Payson's ministry. His congregation was often overwhelmed and reduced to tears by the presence of Christ in their midst. Has that happened in your church lately?

Payson's advice to his colleagues in the ministry was, "Prayer is the first thing, the second thing, and the third thing necessary to a minister. Pray then, my dear brother, pray, pray."

And for us today, it's also true. Pray, pray, pray.

To be much *for* God, we must be much *with* God.

LEONARD RAVENHILL

January 28

See then that you walk circumspectly, not as fools
but as wise, redeeming the time, because the days
are evil.

EPHESIANS 5:15–16 NKJV

We must find time to pray. If we wait until we are
at leisure to pray, we will never have the opportunity
to do so. All who desire to do intercessory work
or to make progress in prayer life must "make" the
time by setting aside a period for prayer. Let us
guard this period and hold fast to it. Let us beseech
God to give us the time to pray. We must pray the
prayer of protection for our prayer time. Pray that
the period of prayer may not be lost. For with any
such loss we will pray no more.

WATCHMAN NEE

Pray About It: At some time or another we all try to
keep track of where our money goes. We put ourselves
on budgets, we watch for sales when shopping, and
we cut expenses where we can. And often the first cuts
are made from the money that we would give God.

So too, many of us find our time slips away as
quickly as our money. And when our time is tight,
what usually gets cut out of the budget first? Very
often it's our time with God. What a mistake this is.

Financially, we quickly learn that it's not wise to
forget to give to God a portion of our income. When
we put Him first financially, we will never be short
of money. Similarly, if we're faithful to God with our

time, He will multiply our hours, just as He did the loaves and fishes given to Jesus.

Let all else go today, but not your prayer time. Guard it zealously. And give Him the firstfruits of your time, not the leftovers.

> When asked what his plans were for the next day, Martin Luther replied, "Work, work from early until late. In fact, I have so much to be done that I shall spend the first three hours in prayer."

January 29

> About noon the following day as they were on their journey and approaching the city, Peter went up on the roof to pray.
>
> Acts 10:9

> Which forms of prayer are best? There is no rule of thumb, for the reason that every thumbprint is different and distinct. Some habit of prayer is clearly wise, for all life is built on habit; but the habit should be under frequent scrutiny lest it harden into a confining shell.
>
> George Buttrick

Pray About It: The secret life of prayer is very personal. Some may pray best on their knees. Others may stand and pace. Yet others feel the need to lay flat on their faces, prostrate before God. Some may, with full passion, pray written prayers that convey their heart's desire. Others will shun written prayers for spontaneous supplications.

The main thing is that prayer be fresh, not hardened "into a confining shell." Today, if you sense that your form of prayer has become simply that — a form — try changing your habit. The result may be a renewal of prayer power.

> No one can prescribe for another. Let each be persuaded in his own mind how to pray, and the Holy Spirit will inspire us and guide us how long to pray. And let us all be so full of the love of God our Savior that prayer, at all times and in all places, may be a joy as well as a means of grace.
>
> A. E. RICHARDSON

January 30

It shall come to pass, that before they call, I will
answer; and while they are yet speaking, I will hear.

ISAIAH 65:24 KJV

There is no danger of the individual Christian being
overlooked amidst the multitude of supplicants who
daily and hourly present their various petitions, for
an infinite Mind is as capable of paying the same
attention to millions as if only one individual were
seeking its attention.

So too the lack of appropriate language, the
inability to give expression to the deepest longing of
the soul, will not jeopardize our prayers, for "It shall
come to pass, that before they call, I will answer;
and while they are yet speaking, I will hear."

ARTHUR PINK

Pray About It: Don't put limitations on God. He can
hear your prayers at the same time your brothers and
sisters are at prayer all around the world. J. B. Phillips
wrote what has become a classic book, entitled *Your
God Is Too Small,* wherein he challenged the limitations that most people put on God.

The one to whom we pray knows the past, the
present, and the future, and nothing is allowed to happen without His knowledge and permission. Thus we
may have firm confidence in God. He is Sovereign.

The prayers you will pray today, God will hear
while you are yet speaking. And even more: before
you call on Him, the answer is on its way!

Your thoughts of God are too human.

MARTIN LUTHER

January 31

My intercessor is my friend
  as my eyes pour out tears to God;
on behalf of a man he pleads with God
  as a man pleads for his friend.

JOB 16:20–21

The greatest and best talent that God gives to any man or woman in this world is the talent of prayer.

ALEXANDER WHYTE

Pray About It: All Christians pray, but some Christians seem to be called to greater prayer than others. These men and women are called "intercessors" and though they are no more righteous or gifted than other Christians, they have a hunger for prayer that not all Christians possess.

Although you and I may not be one of these intercessors, we can learn a lot from them, for we too intercede for others as we pray. When we do, our prayers are at their highest.

Prayer is not a string of words, but a divine piece of work.

RUTH PAXSON

February 1

You are worthy, our Lord and God,
   to receive glory and honor and power,
for you created all things,
   and by your will they were created
and have their being.

REVELATION 4:11

Are you afraid of coming to God too often? You may come too seldom, but you can never come too often to God. Isn't there good occasion for prayer to God both early and late?

Aren't there sins early and late to be pardoned, mercies early and late to be procured, mischiefs early and late to be averted, duties early and late to be performed, afflictions early and late to be endured, and temptations early and late to be broken?

Now, whence comes your health and strength? Is it not from Heaven? And how does it come, but by prayer? Oh above all things, be much in seeking God! You have the very key of heaven, if you have the gift and grace of praying.

ANDREW GRAY

Pray About It: The problem we have is not coming to God too often, but too infrequently. The God we serve is always available to hear our requests. More than that, He's eager for communion with us. Why was man created at all, if not for the pleasure God receives from fellowship with His creation? It was for the very purpose of knowing Him that we were born. It's for knowing Him that you still live. When we're with Him, we fulfill the most basic longings within us. And we fulfill the deepest longing of God—that of our company. There's a special place in the heart of God that only *you* can fill. God is more than willing to be with you today. More than willing to hear your voice.

> God is more willing to be prayed to, and more ready to hear prayer than we are to pray.
>
> MATTHEW HENRY

February 2

Concerning the work of my hands command ye me.
ISAIAH 45:11 KJV

Joshua used this commanding tone when, in the supreme moment of triumph, he lifted up his spear toward the setting sun, and cried, "Sun, stand thou still!"

Elijah used it when he shut the heavens for three years and six months, and again opened them.

Martin Luther used it when, kneeling by the dying man of God whom he loved, Philip Melanchthon, he forbade death to take his prey.

It is a marvelous relationship into which God bids us enter. We can more easily understand the verse which follows: "I have made the earth, and created man upon it: I, even my hands, have stretched out the heavens, and all their host have I commanded." But that God should invite us to command Him, this is a change in relationship which is altogether startling!

What a difference there is between this attitude and the hesitating, halting, unbelieving prayers to which we are accustomed, and which by perpetual repetition lose their edge and point!

How often during His earthly life did Jesus put men into a position to command Him! When entering Jericho, He stood still, and said to the blind beggars:

"What will ye that I shall do unto you?" It was as though He said, "I am yours to command."

Can we ever forget how He yielded to the Syrophoenician woman the key to His resources and told her to help herself even as she would?

What mortal mind can realize the full significance of the position to which our God lovingly raises His little children? He seems to say, "All my resources are at your command. Whatsoever ye shall ask in my name, that will I do."

F. B. MEYER

Pray About It: There is a form of praying given to us whereby we are able to speak boldly our requests to God. We are, after all, seated in the heavenlies and we have the powers of heaven at our command. When circumstances threaten to bury us, we must remember to stay on top, seated in our position in Christ, whereby we are able to command great things in prayer.

How are we able to do this? Isn't this presumption on our part?

Not if we know our true nature as fallen men and women who must rely unceasingly on Christ for everything. When we humbly recognize that any power we have isn't us at all, but Him working through us, we understand that boldness isn't presumption but *obedience*. It's only presumption if we're clothed with the pride that masquerades itself as humility.

Commanding prayer isn't for every occasion. But when it's needed, it's the most powerful weapon in the Christian arsenal.

> Now obviously this in no way can imply that we can force God to do what He will *not* do, not at all. Rather it simply means that we may command Him to do what He *desires* to do. It is because we know God's will that we may say to Him, "God, we want You to do it, we are determined that You do it. You cannot but do it." And thus shall we have strong and powerful prayer.
>
> WATCHMAN NEE

February 3

O LORD, the king rejoices in your strength.
How great is his joy in the victories you give!
You have granted him the desire of his heart
and have not withheld the request of his lips.
Selah

PSALM 21:1–2

One may not get into the spirit of prayer the minute
he goes to prayer, or the second he falls upon his
knees. It may take a little while to get into the spirit
of prayer, to get in touch with the forces of the skies.

Sometimes when we build a fire there is just a
coal or a small chunk of ember. What do we do?
We shave some fine kindlings; place them upon the
coals; then blow lightly until a small blaze leaps up.
Then we put on some more kindling; then we put
on the fuel, and soon there is a roaring fire, and the
room is comfortably warm.

Oftentimes when we've gone to prayer, we were
dry, and the devil did his best to keep us dry, but
we had gone to prayer, and meant to pray clear
through before we quit. We weren't in a hurry. We
had plenty of time for prayer. We would read [some
Psalms and portions of the gospel of John or perhaps the thirteenth chapter of first Corinthians].
We'd testify to His goodness, meditate, reflect, sing
a hymn, pray awhile, praise Him, and keep this up.

Don't quit. Don't get up off your knees. Stay
there until you hear from Heaven. Stay there until
you get into a spirit of prayer. We get what we
want, that is, we get what we pray for. If we want

the spirit of prayer badly enough, and will go down in earnest, it will be ours to enjoy.

W. J. HARNEY

Pray About It: Sometimes the fire of prayer starts with just a spark. When it fails to ignite right away, we give up. It's too much trouble, too hard. Yet the greatest, most productive times of prayer are the result of blowing lightly on the spark and waiting. And then adding a bit of fuel and waiting. Don't be impatient. *The best times you've missed in prayer have been the times you got up and walked away too soon.*

Today, don't get up too soon. Pray until you know you're finished.

Unless I had the spirit of prayer, I could do nothing.

CHARLES G. FINNEY

February 4

Every good and perfect gift is from above, coming down from the Father of the heavenly lights, who does not change like shifting shadows. He chose to give us birth through the word of truth, that we might be a kind of firstfruits of all he created.

JAMES 1:17–18

Saying prayers and praying are two totally different things. A self-righteous Pharisee may excel in the former; none but a converted soul can enjoy the latter.

The spirit of prayer is the spirit of the new man. The language of prayer is the distinct utterance of the new life. The moment a spiritual babe is born into the new creation, it sends up its cry of dependence and of trust toward the Source of its birth.

Who would dare to hush or hinder that cry? Let the babe be gently satisfied and encouraged, not ignorantly hindered or rudely silenced. The very cry which ignorance would seek to stifle, falls like sweetest music on the parent's ear. It is the proof of life.

C. H. MACKINTOSH

Pray About It: At your new birth, you were given prayer as a gift. It's expressly for the children of God. Right now, because you belong to God and have His life in you, you have the words to pray mighty prayers. If it seems difficult to pray, just look to God and speak your heart.

The words will come. God has planted them there.

Prayer requires more of the heart than of the tongue.

ADAM CLARKE

February 5

But seek ye first the kingdom of God, and his righteousness; and all these things shall be added unto you.

MATTHEW 6:33 KJV

Many have prayed earnestly for some definite blessing and then, when it failed to come, have grown bitter and even cynical. And one hears from such disappointed hearts the frequent refrain, "I have lost faith in prayer."

The very phrasing of that statement reveals a misunderstanding of the right attitude toward prayer. Faith in prayer is one thing. Prayer in faith is another.

The Christian who starts out with faith in prayer puts too much emphasis upon prayer and not enough upon the God to Whom he prays. He uses prayer as a sort of magic talisman, an "open sesame" to the things he wants, a quick way of getting things he wants from God. Then, when he doesn't get what he asks for, he gives up prayer much as the heathen beats his fetish when he gets into trouble. Prayer is really his god. Instead of being pious, he is, in a sense, idolatrous. Faith in prayer may be a very childish and inadequate attitude.

The object of our faith should be God rather than prayer. Then, prayer in such faith will not fail. We ought first utterly to commit all we are and have into His hands and leave them in His keeping. We ought to realize that while we can see only a tiny segment of life at a time, God sees the length and breadth of it with all its complications and intricacies. That being true, what we think we want may not, in His sight, be our need at all. So, when we pray in faith, faith in God, we first recognize that all things are in His hands and that He has promised to supply our needs. . . .

Faith in prayer may be a cheap thing, bordering on superstition, like knocking on wood. But prayer in faith, faith in God, is a sturdy, rugged confidence that presents humbly, yet boldly, its claims and leaves the rest with God.

VANCE HAVNER

Pray About It: Remember as you pray in faith that your faith must not be in your prayers, but in the God to whom you pray. Prayer isn't akin to luck or superstition. The faith with which true prayer is united is faith that has God the Father as its object. So often we carelessly speak our prayers with no thought of actually directing them to God. Small prayers will accomplish much if they're directed to our very large God.

Today, don't depend upon your prayers. Depend upon your God.

> We have to pray with our eyes on God, not on the difficulties.

OSWALD CHAMBERS

February 6

The kingdom of heaven suffers violence, and the violent take it by force.

MATTHEW 11:12 KJV

How violent Christ was about our salvation! He was in agony; He "continued all night in prayer" (Luke 6:12 KJV). He wept, He fasted, He died a violent death. He rose violently out of the grave.

Was Christ so violent for our salvation, and does it not become us to be violent who are so intimately concerned in it? Christ's violence was not only satisfactory, but exemplary. It was not only to appease God, but to teach us. Christ was violent in dying to teach us to be violent in believing.

THOMAS WATSON

Pray About It: To be effective pray-ers, there must be a violent believing. Taking God solidly at His Word, securing the promises He has given, soundly refusing doubt; these are some of the attributes of violent believing in prayer.

Like most everything else in the Christian life, this kind of praying doesn't necessarily come with ease. Rather, like the exercising of a muscle to make it stronger, so too prayer must be made more effective through regular exercise. Small muscles may grow into large powerful muscles. So too a person of small prayers may, through exercise, grow into a mighty warrior of God.

Today, be violent in taking the kingdom. Jesus has told us to do so.

Satan fears prayer and offsets it at every angle. At every opportunity he stalls the impulse to pray, for he has felt the smart of men who pray in the Holy Ghost. Again and again hell has shuddered because of the onslaughts of men who have taken the kingdom of heaven by violence.

LEONARD RAVENHILL

February 7

> If I had cherished sin in my heart,
>   the Lord would not have listened;
> but God has surely listened
>   and heard my voice in prayer.
> Praise be to God,
>   who has not rejected my prayer
>   or withheld his love from me!

PSALM 66:18–20

Praying which does not result in pure conduct is a delusion. We have missed the whole office and virtue of praying if it does not rectify conduct. It is in the very nature of things that we must quit praying, or quit bad conduct.

E. M. BOUNDS

Pray About It: If we have trouble praying, we should ask ourselves if the problem is known sin in our life. When we willingly and repeatedly sin, we hand over to Satan a poisonous weapon that he will eagerly use against us. Faith is undermined by sin. A clouded conscience can't pray rightly. The irony is that prayer will either keep us from sinning, or sinning will keep us from prayer.

But praise be to God, He will not reject our prayer or withhold His love. As we depart from sin, we remove Satan's weapon and our faith is strengthened.

Search yourself today and be done with any known sin.

> Prayer will make a Christian cease from sin, or sin will entice a man to cease from prayer.
>
> JOHN BUNYAN

February 8

I cried unto the LORD with my voice, and he heard me out of his holy hill. Selah.

PSALM 3:4 KJV

Silent prayers are often true prayers, but there are times, in extreme suffering, when it's helpful to give vocal expression to our soul's agony.

I know some friends who can never pray to their own comfort unless they can hear their own voices; and I believe that it's a good thing for most of us to retire to some private place where we cannot be heard by men, and where we can therefore freely use our voices in prayer.

Very often, the use of the voice helps to keep the thoughts from wandering, and also gives intensity to the desires. You notice that David particularly mentions here that he cried unto the Lord *with his voice*. No doubt many of his prayers ascended to God from his heart without the medium of his voice; but here, the cry with voice went with the desires of his heart.

Charles Haddon Spurgeon

Pray About It: Silent prayers are fine. Sometimes because of where we are, they're the only appropriate prayers to offer. However, in our daily time with God, when we're apart from anyone else, we should speak our prayers audibly. As David did, we should cry aloud with our voice.

Today, pray aloud. He will hear out of His holy hill.

Use me, Lord Jesus, for whatever purpose and in whatever way You desire. Here is my poor heart—an empty vessel—fill it with Your grace. Here is my sinful and troubled soul—quicken it and refresh it with Your love. Take my heart and use it for Your dwelling place. Use my mouth to spread the glory of Your name. Use my love and all my powers for the edifying of my brothers and sisters in Christ. Never allow the confidence of my faith to slacken, so that at all times I can truly say: "Jesus needs me, and I need Him."

Dwight L. Moody

February 9

But shun profane and vain babblings: for they will increase unto more ungodliness.

2 TIMOTHY 2:16 KJV

In this [modern day] we are, more and more, turning from the God-appointed means of intercessory prayer and adopting, instead, merely natural agencies for the carrying on of His work. Intercessory prayer has been shelved. For some reason it is out of date. Our methods, we say, are better, our plans more successful, and so we adopt natural means to bring to pass the supernatural.

My brethren, it can never be done. We may appear successful; the crowds may come; the altar may be full night after night. Reported results may be broadcasted everywhere. Whole cities may be stirred and mightily moved! And yet when it is all over and two or three years have passed, how little will be found to be genuine! And why? Simply because we have been satisfied with a superficial, spectacular work, brought to pass by natural means. Consequently the truly supernatural has been largely lacking. Oh let us get back to intercessory prayer, the highest form of Christian service, and give God no rest until we have a spiritual outcome.

OSWALD J. SMITH

Pray About It: Much of what passes for revival today is a "superficial, spectacular work brought to pass by natural means." And for the most part, we've settled for such man-initiated revivals, rather than hold out for the real thing through prayer—the genesis of all true revival.

But even more, in our own lives, how often have we gone from Christian fad to fad, settling for goosebump spirituality rather than taking the time to grow deep roots that plumb the very depths of God Himself.

Both in the church and personally, we must set aside the superficial and pray for nothing less than the Spirit of God busily at work in our lives and churches.

Remember today, you can never bring about the supernatural through natural means. Don't even try.

> Faith doesn't operate in the realm of the possible. There is no glory for God in that which man can do. Faith begins where man's power ends.
>
> GEORGE MUELLER

February 10

Ye are our epistle written in our hearts, known and read of all men.

2 CORINTHIANS 3:2 KJV

What is the reason that some believers are so much brighter and holier than others? I believe the difference, in 19 cases out of 20, arises from different habits about private prayer. I believe that those who are not eminently holy pray little and those who are eminently holy pray much.

J. C. RYLE

Pray About It: All Christians are God's epistles sent out into the world to be read of all men. All Christians are also, in a sense, pray-ers that can be read of all men. When a pray-er leaves his time with God, he's different from other people, and it shows. A person who has visited with God has become extraordinary.

Today, be an extraordinary Christian. Make Whitefield's prayer your own.

I pray to God this day to make me an extraordinary Christian.

GEORGE WHITEFIELD

February 11

Then Isaiah said, "Prepare a poultice of figs." They did so and applied it to the boil, and he recovered.

2 KINGS 20:7

I would have you understand that prayer must be accompanied by means. It is an outrage to ask God to do a thing while we sit passively. Prayer, to be acceptable, must come not only from the heart, but from the hands. We must work while we pray—devotion and work going together. Luther came to his [dying friend's] bedside and prayed for his recovery, and insisted, at the same time, that he should take some warm soup, the soup being just as important as the prayer.

In the time of the great plague that came to England, the priests prayed all day and all night for removal of the plague, but didn't think of clearing out the dead dogs and cats that lay in the gutters, causing the sickness. We must use means as well as supplication.

If a man prays for good health, and then sits down to a full supper of indigestibles at eleven o'clock at night, his prayer is a mockery. A man has no right to pray for the safety of his family when he knows there is no cover on the cistern.

The Christian man, reckless about his health, ought not to expect the same answer to his prayer as the Christian man expects who retires regularly at a reasonable hour and practices good hygiene.

Paul said to the passengers of the Alexandrian corn-ship that they would get safely ashore, but he told them that they must use means, and that was, "Stick to the old ship!"

God is not weak, needing our help, but God is strong and asks us to cooperate with him that we may be strong too. Pray by all means, but don't forget the fig-poultice.

T. DeWitt Talmadge

Pray About It: Often in prayer, God will give us the means to our prayer's answer. If the need is financial, He may prompt us to a specific job change. Or if a rebellious child is the problem, God may give specific instructions on what to do for the child. Practical advice from God may come from reading a book, hearing advice from a friend, or be revealed to us as we pray. Sometimes, we know full well what to do, but continue to pray, asking God to do what we know we should do.

As you pray, always be asking God, "Is there a fig poultice for this situation?" If yes, then do what you know you must.

See that you do not use the trick of prayer to cover up what you know you ought to do.

Oswald Chambers

February 12

If any of you lacks wisdom, he should ask God, who gives generously to all without finding fault, and it will be given to him. But when he asks, he must believe and not doubt, because he who doubts is like a wave of the sea, blown and tossed by the wind. That man should not think he will receive anything from the Lord; he is a double-minded man, unstable in all he does.

JAMES 1:5–8

I have been driven many times to my knees in the overwhelming conviction that I had nowhere else to go. My wisdom, and that of all about me, seemed insufficient for that day.

If the Lord did not answer prayer I could not stand it. And if I did not believe in a God who works His will with nations, I should despair of the republic.

ABRAHAM LINCOLN

Pray About It: The exact nature of President Lincoln's faith has been often debated. But as the leader of a great nation, he was often sent to his knees when the wisdom of mere men proved insufficient.

Lincoln was right on two counts: God does answer prayer and God does work His will with nations. Pray today that our leaders will have the same spirit of prayer and dependency on God as did Abraham Lincoln.

When God wants me to do something, He always finds a way of letting me know about it.

ABRAHAM LINCOLN

February 13

It is the glory of God to conceal a matter;
to search out a matter is the glory of kings.

PROVERBS 25:2

A crowded gathering of distinguished scientists had been listening intently to the enthralling speech given by acclaimed scientist, Michael Faraday. For an hour he held his brilliant audience spellbound as he demonstrated the nature and properties of the magnet. He brought his lecture to a close with an experiment so novel, so bewildering, and so triumphant that, for some time after he resumed his seat, the house rocked with enthusiastic applause.

And then the Prince of Wales stood to propose a motion of congratulations to Faraday. The resolution was easily seconded and passed with renewed thunders of applause. But the uproar was succeeded by a strange silence. The crowd of scientists waited for Faraday's reply but the lecturer had vanished! What had become of him? Only two or three of his most intimate friends knew of his secret departure.

They knew that the great chemist was something more than a great chemist; he was a great Christian. Michael Faraday served as an elder in a small church nearby that never boasted more than twenty members. The hour at which Faraday concluded his lecture was the hour of the midweek prayer meeting—a meeting that Faraday never neglected. And, under cover of the cheering applause, the great chemist had slipped out of the crowded hall and hurried off to the little meetinghouse.

F. W. BOREHAM

> I can take my telescope and look millions of miles into space; but I can go away to my room, and in prayer, get nearer to God and heaven than I can when assisted by all of the telescopes in the world.
>
> SIR ISAAC NEWTON

Pray About It: We live in an age where science has been given almost religious status. Few modern scientists are openly Christian. What a change this is from their forebears. Many of the most important scientists of the past had a deep faith in God. Many, like Faraday and Newton, were strongly Christian.

There should be no gulf between science and Christianity. Scientists have helped humankind immensely. Many men and women alive today would be dead if not for the achievements of modern medicine. We all benefit daily from the inventions given to us by inventors and scientists.

But what *is* science if not the discovery of laws that God has set in motion? There can be no design without a designer. A scientist merely applies the laws that God has ordained in such a way as to benefit humankind. The great man of science, George Washington Carver, simply asked in prayer, "Mr. Creator, why did You create the peanut?" From the answer to that simple prayer came knowledge that influenced the development of a host of modern conveniences including printer's ink, salad oil, instant coffee, and paints.

What would happen if God were to move dramatically in the hearts and minds of contemporary scientists?

Perhaps a cure for cancer? Perhaps the discovery of ways to grow food with which we could eliminate famine?

Pray for the scientific community. Pray first and foremost that they step back from their microscopes, pause, and consider that the answers they seek are known by God.

May they, like Faraday, Newton, and Carver, have the courage to put God first.

> God is going to reveal to us things He never revealed before, if we put our hands in His.
>
> GEORGE WASHINGTON CARVER

February 14

> The LORD was with Samuel as he grew up, and he let none of his words fall to the ground.
>
> 1 SAMUEL 3:19

Prayer is no magic transformation of words into heavenly language just because we close our eyes. Words are not prayer because we utter them on our knees, nor because we say them in the pulpit, nor because they are breathed within the confines of a church. . . .

We can use words without prayer, and we can pray without using words. We can also pray when words are used. But there is a language of the Spirit beyond words—groanings that cannot be articulated, that defy language, that are above language, that are beyond language, that are the yearnings of the heart of God committed to those who seek to know His will and to care for a lost world and feeble Church.

LEONARD RAVENHILL

Pray About It: Never pray words that "fall to the ground" before reaching God's ears. If necessary, let your heart speak, and your mouth remain shut. Be sensitive to God. You will know when words are the language of the spirit and when silence or the groanings of a yearning heart are appropriate. Today, consider if silence might speak more loudly to God than words.

> Prayer is something deeper than words. It is present in the soul before it has been formulated in words. And it abides in the soul after the last words of prayer have passed over our lips.
>
> OLE HALLESBY

February 15

As for me, far be it from me that I should sin against the LORD by failing to pray for you.

1 SAMUEL 12:23

If I feel myself disinclined to pray, then is the time when I need to pray more than ever. Possible when the soul leaps and exults in communion with God it might more safely refrain from prayer than at those seasons when it drags heavily in devotion.

CHARLES HADDON SPURGEON

Pray About It: We all face days when we just don't feel like praying. We even reason, *if I have to do it legalistically, then it profits me nothing. Surely God doesn't want me to pray when my heart's not in it.*

That's true, but what usually happens is that if we once make the effort to simply begin to pray, we find that something within us loosens up and we continue on.

If you don't feel like praying, there's probably an urgent, unknown to you reason why you should be praying.

Just start. Don't worry about anything else. Just start.

Deliver me, O Lord, from a slothful mind, from all lukewarmness, and all dejection of spirit. I know these only serve to deaden my love for you. Mercifully free my heart from them and give me a lively, zealous, active, and cheerful spirit, so that I can vigorously do all that you've assigned to me.

JOHN WESLEY

February 16

Trust in the LORD with all your heart
    and lean not on your own understanding;
in all your ways acknowledge him,
    and he will make your paths straight.

PROVERBS 3:5–6

I want to share with you a growing conviction with me, and that is that as we obey the leadings of the Spirit of God, we enable God to answer the prayers of other people. I mean that our lives, my life, is the answer to someone's prayer, prayed perhaps centuries ago. . . .

I have the unspeakable knowledge that my life is the answer to prayers, and that God is blessing me and making me a blessing entirely of His sovereign grace and nothing to do with my merits, saving as I am bold enough to trust His leading and not the dictates of my own wisdom and common sense.

OSWALD CHAMBERS

Pray About It: Have you ever thought about how your life may be the answer to someone else's prayer, perhaps someone you never even met? I can fully imagine my great-great-grandfather, more than 150 years ago, praying for his descendants in the twenty-first century. Or perhaps it was the Christian woman who lived in our neighborhood when I was a boy. Maybe that first Sunday school teacher who told me the story using her flannel board.

The above words from Oswald Chambers were part of a letter he wrote, dated February 16, 1907.

Sometimes I wonder if God lets those who have gone on to heaven see how their words, lives, and prayers are still having an impact many years after they've left this world.

I'd like to think that my great-great-grandpa (or whoever it was who prayed for me) knows that I thank him for praying for me.

Think back. Whose answer to prayer might you be?

Who might you pray for today in the same manner? A future descendant? A friend? A neighbor?

> How long will it take us to learn that the shortest route to the man, woman, or child next door is by way of God's throne!
>
> A. T. PIERSON

February 17

My tongue will speak of your righteousness
and of your praises all day long.

PSALM 35:28

You must learn a kind of prayer which can be made at all times, which doesn't divert from your outward business, and which princes, kings, prelates, priests, magistrates, soldiers, children, artisans, laborers, women and sick persons, may all perform.

This kind of prayer isn't from the head, but from the heart. It's not a prayer of thought only, because the spirit of man is so bound that while he thinks on one thing he cannot fully think on another; but it's the prayer of the heart, which isn't at all interrupted by all the occupations of the mind. Nothing but abnormal affections can interrupt the prayer of the heart, and it's almost impossible for the soul which has once tasted God and the sweetness of His love, to relish anything else but Him.

MADAME GUYON

Pray About It: There is, of course, the prayer we pray in our prayer closets; but that can't be the only time we pray. If we leave our homes in the morning, having spent time with God, we will, throughout the day, carry that spirit of prayer with us. And no matter what we do — our office jobs, our sales calls, our college classes, our teaching, our reading, our parenting — can all be occasions for yet more prayer. How? By allowing our "prayers of the heart" to constantly be in communion with God. Such prayers are "not at all interrupted by all the occupations of the mind."

God will be with you all day today. See if you can't find time to remember Him throughout the day and offer a short prayer of the heart.

> What can be more agreeable to God than to withdraw thus many times a day from the things of the world to retire into ourselves and adore Him interiorly?
>
> BROTHER LAWRENCE

February 18

But when ye pray, use not vain repetitions, as the heathen *do:* for they think that they shall be heard for their much speaking.

Matthew 6:7 KJV

The prayer life doesn't consist of the perpetual repetition of petitions. The prayer life consists of a life that is always upward and onward and Godward.

George Campbell Morgan

Pray About It: There is a fine line between persistence in prayer and repetition of prayers. If our burden is of God, we'll find it fresh every day. But if we are constantly repeating the same words for the same request, day after day, how can our heart be in it?

Our prayers must be vital, fresh, and living. They must be always "upward and onward and Godward." Like dominoes falling with continuing forward momentum.

Today, only pray for that which God prompts you to seek. Leave the dry lifeless prayers by the wayside.

Prayer must be aflame. Its passion must consume. Prayer without fervor is like the sun without light or heat or like flower without fragrance or beauty.

E. M. Bounds

February 19

Come unto me.

MATTHEW 11:28 KJV

There are none of us so close to Christ but that we can't come nearer, and the secret of our daily Christian life is all wrapped up in that one word of invitation from Jesus, "Come."

That nearness is what we are to make daily efforts after, and that nearness is one capable of indefinite increase. We know not how close to His heart we can lay our aching heads. We know not how near to His fullness we can bring our emptiness. We have never yet reached the point beyond which no closer union is possible.

ALEXANDER MACLAREN

Pray About It: Prayer is, in its most basic definition, a "coming" to God. Before words are spoken or thoughts organized, the fact that we have come unto Him has established prayer. Each time we enter prayer, there is this same coming to God.

"Come unto me" are the sweetest words of Christ to echo down through the centuries. Can you imagine a finer invitation? Today, as you pray, realize just who it is that invites you to come. It was He who first loved us.

God is always near you and with you. Leave Him not alone.

BROTHER LAWRENCE

February 20

Suppose a brother or sister is without clothes and daily food. If one of you says to him, "Go, I wish you well; keep warm and well fed," but does nothing about his physical needs, what good is it? In the same way, faith by itself, if it is not accompanied by action, is dead.

JAMES 2:15–17

When praying for others, we must be willing to be part of the answer if necessary. If we aren't willing to be used to answer our own prayers, we aren't cooperating with God. As a result, He won't cooperate with us; He won't answer our prayers. Why? Because these are prayers of isolation and separation. We are saying, "God, I don't want to get mixed up in anyone's problems. *You* take care of that."

Can you imagine Jesus doing that? "Sorry, Bartimaeus, I don't want to get *my* hands dirty." God will not hear our prayers of isolation. If we aren't more interested than that, then He's not interested in our prayers. As long as we ask and do nothing, He will listen and do nothing. If it costs us nothing, we can expect little in return.

Don't pray for more missionaries unless you're willing to go yourself or are willing to send your children. Don't pray for another's financial need unless you're willing to give yourself. And don't pray for the lost unless you're willing to go to them and share what Christ means to you.

CHARLES STANLEY

Pray About It: As you pray today, ask yourself, what can I do for these people for whom I'm praying? Can I call them and tell them I was thinking about them? Can I visit them if they're sick or lonely? Can I send money to support them if they're in need?

If you're praying for a certain country, can you go there as part of an outreach? There are ministries that offer numerous opportunities to get your hands dirty for Christ.

Be available, and willing, if God calls.

> The best way to do ourselves good is to be doing good for others. The best way to gather is to scatter.
>
> THOMAS BROOKS

February 21

> But the greatest of these is love.
>
> 1 CORINTHIANS 13:13

> Prayer doesn't consist in sweet feelings, nor in an excited imagination, nor in an enlightened intellect. All these are external gifts from His hand, in the absence of which love may exist even more purely. Without these things, our soul may attach itself immediately and solely to God, instead of to His gifts.
>
> FRANÇOIS FÉNELON

Pray About It: If we arise from our time of prayer unchanged in our feelings, does that mean God wasn't

present or that we were unsuccessful in our prayers?
No! The measurement of prayer isn't in our feelings,
our imagination, or our intellect. All these may be
present, yet if love is lacking, we profit nothing.

Today, look solely to God as you pray. Don't
worry about your fickle feelings.

> He prays well who is so absorbed with God that he
> does not know he is praying.
>
> FRANCIS DE SALES

February 22

"Lord," Martha said to Jesus, "if you had been here,
my brother would not have died. But I know that
even now God will give you whatever you ask."

JOHN 11:21–22

How many of us have been blind in our prayers? Look
back and think of the prayers you thought had not
been answered but now find that God has answered
with a bigger manifestation than you ever dreamed.
God has trusted you in the most intimate way He
could trust you, with an absolute silence, not of despair
but of pleasure, because He saw you could stand a
much bigger revelation than you had at the time.

Some prayers are followed by silence because
they are wrong, others because they are bigger
than we can understand. Jesus stayed where He

was — a positive staying, because He loved Martha and Mary. Did they get Lazarus back? They got infinitely more; they got to know the greatest truth mortal beings can ever know — that Jesus Christ is the Resurrection and the Life.

It will be a wonderful moment when we stand before God and find that the prayers we clamored for in early days and imagined were never answered, have been answered in the most amazing way, and that God's silence has been the sign of the answer.

OSWALD CHAMBERS

Pray About It: The silence of God in response to our prayers isn't a sign that He has not heard or will not grant our requests. Many pray-ers think that God's silence means they have done something wrong and thus He won't answer. But Martha and Mary had done nothing wrong. Their request of Jesus was good. And He complied — in His own time, not theirs. As a result, their blessing was even greater than their original request.

God's silence may offer proof that the answer has come or will come in a greater way than we suppose. Don't fence God in with your expectations of His action. His silence itself may be the action that grants your prayer.

As you pray today, God may be silent. But the answer you need is on its way, nevertheless.

Prayer is knocking at the door, faith is the expectation that it will be opened.

W. J. HARNEY

February 23

They devoted themselves to the apostles' teaching and to the fellowship, to the breaking of bread and to prayer.

ACTS 2:42

In the early church the prayers were simple, unpremeditated, and united. [No matter who uttered them] — the well-taught apostle, the accomplished scholar, the rough but fervent peasant, the new and zealous convert — their prayers sought God and wrestled with an instant and irrepressible urgency. As such their prayers were an essential part of the beginnings of Christianity, a faith kindled by holy fire and fanned by the daily prayers of the early believers.

WILLIAM ARTHUR

Pray About It: When we pray, we're taking up the mantle of a two-thousand-year-old practice. Prayers, of course, were offered before Christ, but at Pentecost, with the imparting of the Holy Spirit to the church, a new era began. By their "devoting themselves to prayer," the early disciples set in motion a chain of events that have led to this very day, and which are yet to be fulfilled at the return of Christ.

As we pray today, we should see ourselves as part of a relay team of sorts. The baton of prayer has been passed to us. For our entire lives, we live as pray-ers, urging the church on toward God's finish line at the culmination of human history.

Consider the privilege we are granted in being a part of such a holy mission. Thank Him today for your part on God's relay team of pray-ers.

God provides the men and women needed for each generation.

Mildred Cable

February 24

Be self-controlled and alert. Your enemy the devil prowls around like a roaring lion looking for someone to devour. Resist him, standing firm in the faith, because you know that your brothers throughout the world are undergoing the same kind of sufferings.

1 Peter 5:8–9

The concern of the devil is to keep the saints from praying. He fears nothing from prayerless studies, prayerless work, prayerless religion. He laughs at our toil, he mocks at our wisdom, but he trembles when we pray.

Samuel Chadwick

Pray About It: Of all the tools God has given the church, prayer is the most effective. And to Satan it's the most dangerous weapon he faces. Why then should it surprise us that we are so often distracted from wielding this mighty force? Satan does indeed tremble at our prayers. They signal his defeat in our lives.

Don't be distracted today from prayer, nor from the faith that prevails in prayer. Instead, as you pray, proclaim again (and firmly) Satan's defeat.

> Prayer is repeating the victor's name (Jesus) into the ears of Satan and insisting on his retreat.
>
> S. D. GORDON

February 25

> Then Peter began to speak: "I now realize how true it is that God does not show favoritism but accepts men from every nation who fear him and do what is right."
>
> ACTS 10:34–35

> You should think: My prayer is as precious, holy, and pleasing to God as was that of St. Paul or of the most holy saints. . . . God does not regard prayer on account of the person, but on account of His word and obedience thereto. For on the same rock upon which all the saints rested their prayers I, too, rest mine. Moreover I pray for the same thing for which they all prayed; besides, I have just as great a need as did those great saints.
>
> MARTIN LUTHER

Pray About It: Yes, it's true — our prayers are as precious, holy, and pleasing to God as those of any believer — including the apostle Paul. How is this so? Because our prayers are never based on our own personal merit or standing, but on the ground of Christ alone. Apart from Him, we are all sinners. The apostle Paul claimed he was, in fact, the "chief sinner." And yet because of grace we redeemed sinners have authority before God.

Pray today with the same authority with which Paul prayed. Pray mightily.

> There is no leveler like Christianity, but it levels by lifting all who receive it to the lofty tableland of a true character and of undying hope both for now and eternity.
>
> JONATHAN EDWARDS

February 26

> Then Caleb silenced the people before Moses and said, "We should go up and take possession of the land, for we can certainly do it."
>
> NUMBERS 13:30

It is a solemn thing to intercede for the nations of the world! Let us mobilize prayer! We can tip the scales of history. Christians can be the controlling factor in the unfolding drama of today's world—let us not allow ourselves to be chased around by the enemy, but let us go up at once and take the kingdoms of this world for Jesus. . . . He is delighted to give them to us. . . .

In practical terms, may these truths make our prayer lives as individuals, and in prayer meetings, outward-looking, Satan-shaking, captive-releasing, kingdom-taking, revival-giving, Christ-glorifying power channels for God!

> PATRICK JOHNSTONE

Pray About It: In his book, *Operation World,* Patrick Johnstone calls Christians to pray for the nations of the world. Too often we are unaware of the needs of those around the world, many of whom are our brothers and sisters in Christ. If God gives you compassion for a foreign land, learn the names of that country's leaders and pray for them. Find out what missions organizations are operating in that country. Pray for them daily and send them financial support.

If the great commission to preach the gospel to all nations is to be filled, it must be done with powerful praying by compassionate Christians who are willing to be burdened for others.

In this respect, we can all be missionaries on the foreign field.

What country has God laid on your heart? If none, then consider asking God today to point out the country for which you can labor in prayer.

> We ask for toys when we should ask for continents
> and be claiming the world for Christ.
>
> THOMAS PAYNE

February 27

Those who honor me I will honor.

1 SAMUEL 2:30

Take obedience with you into your time of prayer and meditation, for you will know as much of God, and only as much of God, as you are willing to put into practice. There is a great deal of truth in the hymn "Trust and Obey."

ERIC LIDDELL

Pray About It: Not too many people remembered the name Eric Liddell—that is until Hollywood made a movie of his life called *Chariots of Fire*. Mr. Liddell prayed much, but he also followed up his prayers with obedience. With his talent and love of running, he was asked to run on a Sunday, which to him was wrong. He stood in faith by what he believed and God honored him. Who can forget the passing of the note to Liddell with the simple words from 1 Samuel, "He who honors me, I will honor."

Liddell went on to serve as a missionary and died at age 42 in China. Wouldn't he be amazed at the turn of events that made him famous so many years after his death?

Honor God and He will honor you.

> When we walk with the Lord
> In the light of His Word
> What a glory He shed on our way!
> While we do His good will,
> He abides with us still,
> And with all who will trust and obey.
>
> J. H. SAMMIS

February 28

I thank my God every time I remember you.

PHILIPPIANS 1:3

What a blessed habit I have found my prayer list; morning by morning, it takes me via the Throne of all Grace straight to the intimate personal heart of each one [listed], and I know that He who is not proscribed by time and geography answers immediately.

OSWALD CHAMBERS

Pray About It: Many Christians benefit from keeping a written list of their requests, possibly in a journal. This serves two purposes. First, it can help us remember those we want to pray for or those for whom we have promised to pray. Second, as we see answers to prayer, we can enter the dates and the way that God answers. As such, it can be a great faith builder.

One word of caution: don't be so dependent on the list that you rattle off your prayers as though you were simply reading it—or worse, that on a day of discouragement, you don't do what one fellow reportedly did—he simply held up his prayer list and said, "God, I'm too tired to pray today. Here, read this!"

A most beneficial exercise in secret prayer before the Father is to write things down exactly so I see exactly what I think and want to say. Only those who have tried these ways know the ineffable benefit of such strenuous times in secret.

OSWALD CHAMBERS

February 29

Evening and morning and at noon I will pray and cry aloud, and He shall hear my voice.

PSALM 55:17 NKJV

The whole life of the believer should be prayer driven. Prayer should be the summary and the conclusion of our every act, every word, every wish. The act that is not prayer in the ultimate sense, and the word which is not prayer in the last analysis, and the wish that is not prayer in the profoundest depth are to be put away; they do not become the life of faith. They are things that produce fainting.

GEORGE CAMPBELL MORGAN

Pray About It: When you stop to think about it, our life is like a wheel, with prayer as the hub. Our finances, our daily bread, our relationships, our health, are all, in the first and last place, dependent on God's provision. And anything dependent on God's provision is bound up inseparably with prayer.

As you pray today, remind yourself that this lone activity is your starting place for everything you are.

I live in the spirit of prayer. I pray as I walk about, when I lie down and when I rise up. And the answers are always coming.

GEORGE MUELLER

March 1

His divine power has given us everything we need for life and godliness through our knowledge of him who called us by his own glory and goodness. Through these he has given us his very great and precious promises, so that through them you may participate in the divine nature and escape the corruption in the world caused by evil desires.

2 PETER 1:3–4

In our private prayers and in our public services we are forever asking God to do things that He has already done or cannot do because of our unbelief. We plead for Him to speak when He has already spoken and is at that very moment speaking. We ask Him to come when He is already present and waiting for us to recognize Him. We beg the Holy Spirit to fill us while all the time we are preventing Him by our doubts.

A. W. TOZER

Pray About It: One caution in your prayers: there's no use asking God for what He's already given us. For instance, if we have accepted the Lord Jesus Christ as our Savior, why would we continue to pray for our salvation? To do so is an affront to God, in that it demonstrates our great lack of faith in His Word. Many times we find ourselves asking God for something that He gave us long ago, which we need only to appropriate by faith.

What are some of these things we already have? Salvation, the Holy Spirit, eternal life, deliverance, victory over the enemy, the mind of Christ. To learn about these gifts God has already given us, we only need to turn to His Word, read His promises, and appropriate them.

It has been well said that Bible study is simply an exploration of the promises God has made to His people. Prayer is appropriating them.

> Faith is to believe on the Word of God, what we do not see. And its reward is to see and enjoy what we believe.
>
> AUGUSTINE

March 2

> Likewise the Spirit also helpeth our infirmities: for we know not what we should pray for as we ought: but the Spirit itself maketh intercession for us with groanings which cannot be uttered.
>
> ROMANS 8:26 KJV

Prayer is an impossible task without the Holy Ghost. We know not what we should pray for as we ought, but the Spirit helps our infirmities. The Spirit instructs and inspires prayer, gives intelligence and intensity to intercession, and brings reality and joy to communion with God. Spirit-filled people love to pray, and prayer that is in the Spirit must prevail.

SAMUEL CHADWICK

Pray About It: The best way for us to pray is to let the Holy Spirit within us pray through us. He knows the will of God in a given matter and thus we can never pray wrong when our prayers are from Him and to Him. We simply are vessels God uses to accomplish His will through prayer.

Pray in the Spirit today and pray in pure joy.

When we pray in the Spirit, we will pray for the right things and in the right way. There will be joy and power in our prayer.

R. A. TORREY

March 3

Praying always with all prayer and supplication in the Spirit, and watching thereunto with all perseverance and supplication for all saints.

EPHESIANS 6:18–19 KJV

Authoritative prayer begins in heaven and ends on earth. In short, authoritative prayer is a praying from heaven to earth.

All who know how to pray know what is meant by praying upward and what is meant by praying downward. If a person has never learned how to pray downward, he has yet to discover authoritative prayer. In spiritual warfare this kind of praying downward is exceedingly important.

What is praying downward? It is standing upon the heavenly position Christ has given us and using authority to resist all the works of Satan by commanding that whatever God has commanded must be done.

Suppose, for example, that we are praying for a particular matter. After we have seen what the will of God is and have really ascertained what God has ordered, we should then not pray: "Oh God, I ask You to do this thing"; on the contrary, we should pray: "God, You must do this thing, it must be done this way. God, this thing must so be accomplished." This is commanding prayer — prayer of authority.

The meaning of "amen" is not "let it be so" but "thus shall it be." When I say amen to your prayer I am affirming that thus shall the matter be, that what you pray shall so be accomplished. This is the prayer of command, which comes out of faith. The reason we may so pray is because we have the heavenly position. We are brought into this heavenly position when Christ ascends to heaven. As Christ is in heaven so we too are in heaven, just as when Christ died and was resurrected, we also died and were resurrected. We ought to see the heavenly position of the church. Satan commences his work by causing us if he can to lose our heavenly position. For the heavenly is the position of victory. As long as we *stand* in that position, we are victorious. But if by Satan we are dragged down from heaven, we are defeated.

WATCHMAN NEE

Pray About It: Because God has seated us with Christ in the heavenlies, we have great authority. By praying downward, rather than upward, it means that we are praying from that high position. We are able to exercise the authority we have as believers, rather than passively praying upward.

Regarding your present circumstances, instead of praying vaguely upward, today try using your authority as a Christian and pray downward. This should be our normal attitude in prayer, not a passing fad. To mature properly as an effective pray-er, we must learn to pray with authority. We must pray downward.

> If we listen in the stillness till our hearts begin to respond to what He is thinking and feeling about the matter in question, whether it concerns ourselves or others, we can, from that moment, begin praying downwards from the Throne, instead of praying upwards from ourselves.
>
> LILIAS TROTTER

March 4

For in Christ all the fullness of the Deity lives in bodily form, and you have been given fullness in Christ, who is the head over every power and authority.

COLOSSIANS 2:9–10

There is no other way to power but by prayer. Hidden prayer is like heat smoldering in the bowels of the earth far beneath the still cone of a volcano. Though to the eye there may be years of inactivity, sooner or later there will be an explosion. So it is with prayer in the Spirit. It never dies. There may be a long birth pain in the Spirit, but birth there will be.

LEONARD RAVENHILL

Pray About It: More than forty years ago, a young Assembly of God pastor was challenged by God to pray for two hours every night. So every night at midnight, the young man stepped into his office, closed the door and prayed. At first the time seemed to drag and he grew restless. But then he combined his prayer time with Bible reading. He also began to offer praises to God in addition to his petitions.

Then one evening he seemed fidgety. He had been praying for quite a while and though he felt close to God, a great sadness seemed to overtake him. "I felt uneasy, as though I had received orders but couldn't make out what they were," he said. He asked God about this uneasiness but received no answer. He then began walking around his study. On his desk lay a copy of *Life* magazine. He started to pick it up, then thought, *No, I'm not going to fall into that trap, reading a magazine when I'm supposed to be praying.* But each time he tried to pray, his attention was drawn to the magazine on his desk.

Finally, he opened the magazine and saw a pen drawing of seven boys who were gang members in New York City. The next thing he knew, the young pastor was in tears. The volcano had erupted.

Though few in his small congregation understood their pastor's burden for these gang members, *he* knew it was from God. A short time later, this skinny young pastor put feet to his prayers and moved to the inner city of New York City and started a work that would become Teen Challenge. The young man was David Wilkerson and many Christians have read the exciting story of how that man's two-hour commitment to prayer ultimately saved many young teens from the gang life, in the now classic book *The Cross and the Switchblade.*

That same volcano builds in the life of every Christian pray-er until it eventually erupts into service to God in some form. It may be in teaching Sunday school (powerfully) or in being a doctor, nurse, attorney, mother, father, or grandparent. Or you may even be called to an inner-city ministry as was David Wilkerson.

But whatever you do will be a result of your commitment to prayer and the volcanic power those prayers unleash to propel you forward in God.

My life has not been the same since.

DAVID WILKERSON

March 5

But the very hairs on your head are all numbered.

MATTHEW 10:30

[When Oswald Chambers was en route to Egypt, he made the following entry in his journal:]

I had a great time yesterday praying before God for all these passengers and crew and those I come in contact with. I do believe this is where my real ministry lies, in intercessory prayer. It is such an inspiration to take human stuff as it actually is and drop the categorizing to which more or less we are all so liable, dealing with human beings as types. I do not believe in the type hunt. Every human being is his own type, therefore take him as a fact, not as an illustration of a prejudice.

Pray About It: Even the Christian who would pray only minimally must have a love for people. Those who would pray diligently must be even more compelled to intercede because of the love they have for others — especially those who are hard to love.

Today, take a lesson from Oswald Chambers. Those people who pass you on the street, who ride with you in the elevator, who stand ahead of you in the grocery checkout line — every one of them is unique. Every one of them has been carefully designed by God and is loved by God. Pray today for those with whom you come in contact. Look past the circumstances that brought them you way and see them as the wonderful "human stuff" that Chambers speaks of. Never lump people into stereotypical groups. In God's eyes, there are no stereotypes—only his magnificent creations.

True, whole prayer is nothing but love.

AUGUSTINE

March 6

For our struggle is not against flesh and blood, but against the rulers, against the authorities, against the powers of this dark world and against the spiritual forces of evil in the heavenly realms.

EPHESIANS 6:12

When the devil sees a man or woman who really believes in prayer, who knows how to pray, and who really does pray, and, above all, when he sees a whole church on its face before God in prayer, "he trembles" as much as he ever did, for he knows that his day in that church or community is at an end.

R. A. TORREY

Pray About It: Why have so many churches grown cold? Why are so many of our communities spiritually desolate? In some cities you can sense a cloud of evil or materialism that quenches righteousness. The enemy has gained a stronghold in these communities and until churches and individual Christians stand in the gap for these areas, Satan will continue to destroy lives. But his influence can be reversed. A band of believing Christians who covenant to pray for their community can bring dramatic results in a short time.

How is it in your town? Are you aware of what's happening spiritually? Does righteousness prevail? Are the schools and streets safe? Does drug use, pornography, crime, violence, and abortion have a foothold? Or perhaps your community is plagued by materialism, greed, broken family relationships, alcoholism, and "white-collar" sin. Christians have the power to halt sin in their localities through vigorous, sustained prayer.

Today, think about your community, identify the major problems, and begin to pray against the work of the enemy. Pray for the churches. Pray for renewal among the Christians. Pray for the children.

> Wherever the church is aroused and the world's wickedness arrested, somebody has been praying.
>
> A. T. PIERSON

March 7

In God we make our boast all day long,
    and we will praise your name forever. *Selah*

PSALM 44:8

When the Spirit has come to reside in someone, that person cannot stop praying; for the Spirit in him prays without ceasing. No matter if he is asleep or awake, prayer is going on in his heart all the time.

He may be eating or drinking, he may be resting or working; no matter, the incense of prayer will ascend spontaneously from his heart. The slightest stirring of his heart is like a voice which sings in silence and in secret to the Invisible.

ISAAC THE SYRIAN

Pray About It: Prayer is as natural to a Christian as breathing to a living body. We *must* pray if we are Christians. The Spirit within us compels us to pray and we obey. Our prayers aren't always spoken, but they are nonetheless prayers.

To be a Christian is to be a pray-er.

Prayer is like breathing. Stop breathing and you die. Stop praying and your Christian experience will soon fade away.

ERIC LIDDELL

March 8

Great is our Lord, and of great power: His understanding is infinite.

PSALM 147:5 KJV

Let us learn that what we bring to God of ourselves when we come to Him we must leave with Him when we go. He who knows how to cast off to God and leave it there will be delivered.

Once I brought a manuscript to a sister to be copied. I made a special trip to her for that purpose. But when I left I unconsciously brought it back with me. It was obvious she could not copy that manuscript even though she wanted to. This is the way we often pray today. With our mouth we say, "O God, please help me." After prayer, however, we bring ourselves back home.

It is exceedingly important for us to let go.

WATCHMAN NEE

Pray About It: Many times we come to God worried about our past sins, our future worries, and our present problems. And yet God has remedies for all three of these phases of our history. Our past sins are covered with the blood of Christ—forever gone. Our future too is under the strict oversight of God. He will allow nothing to cross our path we can't handle. As for our present, it too is in God's keeping. We need only to leave ourselves with God. *Leave ourselves with God.*

Today when you rise from prayer, be sure that your load is lighter. You will have left all your burdens *there.*

There is nothing too great for God's power, and nothing too small for His love.

CORRIE TEN BOOM

March 9

Since we live by the Spirit, let us keep in step with the Spirit.

GALATIANS 5:25

The major conflict in the believer's life is to maintain an unbroken attitude of reliance upon the Spirit. Only in that way can the Spirit possess and vitalize every human faculty, emotion and choice. We cannot meet tomorrow's issues today. To walk is to take one step after another and this demands a constant appropriation of the power of God. That is spirituality. That is the Spirit-filled life — the unhindered manifestation of the indwelling Spirit.

LEWIS SPERRY CHAFER

Pray About It: One goal of prayer is to aid in maintaining our reliance on the Spirit. As we walk one step at a time, so we need to learn to lean on God one hour at a time.

Remind God today that He has promised His Spirit is will be in us forever — and that includes *today*. And then, throughout the day, keep in step with Him.

Where there is much prayer, there will be much of the Spirit. Where there is much of the Spirit there will be everlasting prayer.

ANDREW MURRAY

March 10

Great is the LORD and most worthy of praise;
    His greatness no one can fathom.

PSALM 145:3 KJV

Little do we know how we wrong ourselves by shutting out of our prayers the praises of God or allowing them so narrow a room as we usually do. Let praises have a larger place in your duties. Consider the excellencies and goodness of the Lord as often as you do your needs, your unworthiness and the mercies that God has given you.

RICHARD BAXTER

Pray About It: Today isn't a day for asking. God knows what you need. Right now, take a few minutes and simply offer praise to Him *for who He is,* not for what He does for you.

At first it may seem difficult not to start asking God to do this or that, but resist the urge for today. Stay on course and confine your words to those of praise and worship. Throughout the day, every time you find yourself asking God for something, stop and turn the request into praise instead. You may be surprised at the results.

Jehovah, the one God, should be the one object of adoration. To give the least particle of His honor to another is shameful treason; to refuse to render it to Him is heartless robbery.

CHARLES HADDON SPURGEON

March 11

Bear ye one another's burdens, and so fulfil the law of Christ.

GALATIANS 6:2 KJV

Have you learned the beautiful art of letting God take care of you, and giving all your thought and strength to pray for others and for the kingdom of God? It will relieve you of a thousand cares. It will lift you up into a noble and lofty sphere, and teach you to live and love like God. Lord save us from our selfish prayers and give us the faith that worketh by love, and the heart of Christ for a perishing world.

A. B. SIMPSON

Pray About It: If we've been in the habit of putting our own needs at the top of our prayer lists, today let's change that. As a matter of intercession and discipline, today, pray not for yourself at all but only for others.

God will remember your needs.

Believers are one body, and ought to pray, not so much for the welfare of their own church or society, but, first of all, for all the saints. This large, unselfish love is the proof that Christ's Spirit and Love is teaching them to pray. Pray first for all and then for the believers around you.

ANDREW MURRAY

March 12

The LORD is far from the wicked but he hears the prayer of the righteous.

PROVERBS 15:29

Oftentimes when we come to God in prayer, we don't feel like praying. What shall we do when this happens? Stop praying until we do feel like it? Not at all. When we feel least like praying is the time when we most need to pray.

We should wait quietly before God and tell Him how cold and prayerless our hearts are, and look up to Him and trust Him and expect Him to send the Holy Spirit to warm our hearts and draw them out in prayer.

It will not be long before the glow of the Spirit's presence will fill our hearts.

R. A. TORREY

Pray About It: If the truth were known, most of the men and women of faith have struggled with prayer. They've not often felt the Spirit of God magnetically pull them to prayer. Rather it's usually *as they pray* that God meets them and thus they continue in prayer.

We depend entirely too much on our feelings as a test of our prayers. We pray if we feel like it, but if something better comes along, our feelings for prayer wane. Feelings can also tempt us to judge God's ability to hear us by how we feel as we pray. Such notions are purely man-centered, not God-centered.

When we pray, God has promised to hear us. That promise is our guarantee of His attention. Today as we pray, rest in the certainty of God's presence and full ear. If you don't feel like praying, just tell God and leave the rest to Him.

Don't pray when you feel like it. Have an appointment with the Lord and keep it.

CORRIE TEN BOOM

March 13

"[Hannah] . . . prayed unto the LORD, and wept sore . . . she spake in her heart."

1 SAMUEL 1:10, 13 KJV

To conduct real business at the mercy-seat of God, give me a homemade prayer, a prayer that comes out of the depths of my heart, not because I invented it, but because God the Holy Ghost put it there, and gave it such living force that I could not help letting it out.

Though your words are broken, and your sentences disconnected, if your desires are earnest, if they are like coals of juniper, burning with a vehement flame, God will not mind how they find expression.

If you have no words, perhaps you will pray better without them than with them. There are prayers that break the backs of words; they are too heavy for any human language to carry.

CHARLES HADDON SPURGEON

Pray About It: Have you ever been desperate for God? I mean *desperate?* So desperate you cried to God without thinking about your words. All you knew was that they were from your heart. And God heard. The prayers we pray best are those with such "living force" that we can't help letting them out.

Our needs come and go, and some days we have no sense of desperation. But God still hears if we remain desperate, even when there is no longer a crisis at hand. At such times, our desperation is simply for *Him*.

> Send a heavy heart up to Christ, it shall be welcome.
> SAMUEL RUTHERFORD

March 14

After they prayed, the place where they were meeting was shaken. And they were all filled with the Holy Spirit and spoke the word of God boldly.

ACTS 4:31

Give me one hundred preachers who fear nothing but sin and desire nothing but God, and I care not a straw whether they be clergymen or laymen; such alone will shake the gates of hell and set up the kingdom of heaven on earth. God does nothing but in answer to prayer.

Pray About It: As Christians we have a calling. We are to "shake the gates of hell" through our prayer and to further God's kingdom on earth. Both of these are done through prayer and the resulting action that follows prayer. For when these violent prayers are heard and answered by God, there comes a parting of the waters, a way for action to take place. It happens all the time. Man prays, God moves, then man moves.

Prayers and pains through faith in Jesus Christ will do anything!

JOHN ELIOT

March 15

These words spake Jesus, and lifted up his eyes to heaven.

JOHN 17:1 KJV

The Son of God came so truly down from Heaven to live among the sons of men, that He lifted up His eyes when He prayed to His Father, just as we ourselves do.

Though He knew that the kingdom of God was within Him, and not in the skies above Him, yet like us, He lifted up His eyes when He prayed. He was in all points made like unto His brethren, and in no point more so than in this point of prayer.

It is built deep into our nature, as we are children of Almighty God, that we are to lift our eyes and look up when we pray. And the Son of God took on our human nature, and prayed as we pray, kneeling down and looking up, falling down and lifting up strong crying and tears.

ALEXANDER WHYTE

Pray About It: We may start our prayers with heads bowed, but before long the magnet of heaven pulls our eyes and our hearts upward.

Today as you pray, look up and praise Him. Look up and be thankful. Look up as Jesus did.

Do everything for God, uniting yourself to Him by a mere upward glance or by the overflowing of your heart towards Him. Never be in a hurry. Do everything quietly and calmly. Don't lose your inner peace for anything whatsoever, even if your whole world seems upset.

FRANCIS DE SALES

March 16

The LORD liveth; and blessed be my rock; and let the God of my salvation be exalted.

PSALM 18:46 KJV

No one who has ever known what it's like to come to God in earnest wrestling about some definite matter, and then receive the answer, can do other than to recognize the blessedness of having to do with the *living* God.

H. A. IRONSIDE

Pray About It: Every generation or so, some theologian with many letters after his name will announce that God is dead. For him, perhaps so. But for those who have prayed and prevailed, the evidence is clear: *Our God lives.*

As you pray remember that God is *alive,* as surely as you are alive. He is the giver and sustainer of all life and He lives to love us.

Meet today with the living God.

The best of all is, God is with us.

JOHN WESLEY

March 17

Apart from me you can do nothing.

JOHN 15:5

Let no one expect to have mastery of his flesh without going, again and again, in his weakness to the Lord for strength. Nor will prayer with others or conversing with the brethren make up for secret prayer.

GEORGE MUELLER

Pray About It: The most successful pray-ers are those who know their own inward weakness. Without God, they have no strength. They know too that the flesh loves to talk to others about our problems, rather than pray. We've all seen this when we've gone to meetings where we ended up talking more than praying. It takes an emptying of self and a total reliance on God to hide oneself away from the brethren and to prevail over our flesh through prayer.

Nothing today will benefit your struggling with the flesh more than spending time with God.

Prayer—secret, fervent, believing prayer—lies at the root of all personal godliness.

WILLIAM CAREY

March 18

These were all commended for their faith, yet none of them received what had been promised. God had planned something better for us so that only together with us would they be made perfect. Therefore, since we are surrounded by such a great cloud of witnesses, let us throw off everything that hinders and the sin that so easily entangles, and let us run with perseverance the race marked out for us.

HEBREWS 11:39 – 12:1

In the eleventh chapter of Hebrews we have a long list of benefits which faith brings to its possessors: justification, deliverance, fruitfulness, endurance, victory over enemies, courage, strength, and even resurrection from the dead. And everything that is attributed to faith might, with equal truth, be attributed to prayer, for faith and true prayer are like two sides of the same coin. They are inseparable.

Men may, and often do, pray without faith (though this is not true prayer), but it is not thinkable that men should have faith and not pray. The biblical formula is "the prayer of faith." Prayer and faith are here bound together by the little preposition *of*, and what God hath joined together, let not man put asunder. Faith is only genuine as it eventuates into prayer.

A. W. TOZER

Pray About It: Prayer and faith are twins that leapfrog us on toward God's will. Prayer begets faith. Faith begets prayer. And thus it goes. If your faith is small, pray. If your prayers are feeble, have faith. The men and women of Hebrews 11 are clouds of witnesses who bear testimony that faith works. They weren't superhuman: They were just like us. Their virtue was that they knew God and believed Him. You too can have that kind of faith, and maybe someday your name may be on God's honor roll of faith.

The possibilities of prayer are the possibilities of faith. Prayer and faith are Siamese twins. One heart animates them both. Faith is always praying. Prayer is always believing.

E. M. BOUNDS

March 19

You are the God who performs miracles;
you display your power among the peoples.

PSALM 77:14

Our gospel belongs to the miraculous. It cannot be maintained but by the supernatural. Take the supernatural out of our holy religion, and its life and power are gone, and it degenerates into a mere mode of morals. The miraculous is divine power. Prayer has in it this same power. Prayer brings this divine power into the ranks of men and puts it to work. Prayer brings into the affairs of earth a supernatural element. Our gospel when truly presented is the power of God.

E. M. BOUNDS

Pray About It: The gospel is supernatural, both in its origin and in its implementation in our lives. Anything relating to God is supernatural. And as we pray, let's remember that no matter how the answer seems to come, whether through miraculous or through natural means, the source of every answered prayer is always supernatural.

The Age of Miracles is forever here!

THOMAS CARLYLE

March 20

Call upon me in the day of trouble;
I will deliver you, and you will honor me.

PSALM 50:15

A prayer for ourselves isn't necessarily a selfish prayer. We may pray for something for ourselves in order that God may be glorified through our receiving the answer. If we could pray more for ourselves, God would be more glorified in us, and we would be a greater blessing to others.

It was well for the world that Jesus spent so much time in prayer for Himself. If we would be fit to pray for others we must spend much time in prayer for ourselves. It is a bad sign when one is always praying for others and never for himself. He is not like his master.

R. A. Torrey

Pray About It: A few days ago we prayed *only* for others. No prayers for self were offered. Today, take time out to pray for yourself. What are your needs? What are your wants? How can God be glorified by blessing you?

Most of our prayers will still be for others, but God knows we too are hungry. Prayers for self don't have to be selfish. Prayer for strength, wisdom, finances, daily bread, mercy, and much more are all legitimate requests.

Today, be bold in asking for yourself. Tell Him exactly what you need. He will hear.

> There is no thought, feeling, yearning, or desire, however low, trifling or vulgar we may deem it, which, if it affects our real interest or happiness, we may not lay before God and be sure of His sympathy. God's nature is such that our often coming does not tire Him. The whole burden of the whole life of every Christian may be rolled on to God and not weary Him, though it has wearied the Christian.

Henry Ward Beecher

March 21

See! The winter is past;
  the rains are over and gone.
Flowers appear on the earth;
  the season of singing has come,
the cooing of doves
  is heard in our land.
The fig tree forms its early fruit;
  the blossoming vines spread their fragrance.
Arise, come, my darling;
  my beautiful one, come with me.

SONG OF SONGS 2:11–13

Lord, end my winter, and let my spring begin. I cannot with all my longings raise my soul out of her death and dullness, but all things are possible with thee.

I need heavenly influences, the clear shinings of thy love, the beams of thy grace, the light of thy countenance; these are the Pleiades to me. I suffer much from sin and temptation, these are my wintry signs, my terrible Orion. Lord, work wonder in me, and for me.

CHARLES HADDON SPURGEON

Pray About It: Spring has arrived. Winter is behind us. Look for the new life of God in nature. Look for His new life in your spirit. We all need the "clear shinings" of His love and the "beams" of His grace.

Welcome spring today with joy to the Father of all seasons. Let the beginning of spring remind you of His resurrection power.

Nature is God's greatest evangelist.

JONATHAN EDWARDS

March 22

And now shall I die for thirst?

JUDGES 15:18 KJV

God's springs burst out in unlikely spots. He is never at a loss. If there is no natural spring, He can create one. If all around, the mighty rocks reflect the sultry heat, and our spirit seems on the point of exhaustion, then in the wilderness He will cause streams to break out. Be of good courage, fainting warrior! The God who made you and has used you knows your frame and knows full well what you need before you even ask.

For your thirst, He can cause the refreshing stream to pour forth from the flinty rocks. He can turn the bitter water sweet for you to drink thereof; He will quench your soul-thirst with the water of life.

F. B. MEYER

Pray About It: That for which you're praying may seem to be the hardest of rocks or the driest of deserts, but wait! It's God's nature to bring forth water from the hard rock and to issue streams in the desert.

Moses saw the water of God as he struck the rock. What do you think he would say about your situation if you could ask him? No doubt he'd urge you to trust and obey. God will come through.

Make us, O blessed Master, strong in heart, full of courage, fearless of danger, holding pain and danger cheap when they lie in the path of duty. May we be strengthened with all might by Thy Spirit in our hearts.

F. B. Meyer

March 23

In all my prayers for all of you, I always pray with joy.

Philippians 1:4

Do let us believe that God's call to much prayer need not be a burden and cause of continual self-condemnation. He means it to be a joy! He can make it an inspiration, giving us strength for all our work, and bringing down His power to work through us in our fellowmen.

Andrew Murray

Pray About It: Sometimes we miss our prayer time. We get busy and go about our day and our prayers are unsaid. It happens. But when it happens, God *never* condemns us nor inflicts guilt on us. We do that ourselves. Prayer is the joyous burden and is meant to add to our lives, not subtract. If you've missed days of praying and have felt condemned, then you must change your thinking.

Pray on in joy and forget your failures. God does.

> Faith cancels all that is past, and there is no condemnation to thee.
>
> John Wesley

March 24

Let your moderation be known unto all men.

Philippians 4:5 kjv

Let our speech and our prayers be under discipline, observing quietness and modesty. Let us consider that we are standing in God's sight. We must please the divine eyes both with the habit of body and with the measure of voice. For as it is characteristic of a shameless man to be noisy with his cries, so, on the other hand, it is fitting to the modest man to pray with moderate petitions.

Cyprian of Carthage

But we more commend our prayers to God, when we pray with modesty and humility. The sounds of our voice likewise should be subdued; else, if we are to be heard for our noise, how large windpipes should we need!

TERTULLIAN

Pray About It: It's always wise to listen to our elders. In this case, Cyprian (200–258) and Tertullian (160–225) were early church fathers. They knew about prayer. And in their exhortation, they encourage discipline, modesty, and moderation.

God isn't hard-of-hearing. Our voices can reach to heaven just fine without resorting to noise. We can pray in an orderly fashion, not hit-or-miss at random. A loud, undisciplined pray-er will find disorder in the rest of his life as well.

Today, respect the order of prayer that was used by the early church. Pray with modesty and humility.

March 25

One thing I know, that whereas I was blind, now I see.

JOHN 9:25 KJV

The more time we spend on our knees in communion with God, the better we shall comprehend His wonderful nature.

ELIZABETH PRENTISS

Pray About It: Spiritual truth can only be understood by spiritual people. That's why the gospel is foolishness to those who don't know God. As we puzzle over the great mystery of God and His attributes, we can begin to see how it all fits together as we pray.

Those who pray to God know Him better than those who don't. And as they pray, what used to be confusing or unknowable about God becomes a secret knowledge between them and their God.

As you pray, consider that you're getting to know more about your heavenly Father than ever before.

Animated, comforted, invigorated with hope and joy, the Christian draws nearer and nearer to God and beholds Him in clearer and brighter view.

TIMOTHY DWIGHT

March 26

I tell you the truth, if you have faith as small as a mustard seed, you can say to this mountain, "Move from here to there" and it will move. Nothing will be impossible for you.

MATTHEW 17:20

The prayer of the feeblest saint who lives in the Spirit and keeps right with God is a terror to Satan. The very powers of darkness are paralyzed by prayer; no spiritualistic séance can succeed in the presence of a humble praying saint. No wonder Satan tries to keep our minds fussy in active work till we cannot think in prayer.

OSWALD CHAMBERS

Pray About It: No matter how weak you think you are, you have the power to paralyze Satan. The attacks that he has made on you can be reversed. If your past has been cursed, your future can be blessed. Why? Because the power to paralyze Satan is unleashed as we lean hard on God. He has given us authority over the enemy and the way we exercise that authority is through prayer. Satan thus works day and night to keep us away from prayer. He will even try to convince us that our Christian work will suffer if we pull away to pray.

Today, realize your power in Christ. Stand firm against the enemy. Allow him no ground.

If we would therefore behave like good soldiers of Jesus Christ, we must be always upon our guard, and never pretend to lay down our spiritual weapons of prayer and watching, till our warfare is accomplished by death; for if we do, our spiritual enemy will quickly prevail against us.

GEORGE WHITEFIELD

March 27

If ye abide in me, and my words abide in you, ye shall ask what ye will, and it shall be done unto you.

JOHN 15:7

Believer, abide in Christ, for there is the school of prayer—mighty, effectual, answer-bringing prayer. Abide in Him, and you shall learn what to so many is a mystery: That the secret of the prayer of faith is the life of faith—the life that abides in Christ alone.

ANDREW MURRAY

Pray About It: The picture Jesus gave to us describing how to abide was that of a vine and a branch. The latter has no life in itself. Its life is dependent on the vine upon which it feeds. So too the believer has no life in himself, but must feed on Christ. In Him is the power for prayer. The kind of power that brings answers.

Today as you pray, remember to abide in Him.

It is as though He were to say, "Children, I am leaving you: There are many things I desire for you, many commands to utter, many cautions, many lessons; but I am content to leave all unsaid, if only you will remember this one all-inclusive bidding—Abide in Me, remain in Me; stay where God has put you; deepen, emphasize, intensify the union already existing between you and Me. From me is your fruit found. Without Me you can do nothing. Abide in Me, and I in you. Grow up into Me in all things, which am the Head; rooted and built in Me, and established by your faith, even as you were taught."

F. B. MEYER

March 28

According to the riches of his glory, to be strengthened with might by his Spirit in the inner man; That Christ may dwell in your hearts by faith.

EPHESIANS 3:16–17 KJV

An old friend of mine used to startle and amuse and challenge me by crying out: "All Heaven is free plunder to faith!" And in my early-morning prayer times I began to feel that it was so.

And now that prayer had brought me into God's treasure-house, I continued to examine, and I found Paul praying for the Ephesians that God would grant "according to the riches of His glory, to be strengthened with might by His Spirit in the inner man; that Christ may dwell in your hearts by faith." And that was just what I felt God was doing for me. I felt no longer dull and depressed, but fully alive toward God and man, and ready for service or suffering or sacrifice.

And then I read that this was all wrought, not by some new, strange power which I had not known before, but "according to the power that worketh in us"—the power that convicted me and brought me to Jesus and pardoned my sins and led me on into "the holy of holies," into the blessing of a clean heart and a life hid with Christ in God.

And what is that power? The same power that wrought in Jesus when God "raised Him from the dead, and set Him at His own right hand in the heavenly places, far above all principality, and power, and might, and dominion, and every name that is named, not only in this world, but also in that which is to come" (Eph. 1:20, 21). Matchless, exhaustless power! And this power was working in me!

SAMUEL LOGAN BRENGLE

Pray About It: The secret of living the Christian life is the same secret for successful prayer—living not by our flesh, but by "the power that worketh in us." This is the same power that raised Christ from the dead and will raise us in the day of resurrection. That power lives in us today and is the power through which we pray.

Today, pray in the power of the Spirit. Plunder heaven.

> Who among us has the Spirit of prayer? They are mighty who have this Spirit, and weak who have it not.
>
> J. HUDSON TAYLOR

March 29

He maketh my feet like hinds' *feet*, and setteth me upon my high places.

PSALM 18:33 KJV

On the mountain, torrents of water flow right along, cutting their own courses. But on the plains, canals have to be cut out painfully by men so that the waters may flow.

So among those who live on the heights with God, the Holy Spirit makes His way through of His own accord, whereas those who devote little time to prayer and communion with God, have to organize painfully.

SADHU SUNDAR SINGH

Pray About It: Has your life been one of plowing the canals through which your spiritual life must flow? Then come to the heights where the torrents flow in courses cut by the Spirit. God's good news is an invitation to rest and let the river of God's Spirit wash through us. Set aside your own efforts at prayer. Let Him pray through you.

> You cannot live this life, but Christ can. Christ in us can live this life anywhere and everywhere. He lived it on earth in a home where He was misunderstood and maligned; among people who ridiculed, scoffed, opposed, and finally crucified Him. We, then, do not have to live this life; Christ is willing and able to live it in us.

RUTH PAXSON

March 30

And when he had taken it [the scroll], the four living creatures and the twenty-four elders fell down before the Lamb. Each one had a harp and they were holding golden bowls full of incense, which are the prayers of the saints. And they sang a new song:

"You are worthy to take the scroll
  and to open its seals,
because you were slain,
  and with your blood you purchased men for God
  from every tribe and language and people and nation.
You have made them to be a kingdom and priests
to serve our God,
  and they will reign on the earth."

REVELATION 5:8–10

On the ground of our own goodness we cannot expect to have our prayers answered. But Jesus is worthy, and for His sake we may have our prayers answered. There is nothing too choice, too costly, or too great for God to give Him. He is worthy. He is the spotless, holy Child, who under all circumstances acted according to the mind of God. And if we trust in Him, if we hide in Him, if we put Him forward and ourselves in the background, depend on Him and plead His name, we may expect to have our prayers answered.

GEORGE MUELLER

Pray About It: Never approach God on the grounds of your own righteousness or need. Our access to God is dependent totally on the work of Christ. In Him, and in no other, we have access. There are many religions that practice prayer, but their prayers are largely dependent on their good works or sacrifices for God. As such their prayers are void.

There is no other name by which man may be saved than that of Christ, and there is no other ground upon which we may offer our prayer than that of Christ.

Today, reflect on the worthiness of Christ, both for God's approval and for our adoration.

In the name of my Master, I ask you, *Have you forsaken all your own righteousness?* You have heard that salvation is not of works. Are you completely divorced from your own righteousness and have laid hold on Christ's righteousness? Then . . . look up to heaven, and say, Father, I forsake all for Christ.

ROBERT MURRAY MCCHEYNE

March 31

. . . that all of them may be one, Father, just as you are in me and I am in you. . . .

JOHN 17:21

Many can do nothing but pray, and prayer is perhaps the one thing in which Christians of all denominations can cordially and unreservedly unite and in this we may all be one.

Were the whole body thus animated by one soul, with what pleasure would believers fulfill all their duties as Christians, and with what delight would their ministers attend to their duties as shepherds of God's flock.

WILLIAM CAREY

Pray About It: Although Jesus prayed often, we don't know the content of many of those prayers. However, in John 17, we hear Jesus pray for several things, primarily unity among His people. This is something for which we should continue to pray, because Satan's number one strategy against the church is to create division.

William Carey was one of the pioneer missionaries in the church. He lived a hard, hard life in India. But he was a mighty prayer warrior. His motto was "Expect great things from God. Attempt great things for God."

The first portion of his motto has to do with the way we pray. We should expect that God will give us great answers to prayer. The second part of Carey's motto has to do with action. Having prayed, will we then attempt to do great things for God, trusting Him to lead the way? Even the hard way that Carey was called to follow?

It may be hard for us to think that such a motto can apply to us. But it can. Pray today for your expectations of God to increase. Pray in unity with the rest of God's church.

Remember:

Expect great things from God. Attempt great things for God.

WILLIAM CAREY

April 1

This day is sacred to our Lord. Do not grieve, for the joy of the LORD is your strength.

NEHEMIAH 8:10

Prayer is the nearest approach to God and the highest enjoyment of Him that we are capable of in this life.

WILLIAM LAW

Pray About It: When we think of enjoying God, we often think about the goose-bump emotions that can result in some highly charged worship services. But to Christians who know better, emotions are never a measurement of the spiritual life. The true enjoyment of God is deeper than our emotions and is only known by those who meet God in prayer.

Even a brief time of enjoying God is priceless and far more sustaining than all the goose-bumps you can muster.

Today is an opportunity for you to enjoy your God. And by the way, He will enjoy you too.

A calm hour with God is worth a whole lifetime with man.

ROBERT MURRAY MCCHEYNE

April 2

"Present your case," says the Lord. "Bring forth your strong reasons," says the King of Jacob.

ISAIAH 41:21 NKJV

It is possible that some who read these words may have a complaint against God. A controversy of long standing has come between your soul and His grace. If you were to utter the word that is trembling on your lips, you would say to him, "Why hast Thou dealt thus with me?" Then dare to say, with reverence and with boldness, all that is in your heart. Carry your grievance into the light of His countenance; charge your complaint home. Then listen to His answer. For surely, in gentleness and truth, He will clear Himself of the charge of unkindness that you bring against Him. And in His light you shall see light. But, remember, that this is a private matter between you and your Lord, and you must not defame Him to any one.

DAVID MACINTYRE

Pray About It: Honesty with God is essential in the life of a pray-er. God knows your anger, your confusion, your questions about how He's arranged the circumstances of your life. Now is the time to open up to God and spread your case before Him. *He can take it, my friend.* God will listen to all you have to say—the bad and the good.

David, a man after God's heart, questioned God's actions. Jesus asked why His Father had forsaken Him. Jonah was bitter when God called him to preach to Nineveh. Job, the most righteous man in the land, was devastated by his losses. The list goes on. Men and women who love God are often put through trials that try their very souls. God knows, watches, and understands. It's no sin to lay out your case before God.

Pray from your heart—no matter what's there.

Honest dealing becomes us, when we kneel in His pure presence.

DAVID MACINTYRE

April 3

Follow my example, as I follow the example of Christ.

1 CORINTHIANS 11:1

Come near to the holy men and women of the past and you will soon feel the heat of their desire after God. They mourned for Him, they prayed and wrestled and sought for Him day and night, in season and out, and when they had found Him, the finding was all the sweeter for the long seeking.

A. W. TOZER

Pray About It: To be an effective pray-er is to join a long list of holy men and women of the past who have set a challenging pace as they pushed hard after God.

Today as you pray, remember that you're a link in a two-thousand-year-old prayer chain. I like to think of it as an orchestra in which all Christians past and present have played and are playing the same beautiful music by their prayers and praises. The harmony we have with our predecessors and with each other keeps the melody going strong.

You can make a difference for the kingdom of God as you play your part, just as all who have gone before you, have done and those who will come after us as well.

Has it ever occurred to you that one hundred pianos all tuned to the same fork are automatically tuned to each other? They are of one accord by being tuned, not to each other, but to another standard to which each one must individually bow. So one hundred worshippers meeting together, each one looking away to Christ, are in heart nearer to each other than they could possibly be were they to become "unity" conscious and turn their eyes away from God to strive for closer fellowship.

A. W. Tozer

April 4

"Do not come any closer," God said. "Take off your sandals, for the place where you are standing is holy ground."

Exodus 3:5

Here is the secret of a life of prayer: Take time in the inner chamber to bow down and worship; and wait on Him until He unveils Himself, and takes possession of you, and goes out with you to show how a man can live and walk in abiding fellowship with an unseen Lord.

Andrew Murray

Pray About It: Begin your prayer time with worship. It sets the tone for all that will follow. The unseen Lord will inhabit the praises of His pray-ers and you will be standing on holy ground. Allow the Lord to thus take possession of you as you pray.

When you go on about the day's business, you will be confident and His Spirit will live through you. Others will see and be blessed.

> Worship should never be pursued as a means to achieving something other than worship. Worship is never a step on our way up to any other experience. It is not a door through which we pass to get anywhere. It is the end point, the goal.
>
> JOHN PIPER

April 5

Be careful, or your hearts will be weighed down with dissipation, drunkenness and the anxieties of life, and that day will close on you unexpectedly like a trap. For it will come upon all those who live on the face of the whole earth. Be always on the watch, and pray that you may be able to escape all that is about to happen, and that you may be able to stand before the Son of Man.

LUKE 21:34–36

According to this passage there is only one way in which we can be prepared for the coming of the Lord when He appears, that is, through much prayer.

The coming again of Jesus Christ is a subject that is awakening much interest and much discussion in our day, but it's one thing to be interested in the Lord's return, to read books about it, and to talk with others about it, and quite another thing to be prepared for it.

We live in an atmosphere that has a constant tendency to unfit us for Christ's coming. The world tends to draw us down by its gratifications and by its cares.

There is only one way by which we can rise triumphant above these things—by constant watching unto prayer. The Christian who spends little time in prayer, who is not steadfast and constant in prayer, will not be ready for the Lord when He comes. But we may be ready. How?

Pray! Pray! Pray!

R. A. Torrey

Pray About It: Do you believe in the soon return of Christ? Are you ready? The way to readiness is through prayer. It may be interesting to read books and watch movies about what the end times will be like, but the bottom line isn't knowledge of His coming, it's preparedness.

Before His return, there will be an increase in evil all around us. We can see it happening now. Sadly, many Christians are overtaken by the wickedness that is being unleashed. But through prayer, we can stand firm. Prayerfulness is like the virgins who had oil in their lamps when the bridegroom came. Prayerlessness is to be without oil.

Today, fill your lamp to the brim with oil of the Holy Spirit. Be ready. Be prayed up.

The Lord is near. He comes softly while the virgins slumber.

ANDREW A. BONAR

April 6

Call unto me, and I will answer thee, and show thee great and mighty things, which thou knowest not.

JEREMIAH 33:3 KJV

God explicitly says, "Call unto me, and I will answer." There are no limitations, no hedges, no hindrances in the way of God fulfilling the promise. His word is at stake. God solemnly engages to answer prayer. Man is to look for the answer and be inspired by the expectation of the answer. God, who cannot lie, is bound to answer. He has voluntarily placed Himself under obligation to answer the prayer of him who truly prays.

E. M. BOUNDS

Pray About It: God has gone out on a limb for us—and gladly so. He wants us to come to Him and ask, so in His answering, He proves Himself to us again and again.

Call to Him today and He will answer. Ask Him what you will. His reputation is at stake.

Whether we like it or not, asking is the rule of the Kingdom.

CHARLES HADDON SPURGEON

April 7

The harvest is plentiful, but the workers are few. Ask the Lord of the harvest, therefore, to send out workers into his harvest field.

LUKE 10:2

Prayer puts one in touch with a planet. I can as really be touching hearts for God in far away India or China through prayer as though I were there. A man may go aside today, and shut his door, and as really spend a half hour in India for God as though he were there in person.

S. D. GORDON

Pray About It: Where might God send you today as you pray? There are needs all around the globe — maybe you're aware of some of them. There is hunger, war, paganism, disease, all of which God hates. Pray for missionaries around the world, support them with your money — and be willing to go yourself if He should so lead.

Lord, awaken a sleeping church. Help us to do what we could if we only cared. Help us, in this generation, to obey Thy command to preach the gospel to every creature.

CHARLES E. COWMAN

April 8

He brought me to the banqueting house, and his banner over me was love.

SONG OF SOLOMON 2:4 KJV

Christ is not only a remedy for your weariness and trouble, but He will give you an abundance of the contrary: joy and delight. They who come to Christ, do not only come to a resting place after they have been wandering in a wilderness, but they come to a banqueting house where they may rest, and where they may feast. They may cease from their former troubles and toils, and they may enter upon a course of delights and spiritual joys.

JONATHAN EDWARDS

Pray About It: Today is the day to leave all your troubles *outside* your prayer closet. You've been invited to a banquet where you will find your fill of joy and feasting. Best of all, you will find rest. Close the door to the wilderness. Eat and drink your fill at the banqueting table prepared for you.

This is the hour of banquet and song;
This is the Heavenly table spread for me;
Here let me feast, and feasting still prolong
The brief, bright hour of fellowship with Thee.

HORATIUS BONAR

April 9

Why are you downcast, O my soul?
   Why so disturbed within me?
Put your hope in God,
   for I will yet praise him,
   my Savior and my God.

PSALM 42:5–6

However great may be the temptation, if we know how to use the weapon of prayer well we shall come off as conquerors at last, for prayer is more powerful than all the devils. He who is attacked by the spirits of darkness needs only to apply himself vigorously to prayer and he will beat them back with great success.

BERNARD OF CLAIRVAUX

Pray About It: The best antidote to spiritual depression is prayer. When we enter into communion with God, despair and hopelessness must go. Never fear the darkness. Overcome it through the power of prayer. Commune with the Lord Jesus who, though a "man of sorrows," was also "anointed with gladness more than [His] companions," (Hebrews 1:9). Truly the Christian's strength is the *joy* of the Lord. Where His joy rests, hopelessness can't remain.

If you're one of those blessed with a sunny temperament, remember to pray for those who battle a seeming perpetual sadness.

If you have no joy in your religion, there's a leak in your Christianity somewhere.

WILLIAM A. "BILLY" SUNDAY

April 10

Do not love the world or anything in the world. If anyone loves the world, the love of the Father is not in him. For everything in the world—the cravings of sinful man, the lust of his eyes and the boasting of what he has and does—comes not from the Father but from the world.

1 JOHN 2:15–16

Friends, it seems to me that I can see two hands outstretched to grip the throat of Christians and to strangle prayer. One is the hot, feverish, restless hand of worldliness; the other the cold, nervous hand of ceaseless activity. Has either gripped your throat and all but stopped your prayer?

RUTH PAXSON

Pray About It: We can be one with Christ or one with the world, but we cannot be one with both. If the love of the world is clutching at your throat, it will surely strangle your prayer life.

Ceaseless activity, even good activity in the name of Christ, will also thwart our prayerfulness. Better to step aside from worldliness and busyness and retain our prayer life than to lose the latter and be devoid of the Spirit.

Watch today for those two outstretched hands that are reaching for your throat. Refuse their pull and stay close to God.

God cannot hear the prayers on our lips often because the desires of our heart after the world cry out to Him much more strongly and loudly than our desires for Him.

ANDREW MURRAY

April 11

Come to me, all you who are weary and burdened, and I will give you rest. Take my yoke upon you and learn from me, for I am gentle and humble in heart, and you will find rest for your souls. For my yoke is easy and my burden is light.

MATTHEW 11:28–30

To every toiling, heavy-laden sinner, Jesus says, "Come to me and rest." But there are also many toiling, heavy-laden believers. For them this same invitation is offered. Note well the words of Jesus, if you are heavy-laden with your service, the message isn't to "labor on," as perhaps you imagine. On the contrary, it is to stop, turn back and, "Come to me and rest." Never, never did Christ send a heavy-laden one to work; never, never did he send a hungry one, a weary one, a sick or sorrowing one, away on any service. For such the Bible only says, "Come, come, come."

J. HUDSON TAYLOR

Pray About It: When we bear a heavy load, we need to hear the invitation to "come and rest." The burdens that weigh you down aren't from God, for His burden is light—so says Jesus. To God, *you* are more important than the work He's given you. Today, come to Him and exchange your heavy load for His featherweight burden.

The worker is far more important to our Lord than the work.

MRS. CHARLES E. COWMAN

April 12

Some trust in chariots and some in horses,
   but we trust in the name of the LORD our God.
They are brought to their knees and fall,
   but we rise up and stand firm.

PSALM 20:7–8

How shall we pray? In our Lord's day men often stood to pray. . . . When we are holding adoring and loving communion with the Lord God Almighty, it seems appropriate either to kneel or to stand reverently before Him. Especially do I urge a commitment of oneself to God the very first thing in the morning. It is a real help just to stand before our adorable Lord in the stillness of that early hour and say—at the very least—"Glory be to the Father and to the Son and to the Holy Ghost."

A. E. RICHARDSON

As regards praying aloud, I rarely allow myself to pray silently in secret. I find the wanderings of the mind very much limited and controlled by even the faintest audible vocalizing of my thoughts.

As regards to attitude, I seldom venture to kneel at prayer in secret. At night it leads almost invariably, and very speedily to sleeping on my knees, and even in the morning, my concentration of mind and heart are usually quickened by a reverent standing before the visible Lord and Master, or by walking up and down either indoors or, as I love to do when possible, in the open air.

H. C. G. MOULE

Pray About It: We may be used to kneeling in prayer or perhaps just sitting in a chair or at a desk, but standing in prayer is a position used often in the Bible.

Of course God hears us in any position, but sometimes it helps to stand as we pray—or even to pace a bit. Today, as you pray, start in any position you wish, but at some point stand up, look up, and offer your prayers to God.

Stand before Him in awe.

April 13

Do not be afraid, Daniel. Since the first day that you set your mind to gain understanding and to humble yourself before your God, your words were heard, and I have come in response to them. But the prince of the Persian kingdom resisted me twenty-one days. Then Michael, one of the chief princes, came to help me, because I was detained there with the king of Persia.

DANIEL 10:12–13

What mystery is here! An angel was sent from the throne of God in immediate answer to the prophet's prayer, but for 21 days he couldn't reach Daniel! Who could believe this if it were not so plainly written in the Word of God?

For three weeks this angel-messenger had been in conflict with that particular "world-ruler of this darkness" who was evidently appointed by Satan to control, if possible, the king of Persia and prevent the carrying out of God's plan.

The mystery deepens as we learn that Michael the archangel had to come to assist the first messenger, before the evil angel was defeated. May we not learn from this why answers to many of our prayers seem to be long delayed? May it not be that God answered at once, but there may be something to be settled, to us unseen, before the answer can reach us?

Let us not then be discouraged, nor accuse God of turning a deaf ear to our agonized cry. The answer may already be on the way, but Satan and his evil hosts are battling against it. But God is faithful, and in His due time He will see that the prayer we have made in accordance with His will is wonderfully answered to His praise and glory and to our eternal blessing.

H. A. Ironside

Pray About It: Has it occurred to you that the answer for which you continue to pray may already be on its way? God has heard and attended to it. Don't be discouraged by the delay. God is faithful. Keep watching expectantly.

Today, don't ask God. Thank Him for the answer that's already on the way. Whenever you think of that request, just say, "Thank You, God, that You've heard my prayer and that the answer is on the way!"

No breath of true prayer is lost. The longer it waits, the larger it becomes.

A. B. Simpson

April 14

Greater love has no one than this, that he lay down his life for his friends. You are my friends if you do what I command.

JOHN 15:13–14

When we love an earthly friend, we aren't satisfied with only a few minutes' conversation at a time; nor can we come to know that person's true character or appreciate the deeper parts of one's nature, even if those passing words should occur every few minutes. Neither can we know God in this way.

How often we say of our earthly friends, "How I long to have a good, long, quiet talk with you!" And shall we not have the same with our heavenly Friend, so that we may really get to know Him?

HANNAH WHITALL SMITH

Pray About It: God is our best friend. We are His dear companions. And when two good friends get together for fellowship, the time spent together is rich with love, sharing, and refreshment. Let your time today be like that. Know that you're spending time with the One who knows you the best and loves you the most.

God alone is a thousand companions. He alone is a world of friends. That Christian never knew what it was to be familiar with God, who complains of the want of friends while God is with him.

THOMAS À KEMPIS

April 15

"Have faith in God," Jesus answered.

MARK 11:22

Faith says, "If 'impossible' is the only objection, it can be done!"

Faith brings God into the scene, and therefore it knows absolutely nothing of difficulties—it laughs at impossibilities.

In the judgment of faith, God is the grand answer to every question—the grand solution of every difficulty. It refers all to Him; and hence it matters not in the least to faith whether the need be $600,000 or $600,000,000. No matter, it knows that God is all-sufficient. It finds all its resources in Him.

Unbelief says, "How can such and such things be?" It is full of "Hows"; but faith has one great answer to ten thousand "hows," and that answer is—God.

C. H. MACKINTOSH

Pray About It: Why is it harder to have faith that God can (or will) answer our *impossibilities* rather than our *possibilities?* We pray for a clear day tomorrow for our outing, knowing that no rain is expected. Faith in such a case is easy. But if we have a more urgent need, such as finances, health, a wayward child, an unbelieving spouse, we find it harder to believe. It's no harder for God to answer the tough prayers than the easy ones. The problem is in our limited thinking. With God nothing shall be impossible.

Faith sees the invisible, believes the unbelievable, and receives the impossible.

CORRIE TEN BOOM

April 16

Is anything too hard for the LORD?

GENESIS 18:14 KJV

I have heard this verse used as a plea in asking for something very much desired which appeared to be for the glory of God. But I think we sometimes forget that the question refers to something God had said was to happen. It was not that Abraham said, "Lord, do such and such things for me. Surely they would be for Thy glory? Is anything too hard for the Lord?" but that God Himself was speaking of something which He had appointed to be — a son born to Abraham and Sarah in their old age.

Again and again I have been saved from disappointment in prayer by remembering this.

AMY CARMICHAEL

Pray About It: Some of the things we most ardently ask for are not for our good, as God well knows. But we claim it anyway, offering what we call faith, but what God might call wishful thinking or presumption. God is not Santa Claus. He will give what He has promised, but He will not give what you have mistakenly assumed you could have merely because you wanted it and found a verse to substantiate your desire.

No, God loves you too much. He would no more grant a foolish request than you would give a razor blade to a toddler who asked for it.

What you may wish to receive, but would misuse, God in His mercy refuses to bestow. Nay, more, if a Christian asks for something that would, if answered, only prove injurious, it's better that God would withhold it in His kindness, rather than grant it in His anger.

Augustine

April 17

Lord, save us: we perish.

Matthew 8:25 KJV

Many words in our prayer come from our flesh. Our prayer may be long-drawn-out with many words which are not real or effective. Frequently, in our time of prayer we circle around the world several times, using up time and energy without obtaining any answer to real prayer. Though you have prayed much, your prayer will not be answered nor will it be effective. You simply expend your time and strength ill-advisedly. Prayer need not be too long. There is no necessity to insert many speeches into it. Be careful lest you have too much argument in your prayer. We need only to present our heart desire before God. That alone is enough.

Watchman Nee

Pray About It: Today, let your words of prayer be few. Use only the words that come directly from your heart aimed squarely at the heart of God. God can answer short prayers as easily as long ones. "Lord, save us: we perish" was a pretty short prayer, but it caused Jesus to rebuke the storm that threatened the disciples.

> True prayer is measured by weight, not by length. A single groan before God may have more fullness of prayer in it than a fine oration of great length.
>
> CHARLES HADDON SPURGEON

April 18

Do not be anxious about anything, but in everything, by prayer and petition, with thanksgiving, present your requests to God. And the peace of God, which transcends all understanding, will guard your hearts and your minds in Christ Jesus.

PHILIPPIANS 4:6–7

Cultivate a holy calm as a preparation for private prayer. As a lake while it is ruffled, can not reflect the over-arching heavens; so your heart while disturbed and distracted, can not reflect the face of God. Wait before God until you are at peace.

ARTHUR T. PIERSON

Pray About It: If we rush into God's presence with the cares of the world attached to our hearts, we won't be able to enter God's presence. He is a calm God and responds to us best when we are at peace. Take a minute before you pray and be silent. The old-time Quakers used to call this "centering." It means getting to the place where God has your full attention. For this, there must be calm.

Today, center on God.

> Keep the inward watch, keep a clear soul and a light heart. Mind an inward sense upon doing anything.
>
> WILLIAM PENN

April 19

My expectation is from Him.

PSALM 62:5 NKJV

Every true prayer is not only an acknowledgment of God as the only sufficient One, but it demands an attitude of entire expectation from Him on the part of the pray-er. This is essential if normal relations are to exist between God and man. An answer to prayer, when the expectation is not wholly toward God, would only divert the confidence of the pray-er, and foster a false trust in his mind.

It is necessary for the Christian, therefore, in the interests of his own understanding of God and truth, to come directly to God, acknowledging His omnipotence, and looking to Him as alone sufficient to do the thing for which he is praying.

LEWIS SPERRY CHAFER

Pray About It: Our expectation in prayer must be from Him alone. Don't look to the natural means to your answer, for you may be disappointed. God will work on your behalf when you depend on Him alone.

If the Christian looks for anything from the world, it is a poor expectation indeed. But if he looks to God for the supply of his wants, whether in temporal or spiritual blessings, his expectation will not be a vain one.

CHARLES HADDON SPURGEON

April 20

They overcame him
  by the blood of the Lamb
  and by the word of their testimony;
they did not love their lives so much
  as to shrink from death.

REVELATION 12:11

I am God's wheat. May I be ground by the teeth of the wild beasts until I become the fine wheat bread that is Christ's. My passions are crucified, there is no heat in my flesh. A stream flows murmuring inside me; deep down in me it says: Come to the Father.

IGNATIUS OF ANTIOCH

Pray About It: These are the words of prayer that Ignatius spoke just before his martyrdom in A.D. 107. In the past century there have been more Christian martyrs than in all previous centuries combined. The extreme privilege of dying for faith in Christ is a blessing, not a curse. In America, many young Christians are ridiculed for their faith. Some are killed. At Columbine High School on April 20, 1999, several Christians died after admitting to their faith in Christ.

Such tragedies should serve as wake-up calls to God's people, particularly those who are pray-ers.

We must invest in the next generation of believers by holding them up in prayer and believing God to do great things through them.

Today, pray for our youth. They have temptations that many older Americans never faced. Pray for boldness for our young Christians. Pray with great compassion for our youth who have never heard of Christ. The waning influence of Christianity in our culture has left many empty young men and women spiritually bankrupt. They need Christ desperately.

Also today, pray for the persecuted church around the world. They *covet* your support.

> Pray for the rising generation, who are to come after us. Thing of the young men and young women and children of this age, and pray for all the agencies at work among them; that in associations and societies and unions, in homes and schools, Christ may be honored, and the Holy Spirit get possession of them. Pray for the young of your own neighborhood.
>
> ANDREW MURRAY

> Eternity is in your hands. . . . Change it!
>
> RACHEL JOY SCOTT,
> A YOUNG CHRISTIAN TEENAGER KILLED AT
> COLUMBINE FOR HER FAITH IN CHRIST

April 21

I remember you in my prayers at all times.

ROMANS 1:9–10

Never say you will pray about a thing; pray about it.

OSWALD CHAMBERS

Pray About It: The enemy of our prayers may actually be the lighthearted attitude we sometimes take. How often have we said in passing, "I'll pray for you." Or maybe we've asked others to pray for our need. But do we follow through? Do we really pray much more than a simple bullet prayer to heaven? When we promise to pray for someone, we should consider this as paramount as if we had exchanged a large sum of money. God hates it when prayer, the most powerful weapon He's given us, and the means by which we are to fellowship with Him, is taken lightly by His people.

Prayer is serious. To casually bandy about promises to pray for someone without earnest follow-through undermines our faith.

Take prayer seriously. Today, who have you promised to pray for?

Do it.

Give yourself wholly to God for people, and amid all your work, your heart will be drawn out to people in love, and drawn up to God in dependence and expectation. To a heart thus led by the Holy Spirit, it is possible to pray always and not to faint.

ANDREW MURRAY

April 22

So God created man in his own image,
in the image of God he created him;
male and female he created them.

GENESIS 1:27

Why has God established prayer?

BLAISE PASCAL

Pray About It: Pascal answered his own question by maintaining that God wants to "communicate to His creatures the dignity of causality." In other words, He wants us to enjoy a taste of what it's like to be a creator. By praying for what God puts on our hearts, we actually see something come into being that wasn't there before. Perhaps it's restored health, a mate, a child, a job, or some other such need. By being made in God's image, we, like Him, enjoy watching things happen through our "causality." And although prayer causes God to bring about our answer, we still see how God has given us a part in ushering it into being.

Has God given you something to create through prayer? Perhaps not yet, but maybe soon. Watch and see.

God will either give you what you ask, or something better.

ROBERT MURRAY MCCHEYNE

April 23

Come, let us sing for joy to the LORD;
　　let us shout aloud to the Rock of our salvation.
Let us come before him with thanksgiving
　　and extol him with music and song.

PSALM 95:1−2

The heart must have in it the grace of prayer to sing the praise of God. Spiritual singing is not to be done by musical taste or talent, but by the grace of God in the heart. The conscious presence of God inspires song.

The angels in heaven don't need conductors to lead them, nor do they care for paid choirs to chime in with their heavenly doxologies of praise and worship. They are not dependent on singing schools to teach them the notes and scales of singing. Their singing involuntarily breaks forth from the heart.

God is immediately present in the heavenly assemblies of the angels and the spirits of men made perfect. His glorious presence creates the song, teaches the singing, and impregnates their notes of praise. It is so on earth. God's presence begets singing and thanksgiving, while the absence of God from our congregations is the death of song, or, which amounts to the same, makes the singing lifeless, cold and formal. His conscious presence in our churches would bring back the days of praise and would restore the full chorus of song.

Where grace abounds, song abounds. When God is in the heart, heaven is present and melody is there, and the lips overflow out of the abundance of the heart. This is as true in the private life of the believer as it is so in the congregations of the saints. The decay of singing, the dying down and out of the spirit of praise in song, means the decline of grace in the heart and the absence of God's presence from the people.

The main design of all singing is for God's ear and to attract His attention and to please Him. It is "to the Lord," for His glory and to His honor.

E. M. Bounds

Pray About It: How is your singing voice? No matter how bad you may think it, to God, your voice is beautiful. Singing is a gift God has given us to glorify Him. Our prayer times should often include a song to God. For Luther such songs were especially important when he couldn't pray.

But don't wait until then. Sing today a new song unto our God. Sing out boldly. No one hears but God.

When I cannot pray, I always sing.

Martin Luther

April 24

Teach us to number our days aright,
that we may gain a heart of wisdom.

Psalms 90:12

Every Christian's life is full of days to be remembered. Let them be remembered with deliberation and resolution and determination. Get alone and make a review of your past life and at the same time consider your future and your approaching day of death.

Such thinking will turn all of the evil of your past life to good and will take all the sting out of death. Pray with deliberation and see!

ALEXANDER WHYTE

Pray About It: God has numbered the days of every Christian. Your past is known by God, your present situation is under His care, and your future, including your day of departure from this earth, is all arranged by God.

God doesn't want us to take our days for granted. We must appreciate our past, our present, and our future. Take some time today and reflect on your life. Consider how God brought you to where you are today, how He saved you, how He touched you, how He cares for you. The result should be a grateful heart and awe at what God has done.

His faithfulness to you in the past should give you courage for the future.

> Our days are numbered: let us spare
> Our anxious hearts a needless care:
> 'Tis thine to number our days;
> 'Tis ours to give them to Thy praise.

MADAME GUYON

April 25

You cast off fear, And restrain prayer before God.

JOB 15:4 KJV

He that leaves off prayer leaves off the fear of God. A man that leaves off prayer is capable of any wickedness. When Saul had given up inquiring of God he went to the witch of Endor.

THOMAS WATSON

Pray About It: Do you think that you're not capable of turning away from God? A prayerless Christian can very easily be turned to error. A simple reading of the horoscope in the newspaper or idle curiosity at those psychic readers advertised on television or a movie with occult themes are all ready to influence us ever so subtly.

Few Christians today talk about the fear of the Lord, but as we pray and read His Word, we see that the reason it's so seldom talked about is that so few people really regard God as someone to be feared. But the fear of God is good, cleansing the soul.

Prayer cultivates the fear of the Lord. Prayerlessness casts it off.

The fear of God kills all other fears.

HUGH BLACK

April 26

My house will be called
a house of prayer for all nations.

ISAIAH 56:7

Last night I had a unique experience. I awoke intensely oppressed and as I lay under the dead weight of it, it dawned on me that it meant I was to pray, so I got to work to pray for the men who have just gone off to the fighting line, and in a marvelous way the oppression left and peace ineffable came, and the words emerged, "a house of prayer for all nations." It is a good thing to stake your confidence on the ground of the perfected Redemption and pray from that basis.

OSWALD CHAMBERS

Pray About It: The men who went off to the firing line were soldiers during World War I. God woke Oswald Chambers up to pray for these men. This is a common occurrence among regular pray-ers. Don't be surprised if God comes to you in the middle of the night and asks you to pray. You may never see the answer, but others will. And perhaps someday in eternity, God will let you see too.

The great battles, the battles that decide our destiny and the destiny of generations yet unborn, are not fought on public platforms, but in the lonely hours of the night and in moments of agony.

SAMUEL LOGAN BRENGLE

April 27

[Epaphras] is always wrestling in prayer for you, that you may stand firm in all the will of God, mature and fully assured.

COLOSSIANS 4:12

Epaphras laid himself out with the exhaustive toil and strenuous conflict of fervent prayer, that the Colossian Church might "stand firm in all the will of God." Everywhere, everything in the early church was dependent on the maturity and unity of the people of God. It was imperative that they all came "in the unity of the faith, and of the knowledge of the Son of God, unto a perfect man, unto the measure of the stature of the fullness of Christ" (Ephesians 4:13).

No premium was given to spiritual dwarfs; no encouragement to an old babyhood. The infants were to grow; and the older believers, instead of feebleness and infirmities, were to bear fruit in old age, and be fat and flourishing.

E. M. BOUNDS

Pray About It: Someday in heaven, we may be honored to meet Epaphras, this great prayer warrior who agonized for the Colossian church. God is looking for men and women today who will carry on the work of Epaphras. His reward, and ours if we pray, is the promise of standing "firm in the will of God, mature and fully assured."

Today, seek that reward. Pray like Epaphras.

Painful and difficult prayer is more pleasing to God than that which is easy and tranquil. The grief and pain of one who tries to pray in vain, lamenting his inability to do so, makes him a victor in God's sight and obtains for him abundant graces.

HENRY SUSO

April 28

The prayer of a righteous man is powerful and effective.

JAMES 5:16

When a burden comes upon your soul, or the Spirit leads you out along any line in prayer, take time, plenty of time to get alone with God in prayer. Stay there. Don't get up. Don't be in a hurry. Don't get nervous. Don't look at your watch. Never stop until you get the mind of God. It is dangerous to your own soul; it is destructive to God's cause committed to you. It will cause you to lose the blessed spirit of prayer, when He leads you out, and you fail to follow; fail to stay upon your knees; fail to pray clear through. God would not burden your heart, God would not make you hungry, lead you out, lead you to wrestle, to agonize, to fast and pray, unless He meant to answer. It's proof of the fact when the burden continues, and the Spirit continues to lead you out, that there's an answer, and God wants you to pray clear through.

W. J. HARNEY

Pray About It: If you're in a hurry to pray, better postpone your prayer time. You can't get the mind of God when you're constantly looking at your watch or mentally organizing your day as you pray.

That's why the most productive times of prayer are scheduled times of prayer, when you set aside a specific time in which to do nothing but meet with God. Then He can give you a burden to "pray clear through."

Take your time in prayer today. Get your answer from God.

> Oh, how few find time for prayer! There is time for everything else—time to sleep and time to eat, time to read the newspaper and the novel, time to visit friends, time for everything else under the sun, but no time for prayer, the most important of all things, the one great essential.
>
> OSWALD J. SMITH

April 29

Be joyful in hope, patient in affliction, faithful in prayer.

ROMANS 12:12

I am now, in 1864, waiting upon God for certain blessings, for which I have daily besought Him for 19 years and 6 months, without one day's intermission. Still the full answer is not yet given concerning the conversion of certain individuals.

In the meantime, I have received many thousands of answers to prayer. I have also prayed daily, without intermission, for the conversion of other individuals about ten years, for others six or seven years, for others four, three, and two years, for others about eighteen months; and still the answer is not yet granted, concerning these persons (whom I have prayed for nineteen and a half years). . . . Yet I am daily continuing in prayer and expecting the answer. . . .

Be encouraged, dear Christian reader, with fresh earnestness to give yourself to prayer, if you can only be sure that you ask for things which are for the glory of God.

GEORGE MUELLER

Pray About It: In this reading does Mueller sound the least bit discouraged that he's still waiting for an answer to a prayer that he's offered daily for nearly twenty years? No, and in the other delayed answers he mentions, Mueller is still expectant. He convicts us of our unbelief when God doesn't answer in just a few days or weeks. If we would have God's miracle, we must be willing to wait.

George Mueller got all that he prayed for. Yes, that request he waited so long for was eventually answered. And because Mueller was a steadfast prayer, he prevailed with God. And so can we.

It is a happy way of smoothing sorrow, when we can say, "We will wait only upon God." Oh, ye agitated Christians, don't dishonor your religion by always wearing a brow of care; come, cast your burden upon the Lord. I see ye staggering beneath a weight which He would not feel. What seems to you a crushing burden, would be to him but as the small dust of the balance. See! The Almighty bends his shoulders, and he says, "Here, put thy troubles here." What! Wilt thou bear thyself what the everlasting shoulders are ready to carry?

CHARLES HADDON SPURGEON

April 30

Seeing he ever liveth to make intercession for them.

HEBREWS 7:25 KJV

As Christ began to pray for His own while He was yet here in the world, so He has continued to pray for them, and will continue to pray for them, in heaven.

Who can measure the security of the children of God when they are the objects of the ceaseless intercession of the Son of God, whose prayer can never be denied?

LEWIS SPERRY CHAFER

Pray About It: Do you think God will turn a deaf ear to the ceaseless intercessions of His Son for His bride? Never! You and I are in good hands. We are possessors of the most blessed security conceivable as children of God.

Praise God, He will answer the prayers of His Son on our behalf. Today, we must rejoice at the security we have in an ever interceding Risen Savior.

Since Christ is our Intercessor, I infer that believers should not rest at the cross for comfort . . . but, being justified by His blood, they should ascend up after Him to the throne.

At the cross you will see Him in his sorrows and humiliations, in His tears and blood; but follow Him to where He is now, and then you shall see Him in His priestly robes, and with His golden girdle about His paps. Then you shall see Him wearing the breastplate of judgment, and with all your names written upon His heart. Then you shall perceive that the whole family in heaven and earth is named by Him, and how He prevaileth with God the Father of mercies, for you.

Stand still awhile and listen; yea, enter with boldness into the holiest, and see your Jesus as He now appears in the presence of God for you; what work He makes against the devil and sin, and death and hell, for you. . . .

This, then, is our High Priest, this His intercession, these the benefits of it!

John Bunyan

May 1

In the name of the Father and of the Son and of the Holy Spirit . . .

MATTHEW 28:19

When a believer prays, he is not alone — there are three with him: the Father seeing in secret, His ear open; the Son blotting out sin, and offering up the prayer; the Holy Ghost quickening and giving desires.

ROBERT MURRAY MCCHEYNE

Pray About It: True prayer involves all three parts of the Godhead — the Father, the Son, and the Holy Spirit. Each has his place in prayer, without which prayer cannot happen. In prayer we pray to the Father, in the name of the Son by whom we have access, through the power of the Holy Spirit.

Some Christians pray *to* the Holy Spirit, and yet nowhere is this found in the New Testament. How can you pray to One who lives in you? Nor is praying to the Holy Spirit found after the Day of Pentecost. The early church had the attitude of *welcome* to the Holy Spirit, rather than that of invocation.

Today, acknowledge the presence and purpose of all three aspects of the Trinity and their role in prayer.

When the Spirit takes possession of the soul, He becomes essentially the Spirit of intercession and the heart is drawn out in earnest prayer, the Spirit helping our many weaknesses.

W. H. GRIFFITH THOMAS

May 2

Delight thyself also in the LORD;
  and he shall give thee the desires of thine heart.
Commit thy way unto the LORD;
  trust also in him; and he shall bring it to pass.

PSALM 37:4–5 KJV

Prayer is an offering up of our desires unto God, for things agreeable to his will, in the name of Christ, with confession of our sins, and thankful acknowledgment of his mercies.

WESTMINSTER CATECHISM

Pray About It: This brief definition of prayer has been memorized and repeated by millions of Christians down through the past centuries. For many it may have become a meaningless phrase for which they were awarded Sunday school points. But in truth, this is the essence of prayer.

Prayer is our offering to God, as important as the sacrifice of praise.

Today, see your prayers as an offering and lift them up to your heavenly Father. He will receive them joyfully.

Will you not, before venturing away from your early quiet hour, commit your works to Him definitely, the special things you have to do today, and the unforeseen work which He may add in the course of it?

FRANCES HAVERGAL

May 3

And Mary said, "Behold the handmaid of the Lord; be it unto me according to thy word."

LUKE 1:38 KJV

Carnal reason is an enemy to faith: it is ever crossing and contradicting it. It will never be well with thee, Christian, so long as thou art swayed by carnal reason, and you rely more upon your five senses, than upon the four gospels. As the body lives by breathing, so the soul lives by believing.

THOMAS BROOKS

Pray About It: Beware of allowing natural reason to assault your faith. The things for which we pray are very often unreasonable, unfathomable to the natural human eye. But no matter, to God all things are possible.

In truth, prayer is compatible with reason — God's reason. Submit to His divine reason and allow your own reason to exercise itself only on earthly matters, not heavenly.

Prayer is simple, prayer is supernatural, and to anyone not related to our Lord Jesus Christ, prayer is apt to look stupid.

OSWALD CHAMBERS

May 4

I will delight myself in thy statutes: I will not forget thy word.

PSALM 119:16 KJV

Conversation between God and mankind in this world is maintained by God's Word on His part, and by prayer on ours. By the former, He speaks and expresses His mind to us; by the latter, we speak and express our minds to Him.

JONATHAN EDWARDS

Pray About It: There is a remarkable intertwining between God's Word and prayer that many Christians miss. Just as our prayers express our heart to God, so His Word expresses His heart to us. As we read God's thoughts through His Word, we know Him better. And to know Him better is to pray better.

Today, read Psalm 91 and see in the words God's message for you. Return often to His Word to hear Him speak to you again and again.

The Bible is God's chart for you to steer by, to keep you from the bottom of the sea, and to show you where the harbor is, and how to reach it without running on rocks and bars.

HENRY WARD BEECHER

May 5

But without faith it is impossible to please him: for he that cometh to God must believe that he is, and that he is a rewarder of them that diligently seek him.

HEBREWS 11:6 KJV

God's best gifts, like valuable jewels, are kept under lock and key, and those who want them must, with fervent faith, importunately ask for them; for God is the rewarder of them that *diligently* seek Him.

DWIGHT L. MOODY

Pray About It: Think of your prayer as a key to a vast storehouse stocked with riches unimaginable. If you had such a key, you would surely use it. And you do indeed have such a key—and there is actually such a storehouse.

Today, use your key to unlock God's storehouse of spiritual riches. He is a rewarder of those who diligently seek Him.

Prayer is the key that unlocks all the storehouses of God's infinite grace and power. All that God is, and all that God has, is at the disposal of prayer. But we must use the key.

R. A. TORREY

May 6

Set a watch, O LORD, before my mouth; keep the door of my lips.

PSALM 141:3 KJV

No prayer should be spoken more often by us than this prayer of David: "Keep the door of my lips." There is nothing in all of life to which most of us give less attention than to our words. We let them fly from our lips as the leaves fly from the trees when the autumn winds blow. Many people seem to think that words are not important. They watch their acts, their conduct, and then give full license to their tongues. This is not right. A true Christian should have a Christian tongue.

J. R. MILLER

Pray About It: A practical result of using our tongue for prayer is that when we're not at prayer, the taste of God's Spirit still comes from our mouth. It's useless to insist that we will be strong in prayer and live with an unholy tongue. James says that the tongue is full of poison. But from the tongue of a Christian should come only honorable words and humble prayers.

Watch your tongue today. Let it be used to edify others, not criticize them.

Touch the man of God who understands prayer, at any point, at any time, and a full current of prayer is seen flowing from him.

E. M. BOUNDS

May 7

So Peter was kept in prison, but the church was earnestly praying to God for him.

The night before Herod was to bring him to trial, Peter was sleeping between two soldiers, bound with two chains, and sentries stood guard at the entrance. Suddenly an angel of the Lord appeared and a light shone in the cell. He struck Peter on the side and woke him up. "Quick, get up!" he said, and the chains fell off Peter's wrists.

Then the angel said to him, "Put on your clothes and sandals." And Peter did so. "Wrap your cloak around you and follow me," the angel told him. Peter followed him out of the prison, but he had no idea that what the angel was doing was really happening; he thought he was seeing a vision. They passed the first and second guards and came to the iron gate leading to the city. It opened for them by itself, and they went through it. When they had walked the length of one street, suddenly the angel left him.

Then Peter came to himself and said, "Now I know without a doubt that the Lord sent his angel and rescued me from Herod's clutches and from everything the Jewish people were anticipating."

When this had dawned on him, he went to the house of Mary the mother of John, also called Mark, where many people had gathered and were praying. Peter knocked at the outer entrance, and a servant girl named Rhoda came to answer the door. When she recognized Peter's voice, she was so overjoyed she ran back without opening it and exclaimed, "Peter is at the door!"

"You're out of your mind," they told her. When she kept insisting that it was so, they said, "It must be his angel."

But Peter kept on knocking, and when they opened the door and saw him, they were astonished. Peter motioned with his hand for them to be quiet and described how the Lord had brought him out of prison.

ACTS 12:5–17

God, the eternal God of the universe, stands, as it were, like an almighty servant and says: "If you, My child, will only *pray* I will *work;* if you will only be busy with *asking* I will see to the *doing.*" Not only does He bestow at our cry, but He *acts.* Not only does our praying evoke His bounty, it sets in motion His omnipotence.

Wherefore, as we enter into the secret chamber of prayer, nothing will so stir us to mighty intercession, nothing will so soon make us master-pleaders with God for a lost world, as to whisper to our own soul, again and again, this wonderful truth, "*While I am praying GOD is really DOING that which I am asking!*"

JAMES H. McCONKEY

Pray About It: Our prayers move God! Amazing! And yet we pray with such shallowness. Rise up, fellow Christian, and pray today with the knowledge that your prayers motivate God. Whisper — or call out loudly — "While I am praying, God is really doing that which I am asking!" He is here, and He is not silent.

The angel fetched Peter out of prison, but it was prayer that fetched the angel.

THOMAS WATSON

May 8

Great is the LORD, and greatly to be praised in the city of our God, in the mountain of his holiness.

PSALM 48:1 KJV

"Great is the Lord!"

So many people have such a little God! There is nothing about Him august and sublime. And so He is not greatly praised. The worship is thin, the thanksgivings are scanty, the supplications are indifferent.

All great saints have a great God. He fills their universe. Therefore do they move about in a fruitful awe, and everywhere there is only a thin veil between them and His appearing. Everywhere they discern His holy presence, as the face of a bride is dimly seen beneath her bridal veil. And so even the common scrub of the wilderness is aflame with sacred fire: the humble "primrose on the rock" becomes "the court of Deity": and the "strength of the hills is His also"!

Yes, a great God inspires great praise, and in great praise small cares and small meannesses are utterly consumed away. When praise is mean, anxieties multiply. Therefore let me contemplate the greatness of God in nature and in providence, in His power, and His holiness, and His love. Let me "stand in awe" before His glory: and in the fruitful reverence the soul will be moved in acceptable praise.

JOHN HENRY JOWETT

Pray About It: Today is a day of high praise! Great is our God and greatly to be praised! Look and see the work of our great God in nature. See Him in the faces of humankind.

Those troubles about which you want to pray — try praising God today instead. Watch your troubles dwindle and be consumed by your praise of God.

Give God great glory today, for He is worthy!

The purpose of God is to be known and praised and enjoyed and reverenced among all the peoples of the earth. That is why the world exists. That is why the church exists. That is why you exist.

JOHN PIPER

May the peoples praise you, O God; may all the peoples praise you.

PSALM 67:3

May 9

I saw the Spirit come down from heaven as a dove and remain on him.

JOHN 1:32

The instinct of prayer to us is like the wing of a bird to a bird and the fin of a fish to a fish. The wing of the bird demands the air, the fin of the fish demands the water. The instinct of prayer demands GOD. Therefore the only monstrosity of nature, just as much a monstrosity as a wingless bird or a finless fish, is the prayerless man or woman, because the deepest and most real instinct they have is not satisfied.

ARTHUR F. WINNINGTON INGRAM

Pray About It: If you are a Christian, the instinct to pray is natural. You must pray; you're compelled to speak to Him who loves you. To have no desire to pray is to be deformed spiritually. However, this deformity is quickly healed by a fresh understanding of God and His love.

Christian, use your wings today to fly. Use your fin to sail through the water of life with ease. Follow your instinct and pray until you know that you've accomplished your goal.

If the spiritual life be healthy, under the full power of the Holy Spirit, constant prayer will be natural.

ANDREW MURRAY

May 10

And we know that in all things God works for the
good of those who love him, who have been called
according to his purpose.

ROMANS 8:28

The mother of Augustine, in her longing for the
conversion of her son, prayed that he might not
go to Rome, as she feared its dissipations. God
answered her by sending him to Rome to be converted there. Things we call good are often God's
evil things, and our evil is His good. However things
may look, we always know that God must give the
best because He is God and can do no other.

HANNAH WHITALL SMITH

Pray About It: When God sends our son to Rome
though we have prayed otherwise, do we despair and
complain, thinking God hasn't heard our request? Or
do we remember another son who was sent to a land
full of dissipation that God's will might be done?

Never limit God. Give Him room. Though God
may seem momentarily to be moving in a direction
that alarms you, He will make it work for good.

Trusting God is easy when His will aligns with
ours. But when His will leads to Rome, will we
patiently watch for the outcome of His will with joy?
To do so is to display deep trust in God.

Augustine's mother wasted her worry. God had it
all under control, even in Rome. Make the following
prayer by Augustine your own. Pray it aloud.

185

I was nothing. You had no need of me. Even now my service has not even the value of a laborer tilling his master's land, because even if I did not work, you would bring forth the same harvest. I can only serve You and worship You with the good that comes from You. It is from You alone that I receive strength, and without You I am nothing.

May 11

There, in the presence of the LORD your God, you and your families shall eat and shall rejoice in everything you have put your hand to, because the LORD your God has blessed you.

DEUTERONOMY 12:7

There come times when I have nothing more to tell God. If I were to continue to pray in words, I would have to repeat what I have already said. At such times it is wonderful to say to God, "May I be in Thy presence, Lord? I have nothing more to say to Thee, but I do love to be in Thy presence."

OLE HALLESBY

Pray About It: We don't always need to come to God with our list of wants. Sometimes we just feel prayed out, or we sense a need just to be with God, asking nothing, saying nothing. This is good.

Today, simply ask, "May I be in Thy presence, Lord?"

He will say yes.

What would you think of a man who was content to remain in the outer halls of Windsor Castle when he was invited inside to have a feast with the King? That's the way some Christians are: they spend their life exploring the lobbies when the King and the feast are waiting in the upper room!

JOHN HENRY JOWETT

May 12

The LORD thy God in the midst of thee is mighty; he will save, he will rejoice over thee with joy; he will rest in his love, he will joy over thee with singing.

ZEPHANIAH 3:17 KJV

In prayer there must be deliberateness — the secret place, the inner chamber, the fixed time, the shut door against distraction and intruders. In that secret place the Father is waiting for us. He is as certainly there as He is in Heaven. Be reverent, as Moses when he took the shoes from off his feet! Be trustful, because you are having an audience with One who is infinite sympathy and love! Be comforted, because there is no problem He cannot solve, no knot He cannot untie!

F. B. MEYER

Pray About It: The place where you pray — have you considered that God is as certainly there as He is in heaven? If so, you know that it almost makes you want to take off your shoes, for this place of prayer is holy ground. In the presence of God there is joy and laughter. But there is also reverence and solemnity at times.

He is there today, waiting for you in your place of prayer — as surely as He is in heaven. Meet Him there.

> We must not only think of our waiting upon God, but also of what is more wonderful still — of God waiting upon us. If He waits for us, then we are more than welcome in His presence.
>
> ANDREW MURRAY

May 13

> Then you will call upon me and come and pray to me, and I will listen to you. You will seek me and find me when you seek me with all your heart.
>
> JEREMIAH 29:12–13

Prayer must not be our chance work but our daily business, our habit, and vocation. As artists give themselves to their models, and poets to their classical pursuits, so must we addict ourselves to prayer. We must be immersed in prayer as in our element, and so pray without ceasing. Lord, teach us to pray that we may be more prevalent in supplication.

CHARLES HADDON SPURGEON

Pray About It: Painters, poets, musicians, and other talented artists give themselves to their work. To be great they must, in a very real way, be addicted to their art. Michelangelo didn't whip out his *David* in a week. Nor in a month. To be true to your art requires getting it right, no matter how long it takes.

In prayer, getting it right also means being patient and doing it over and over again. Prayer can be likened to an art in that the final result is a wonderful creation wrought through much sweat and labor.

If you are a pray-er, then you are an artist of the finest sort.

To pray rightly is a rare gift.

JOHN CALVIN

May 14

Bear ye one another's burdens, and so fulfill the law of Christ.

GALATIANS 6:2 KJV

When we are linked by the power of prayer, we, as it were, hold each other's hand as we walk side by side along a slippery path; and thus by the bounteous disposition of charity, it comes about that the harder each one leans on the other, the more firmly we are riveted together in brotherly love.

GREGORY THE GREAT

Pray About It: Prayer draws us closer to God, that's true. But it should also draw us closer to each other. Don't be afraid to lean hard on your brother or sister in Christ. And allow them to lean hard on you. Bear one another's burdens.

> Faith, like light, should always be simple and unbending. But love, like warmth, should beam forth on every side and bend to every need of our brethren.
>
> MARTIN LUTHER

May 15

> For this reason I remind you to fan into flame the gift of God, which is in you through the laying on of my hands.
>
> 2 TIMOTHY 1:6

Am I ignitable? God deliver me from the dread asbestos of "other things." Saturate me with the oil of the Spirit that I may be a flame. But flame is transient, often short-lived. Canst thou bear this, my soul—short life? In me there dwells the Spirit of the Great Short-Lived, Whose zeal for God's house consumed Him. "Make me Thy fuel, Flame of God."

> JIM ELLIOT

Pray About It: In 1956, Jim Elliot was a missionary to the Auca Indians of South America. He and the rest of the missions team were murdered by those whom they came to evangelize. Later, many of the Aucas became Christians. This story is told in several books by Jim's widow, Elisabeth Elliot, most notably, *The Shadow of the Almighty*. His words above are inspired by the following poem by another great Christian missionary, Amy Carmichael.

Today, make it your prayer to ask God if you're ignitable. Ask Him to make you His fuel in whatever way He chooses.

> From prayer that asks that I may be
> Sheltered from winds that beat on Thee,
> From fearing when I should aspire,
> From faltering when I should climb higher,
> From silken self, O Captain, free
> Thy soldier who would follow Thee.
>
> From subtle love of softening things,
> From easy choices, weakenings;
> Not thus are spirits fortified,
> Not this way went the Crucified,
> From all that dims Thy Calvary,
> O Lamb of God, deliver me.
>
> Give me the love that leads the way,
> The faith that nothing can dismay,
> The hope no disappointments tire,
> The passion that will burn like fire,
> Let me not sink to be a clod:
> Make me Thy fuel, Flame of God.

Amy Carmichael

May 16

Give attention to your servant's prayer and his plea for mercy, O LORD my God. Hear the cry and the prayer that your servant is praying in your presence.

2 CHRONICLES 6:19

It takes prayer to minister. It takes life, the highest form of life, to minister. Prayer is the highest intelligence, the profoundest wisdom, the most vital, the most joyous, the most efficacious, the most powerful of all vocations. It is life, radiant, transporting, eternal life.

Away with dry forms, with dead, cold habits of prayer! Away with sterile routine, with senseless performances, and petty playthings in prayer! Let us get at the serious work, the chief business of men, that of prayer. Let us work at it skillfully. Let us seek to be adept in this great work of praying. Let us be master-workmen, in this high art of praying. Let us be so in the habit of prayer, so devoted to prayer, so filled with its rich spices, so ardent by its holy flame, that all heaven and earth will be perfumed by its aroma, and nations yet in the womb will be blest by our prayers.

Heaven will be fuller and brighter in glorious inhabitants, earth will be better prepared for its bridal day, and hell robbed of many of its victims, because we have lived to pray.

E. M. BOUNDS

Pray About It: Think about your unique place in God's history. There are things for which you alone can pray. If you were not here to pray—if you had never been born, or had died early—these matters could not be prayed for in the unique way that you can. Take delight in knowing that your calling as a pray-er is unique. Things will happen only because *you prayed*.

> A zealous Christian feels that, like a lamp, he is made to burn. And if he's consumed in burning, he has but done the work for which God appointed him. Such a Christian will always find an outlet for his zeal. If he can't preach or work or give money, he will cry, and sigh, and pray.
>
> J. C. RYLE

May 17

And he said, I will not let thee go, except thou bless me. And he said unto him, What *is* thy name? And he said, Jacob. And he said, Thy name shall be called no more Jacob, but Israel: for as a prince hast thou power with God and with men, and hast prevailed. And Jacob asked him, and said, Tell me,

I pray thee, thy name. And he said, Wherefore is it that thou dost ask after my name? And he blessed him there. And Jacob called the name of the place Peniel: for I have seen God face to face, and my life is preserved. And as he passed over Penuel the sun rose upon him, and he halted upon his thigh.

GENESIS 32:26–31 KJV

I would not taste of death until I have seen *Thee!* Even were I told that death was but translation, I would not taste it till I had seen *Thee!* No chariot of fire can bear me to glory unless the glory be already in my *heart!* In vain Thy crystal river shall sparkle if I have no eye for beauty! In vain Thy choristers shall sing if I have no ear for music! In vain Thy day shall be nightless if I have no thirst for knowledge! In vain Thy sea shall be stormless if I have no wish for expansion! In vain Thy work shall be painless if I have no mission for my hands! In vain Thy city shall be gateless if there be no love imprisoned in my soul! Not to seek Thee in *heaven* would I come; come and seek *me* on *earth!* I would be translated *before* death; I would taste Thy grapes in my desert. Thy Life is *not* beyond the grave; it is here, it is now. I can reach it without dying; I can breathe it without expiring. I need not the wings of a dove to find it; I require not an angel's flight to lead me to its rest. I have heard men say, "Death is the gate of Life." Nay, *Thou* art the gate, and Death is the shady avenue. Not on the other side would I see

Thy face unveiled; meet me on *this* bank of the crystal river! Meet me in the mist and in the rain! Come to me in my cloud! Speak to me in my struggles! Wait for me at the *opening* of the valley! Translate me into Thy presence ere I tread the narrow way! Send me the morning before the evening! Show me heaven ere I die!

GEORGE MATHESON

Pray About It: The deepest goal of prayer is to see God in the way that He allows Himself to be seen by men and women today. The result will be a dramatic change. We cannot see God in this way and remain the same.

Today, worship God and express your extreme hunger and thirst to see Him. Catch the spirit of George Matheson, the great hymn writer. His most famous composition expresses even more of his passion for His Lord:

Oh Love that wilt not let me go.
O Love that wilt not let me go,
I rest my weary soul on Thee;
I give Thee back the life I own,
That in Thine ocean depths its flow
May richer, fuller be.

GEORGE MATHESON

May 18

Some trust in chariots and some in horses,
  but we trust in the name of the LORD our God.
They are brought to their knees and fall,
  but we rise up and stand firm.

PSALM 20:7–8

When we depend upon organization, we get what organization can do; when we depend upon education, we get what education can do; when we depend upon man, we get what man can do; but when we depend upon prayer, we get what God can do!

A. C. DIXON

Pray About It: Organization, education, and man all have their place. They are good. They are necessary. But to receive what really matters in life requires God's blessing.

Today, set aside the good things, the necessary things and go to God. God uses prayer as the genesis of His works on earth. Depend upon prayer—and get what God can do.

God provides for him that trusteth.

GEORGE HERBERT

Behold, how good and how pleasant it is for brethren to dwell together in unity! It is like the precious
ointment upon the head, that ran down upon the
beard, even Aaron's beard: that went down to the
skirts of his garments; As the dew of Hermon, and
as the dew that descended upon the mountains of
Zion: for there the LORD commanded the blessing,
even life for evermore.

PSALM 133 KJV

I am so convinced that [our work as Christians]
is God's work that nothing from without can by
any means harm it, but you must stay very close
together and at the foot of the cross, where there is
none of self but all of Christ.

You can harm it if you allow disunity among
yourselves, looking after your own personal interests
and failing to be true to the vision God has given
us. Read often Psalm 133. . . . Have fervent love
among yourselves. Pray for fresh baptisms of love.
Disunity cannot live in an atmosphere of love.

CHARLES E. COWMAN

Pray About It: When we read the gospel accounts
of Christ's life, we notice that He prayed often.
Although we don't know everything He prayed for,
we can surmise that if Jesus prayed for it, it must have
been important.

One occasion where we're privy to the content of Jesus' prayer is in John 17 where Jesus prays for His disciples, both those present then and those to come in centuries ahead. His prayer was for them, and for us, to be "one." To be in unity. The work of God goes forward when there is unity among believers. Strife, on the other hand, is the result of disunity in the body of Christ and it always stops God's work cold.

Has Jesus' prayer gone unanswered? Not for those who know that the place where unity can be found is at the Cross. It's there that all self, all strife, all division vanishes.

Center your prayer today on the Cross and the unity to be found there with all other Christians — past, present, and future. God will command the blessing.

> Believers who live in love and peace, shall have the God of love and peace with them now, and they shall shortly be with him forever, in the world of endless love and peace. May all who love the Lord forbear and forgive one another, as God, for Christ's sake, hath forgiven them.
>
> MATTHEW HENRY

May 20

We too will serve the LORD, because he is our God.
JOSHUA 24:18

We must wait on our God every day. Servants in the courts of princes have their weeks or months of waiting appointed them, and are obliged to attend only at certain times. But God's servants must never be out of waiting; all the days of our appointed time, the time of our work and warfare here on earth, we must be waiting and not desire or expect to be discharged from this attendance, till we come to heaven, where we shall wait on God, as angels do, more nearly and constantly.

We must wait on God every day.

MATTHEW HENRY

Pray About It: A pray-er is, first of all, a servant. We wait on our God to speak and then we do His bidding. We are bond slaves, bought with a price. We are no longer our own. There is no time off for a Christian, nor do we seek a vacation. As possessors of eternal life, we are His forever.

Today, see your prayers as your service to God. Take on the lowliness of a servant. Acknowledge Him as your Lord.

Is there anyone who is a grateful servant? Let them rejoice and enter into the joy of their Lord.

JOHN CHRYSOSTOM

May 21

Still other seed fell on good soil. It came up and yielded a crop, a hundred times more than was sown.

LUKE 8:8

Prayer is an essential link in the chain of causes that lead to a revival; as much so as truth is. Some have zealously used truth to convert men, and laid very little stress on prayer. They have preached, and talked, and distributed tracts with great zeal, and then wondered that they had so little success. And the reason was, that they forgot to use the other branch of the means, effectual prayer.

CHARLES G. FINNEY

Pray About It: When truth is advanced through prayer, good seed falls on good ground. Our prayers are the plows that break up the soil so that truth can reap a harvest.

Today, pray that truth be established in our culture. Also pray that error, deception, and falsehood be uprooted — especially from the minds of our youth. The result will be revival. We can never pray too much for God to bring revival.

Passionate, pleading, persistent prayer is always the prelude to revival.

W. E. SANGSTER

May 22

Enter his gates with thanksgiving
   and his courts with praise;
     give thanks to him and praise his name.
For the LORD is good and his love endures forever;
   his faithfulness continues through all generations.

PSALM 100:4-5

The Holy Spirit will teach us when to cease from prayer, and turn our petition into thanksgiving, or go out in obedience to meet the answer as it waits before us, or comes to meet us.

A. B. SIMPSON

Pray About It: Knowing when to pray is important, but there's also a time to stop praying. When we know that God has heard and answered, we need ask no more, but can begin giving thanks. Then go out and meet the answer as it comes to meet us.

> Thanksgiving is nothing if not a glad and reverent lifting of the heart to God in honor and praise for His goodness.

J. R. MILLER

May 23

Those who look to him are radiant;
  their faces are never covered with shame.

PSALM 34:5

Would *you* like to be a radiant Christian? You may be. Spend time in prayer. You cannot be a radiant Christian in any other way. Why is it that prayer in the Name of Christ makes one radiantly happy? It is because prayer makes God real. *The gladdest thing upon earth is to have a real God!*

I would rather give up anything I have in the world, or anything I ever may have, than give up my faith in God.

You cannot have vital faith in God if you give all your time to the world and to secular affairs, to reading the newspapers, and to reading literature, no matter how good it is.

Unless you take time for fellowship with God, you cannot have a real God. If you do take time for prayer you will have a real, living God, and if you have a living God you will have a radiant life.

R. A. TORREY

Pray About It: God is very real. There is no falsehood or deception in Him. All who have had deep prayer lives have known this radiant countenance that comes from being with God. Consider Him as He now sits before the Father and you will be radiant.

See there He sits, in heaven, He has led captivity captive, and now sits at the right hand of God, forever making intercession for us. Can your faith picture Him there? Like a great high priest of old, He stands with outstretched arms: there is majesty in His demeanor, for He is no mean cringing suppliant. He does not beat His breast, nor cast His eyes upon the ground, but with authority He pleads enthroned in glory now.

There on His head is the bright shining miter of His priesthood, and look, on His breast are glittering the precious stones whereon the names of his elect are everlastingly engraved; hear Him as He pleads. Can you hear what it is? It is your very prayer that He is mentioning before the throne. The prayer that this morning you offered, Christ is now offering before His Father's throne. The vow which just now you uttered when you said, "Have pity and have mercy,"—he is now uttering there. He is the Altar and the Priest, and with His own sacrifice He perfumes our prayers.

CHARLES HADDON SPURGEON

May 24

Then Moses said to the Israelites, "See, the LORD has chosen Bezalel son of Uri, the son of Hur, of the tribe of Judah, and he has filled him with the Spirit of God, with skill, ability and knowledge in all kinds of crafts—to make artistic designs for work in gold, silver and bronze, to cut and set stones, to work in wood and to engage in all kinds of artistic craftsmanship."

EXODUS 35:30-33

[One of Oswald Chambers' passions was for the gospel of Christ to impact artists, poets, and writers — what he referred to as the "aesthetic kingdom." In an 1895 letter he wrote the following:]

Our Savior, as far as my limited knowledge goes, has no representative to teach, to reprove, to exhort [in the aesthetic kingdom] . . . and oh, Spirit of God, Thou knowest that an ambition, a longing, a love has seized me powerfully and convinced me of the lack. . . .

The kingdom of the aesthetic lies in a groveling quagmire, half fine, half impure. There is a crying need for a fearless preacher of Christ in the midst of that kingdom, for a fearless writer, writing with the blood of Christ, proclaiming His claims in the midst of that kingdom, for a fearless lecturer above pandering to popular taste, to warn and exhort that all the kingdoms of this world are to become Christ's — and that artists, poets, and musicians be good and fearless Christians. . . .

I think I have heard that cry and have seen the beseeching look of Christ toward that kingdom, longing for it to be His own. . . . The duty of ministers is to instruct the people out of their bigoted notions against art.

It is for the artist [who is a Christian] to enter this aesthetic kingdom and live and struggle and strain for its salvation and exaltation.

OSWALD CHAMBERS

Pray About It: There is indeed a need for Christians to have a voice in the arts. In centuries past, lovers of Christ dominated the arts. Today, we have surrendered the aesthetic kingdom to the enemy—and far too often we even partake of the resulting "art" that emanates from hell.

For pray-ers who are artists, musicians, poets, writers or otherwise a member of the "aesthetic kingdom" don't surrender your faith in pursuit of success. Instead, yield your gift to the Master Designer of the universe. Seek your creative edge through Him.

One often forgotten advantage to prayer is that it enhances creativity. It was said that George Frideric Handel fasted and prayed for many days before composing the "Hallelujah Chorus." He later said that as he composed, "I did think I did see all heaven before me, and the great God Himself."

In your prayer time, ask the Greatest Creator of all to sharpen your gifts and to allow you to be a vessel of his originality. If you aren't artistically gifted, pray for those who are.

We desperately need a revival in the arts community.

Holy Spirit, think through me till your ideas are my ideas.

AMY CARMICHAEL

All who are skilled among you are to come and make everything the LORD has commanded.

EXODUS 35:10

May 25

Great peace have they who love your law,
  and nothing can make them stumble.

PSALM 119:165

Let the life of prayer flow into the busiest hours of your busiest days. It will be a defense against temptations. It will give you power in Christian service. It will hallow all our influence. It will give you peace in the midst of dangers, help in weakness, light in darkness, comfort in sorrows, companionship in loneliness, and friendship for your hungry heart.

If we know how to get help in prayer, we need never fail at any point in life, for then God's might is back of us as the ocean is back of the bay.

J. R. MILLER

Pray About It: Failure in the life of a praying Christian is an oxymoron. When God is consulted, obeyed, and followed, the end of the matter can never be failure, no matter what the natural eye sees. Busyness requires all the more prayer, for busyness requires power. Busyness without prayer is a ticket for sure defeat—no matter what the natural eye sees.

God promises to meet all your needs today. And as you pray, He expects you to exercise faith in all He wants to do today.

God's children should pray. They should cry day and night to Him. God hears every one of your cries in the busy hour of the daytime and in the lonely watches of the night.

ROBERT MURRAY MCCHEYNE

May 26

And he saw that there was no man, and wondered that there was no intercessor.

ISAIAH 59:16 KJV

That God seeks intercessors, but seldom finds them, is plain from the pain of His exclamation through Isaiah and His protest of disappointment through Ezekiel: "I sought for a man among them, that should make up the hedge, and stand in the gap before Me for the land . . . but I found none."

NORMAN GRUBB

Pray About It: It seems amazing that there should be something that causes God to "wonder." Sadly, that single cause of God's wonder is that intercessors are not to be found.

Knowing what we do about the joy of prayer, do we not also wonder that there aren't more intercessors?

If God didn't answer prayer or wasn't faithful, then there would be no need to wonder at the empty prayer closets. However, God tells us He delights in our prayers—and delights to answer.

It is indeed a wonder that more intercessors can't be found. Who wouldn't want to sign up? Pray today for God to raise up an army of faithful intercessors who will "make up the hedge"; "stand in the gap" for humankind.

If we ask why there is so little love to be found amongst Christians, why the very characteristic by which every one should know that we are disciples

of the holy Jesus, is almost banished out of the
Christian world, we shall find it, in a great measure, owing to a neglect or superficial performance
of intercession, or imploring the divine grace and
mercy in behalf of others.

GEORGE WHITEFIELD

May 27

Pray without ceasing.

1 THESSALONIANS 5:17 KJV

The word "pray" does not mean to beg or to plead
as if God were unwilling to give—but simply to
expose by faith every situation as it arises, to the all-
sufficiency of the One who indwells you by His life.

Can any situation possibly arise, in any circumstances, for which He is not adequate? Any pres-
sure, promise, problem, responsibility or temptation
for which the Lord Jesus Himself is not adequate?
If He be truly God, there cannot be a single one!

MAJOR IAN THOMAS

Pray About It: We can pray without ceasing by giving
to God every situation as it arises and letting Him be
God. By living united to God, in our affections and
thoughts, our life will become to God like one very
long prayer.

There is nothing today that will escape God's notice. No problem too big or small. Offer all your requests to Him. He is the All-Sufficient One.

> Pray without ceasing; not in mere words, but in so living united to God, in your affections and thoughts, that your life shall be one long and continued prayer.
>
> BASIL

May 28

> To every thing there is a season, and a time to every purpose under the heavens.
>
> ECCLESIASTES 3:1 KJV

Do the Lord's work in the Lord's time. Pray while God hears, hear while God speaks, believe while God promises, and obey while God commands.

JOHN MASON

Pray About It: Often in our childlike anxiety we've gone ahead of God, almost looking back saying, "Hurry up, God, or we'll never get there." Other times, God may see us lagging behind, calling out to us, "Hurry up, My child, or we'll never get there."

God's time is perfect. In praying we can learn to discern His seasons in our life. We'll know that now isn't a good time to change jobs or to buy a new house.

Or we may sense that God is opening up doors that have long been closed to us. This developing sensitivity to God's perfect timing is one of the benefits of prayer. We must learn to do all things in His time.

Those things which seem most contrary the one to the other will, in the resolution of affairs, each take their turn and come into play. The day will give place to the night and the night again to the day. Is it summer? It will be winter. Is it winter? Stay a while, and it will be summer. Every purpose under heaven has its time. The clearest sky will be clouded, joy will succeed sorrow. The cloudiest sky will soon clear up.

MATTHEW HENRY

May 29

While they were worshiping the Lord and fasting, the Holy Spirit said, "Set apart for me Barnabas and Saul for the work to which I have called them." So after they had fasted and prayed, they placed their hands on them and sent them off.

ACTS 13:2–3

Prayer is the walkie talkie on the battlefield of the world. It calls on God for courage (Eph. 6:19). It calls in for troop deployment and target location (Acts 13:1–3). It calls in for protection and air cover

(Matt. 6:13; Luke 21:36). It calls in for fire power to blast open a way for the Word (Col. 4:3). It calls in for the miracle of healing for the wounded soldiers (James 5:16). It calls in for supplies for the forces (Matt. 6:11; Phil. 4:6). And it calls in for needed reinforcements (Matt. 9:38). This is the place of prayer—on the battlefield of the world. It is a war-time walkie talkie for spiritual warfare, not a domestic intercom to increase the comforts of the saints. And one of the reasons it malfunctions in the hands of so many Christian soldiers is that they have gone AWOL.

JOHN PIPER

Prayer is the mightiest of all weapons that created natures can wield.

MARTIN LUTHER

Pray About It: We live in a war zone. Prayer is our lifeline to supply and to orders from our Commander-in-Chief. As you go through your day, see the battle for what it really is. Take your place as a soldier and wield your weapons well.

Pray for new recruits and encourage those who have gone AWOL to return to the front lines.

No Christian is exempt from this warfare. God has no place for spiritual pacifists. He calls every saint to arms.

RUTH PAXSON

May 30

Praise be to God,
who has not rejected my prayer
or withheld his love from me!

PSALM 66:20

Our best prayers are but the echo of God's promises. God's best answers are the echo of our prayers.
As in two mirrors set opposite to each other, the
same image is repeated over and over again, the
reflection of a reflection. So here, within our prayer,
gleams an earlier promise, within the answer is mir-
rored the prayer.

ALEXANDER MACLAREN

Pray About It: A prayer and its answer are inseparable, like the two sides of a coin. Or like the echo
of a voice shouted into a canyon. God conceived the
answer to your prayer before you even asked it—that's
how united the two are. Know for certain that for
every prayer you pray, there is a God-ordered answer.
There are no unanswered prayers.

It is as natural to Him to answer prayer as it is for
us to ask.

A. E. RICHARDSON

May 31

O God, thou art my God; early will I seek thee: my soul thirsteth for thee, my flesh longeth for thee in a dry and thirsty land, where no water is.

PSALM 63:1 KJV

Turn to God with short but frequent outpourings of your heart; admire His graciousness; ask for His help; cast yourself in spirit at the foot of His cross; adore His goodness; be thankful to Him for your salvation; give Him your whole soul a thousand times a day.

FRANCIS DE SALES

Pray About It: Long prayers are often useful, but not at the expense of offering ourselves to God a thousand times a day. Carry Him with you today and as you think of Him, give Him glory, and pour out your heart in secret. Thank Him every time you think of Him. Adore Him.

Everyday we need to whisper in His ear, as though we had never done so before, our heart's love for Him.

NORMAN B. HARRISON

June 1

We pray this in order that you may live a life worthy
of the Lord and may please him in every way: bearing fruit in every good work.

COLOSSIANS 1:10

Here is the secret of great success: Work with all
your might, but don't trust in the least in your work.
Pray with all your might for the blessing of God,
but work at the same time with all diligence, all
patience and all perseverance.

Pray then, and work. Work and pray. And still
again pray, and then work. And so on all the days of
your life. The result will surely be abundant blessing.

GEORGE MUELLER

Pray About It: God has called us to work as well as to
prayer. Sometimes that work is physically demanding
and we get tired. As a result, our work suffers and we
languish. But it doesn't have to be that way.

Think about the hardest thing you must do today.
Maybe it's just your daily routine that seems to take all
your energy. Or maybe today an unexpected situation
will present itself that will require more effort than
you anticipated.

Read the verses from Isaiah below and take a
minute to pray about all that God will send your

way today. As you pray, appropriate, by faith, these
verses for your specific situations. Later, as the pres-
sure mounts, and the unexpected presents itself, recall
the message of these verses, leaning hard on God to
supply strength:

Do you not know?
  Have you not heard?
The LORD is the everlasting God,
  the Creator of the ends of the earth.
He will not grow tired or weary,
  and his understanding no one can fathom.
He gives strength to the weary
  and increases the power of the weak.
Even youths grow tired and weary,
  and young men stumble and fall;
but those who hope in the LORD
  will renew their strength.
They will soar on wings like eagles;
  they will run and not grow weary,
  they will walk and not be faint.

ISAIAH 40:28–31

You can do more than pray after you've prayed, but
you can't do more than pray until you've prayed.

JOHN BUNYAN

June 2

Will you not revive us again,
   that your people may rejoice in you?

The history of revival shows plainly that all movements of the Spirit started in prayer. It is right there
that many of us wilt and falter at the cost. Pentecost
and all subsequent outpourings of the Spirit resulted
from prayer. The same was true during the mighty
spiritual upheavals in Reformation times—Luther,
Knox and the Moravians at Herrnhut in 1727.
Hourly intercession by relays, praying without ceasing, went on for 100 years. It led to the beginning of
modern foreign missions. Why should we not match
the Moravian movement today? Has the Eternal
Spirit grown weary? Not likely. We may count on
it that the blessing is waiting for us if we will only
get down on our knees and ask for it. In latter days
the same principle of prayer holds—revivals under
Wesley, Finney, Spurgeon, Moody, Torrey, and the
Welsh revival—all resulted from prayer.

JONATHAN GOFORTH

Pray About It: All revivals issue from prayer. Perhaps
the greatest prayer movement in history was that
of the Moravians, as Jonathan Goforth mentions.
This great prayer meeting, which began on August
13, 1727, at Herrnhut ("the Lord's watch"), a small
colony founded by Count Nicholaus von Zinzindorf,
lasted around the clock for one hundred years. From it
came the modern missionary movement as more than

a hundred missionaries were sent out from that colony in twenty-five years.

Secular historians won't mention the true reasons for many of the world's major events—but any praying Christian understands the profound influence prayer has on history.

> Christians who pray are helpers and saviors, yea, masters and gods of the world. They are the legs which bear the world.
>
> MARTIN LUTHER

> I have one passion: it is He, He alone.
>
> COUNT NICHOLAUS VON ZINZINDORF

June 3

Be still, and know that I am God.

PSALM 46:10

In order to really know God, inward stillness is absolutely necessary. I remember when I first learned this. A time of great emergency had risen in my life, when every part of my being seemed to throb with anxiety, and when the necessity for immediate and vigorous action seemed overpowering; and yet circumstances were such that I could do nothing, and the person who could, would not stir.

For a little while it seemed as if I must fly to pieces with the inward turmoil, when suddenly the still small voice whispered in the depths of my soul,

"Be still, and know that I am God." The word was with power, and I listened. I composed my body to perfect stillness, and I constrained my troubled spirit into quietness, and looked up and waited; and then I did "know" that it was God, God even in the very emergency and in my helplessness to meet it; and I rested in Him.

It was an experience that I would not have missed for worlds; and I may add also, that out of this stillness seemed to arise a power to deal with the emergency, that very soon brought it to a successful issue. I learned then effectually that my strength was to sit still.

HANNAH WHITALL SMITH

Pray About It: Emergencies prompt us to pray. But often our prayers are tainted by our anxiety. We pray to God, but with one eye still fixed to the trouble at hand. But when we look fully to God in stillness, with both eyes trained on Him, we display our faith.

God knows full well about your current problem. Not once has it been off His mind. And for that reason alone, you can rest and be still about its resolution. In God's mind, the matter has already been settled. Watch and see.

Beloved! Let us take His stillness!

A. B. SIMPSON

June 4

Give me neither poverty nor riches,
  but give me only my daily bread.
Otherwise, I may have too much and disown you
  and say, "Who is the LORD?"
Or I may become poor and steal,
  and so dishonor the name of my God.

PROVERBS 30:8–9

A great many people do not pray because they do not feel any sense of need. The sign that the Holy Spirit is in us is that we realize that we are empty, not that we are full. We have a sense of absolute need. We come across people who try us, circumstances that are difficult, conditions that are perplexing, and all these things awaken a dumb sense of need, which is a sign that the Holy Spirit is there.

  If we are ever free from the sense of need, it is not because the Holy Spirit has satisfied us, but because we have been satisfied with as much as we have. A sense of need is one of the greatest benedictions because it keeps our life rightly related to Jesus Christ.

OSWALD CHAMBERS

Pray About It: We are so accustomed to praying for God to meet our needs, to take them away, to fill us so that we're no longer empty. Today, let's pray that He keep us as needy as necessary to stay in conscious dependence on Him. And that we stay as empty as necessary to hunger for His Spirit.

Oh, Lord, let us never be without need, lest we forget Thee!

The best disposition for praying is that of being desolate, forsaken, stripped of everything.

AUGUSTINE

June 5

For the eyes of the Lord are on the righteous
and his ears are attentive to their prayer,
but the face of the Lord is against those who do evil.

1 PETER 3:12

Consider well before you put any object or person before you in prayer; whether it is according to the will of God; whether you can claim for your request a definite promise, whether it is laid as a burden on your heart by the spirit of prayer, and having so determined, never cease praying till you have the answer, or at least the assurance of answer.

ARTHUR T. PIERSON

Pray About It: We are presented here with three tests for whether to pray for a certain thing. First, is it according to God's will? Second, is there a promise from God's Word that anchors your hope for this request? And third, is this a burden from God? If the answer to all three is yes, then you can pray in confidence.

Rather than offering random prayers with no heart behind them, use your time to pray for that which God will answer.

God does not mean, in hearing prayer, to abdicate His throne, or to substitute our judgment for His. So, He requires us to ascertain, as much as possible, what His judgment is, and to conform our prayers to it.

JOHN PATON

June 6

Very early in the morning, while it was still dark, Jesus got up, left the house and went off to a solitary place, where he prayed.

MARK 1:35

God seems to place a special value on prayer when it costs us something. Those who rise early in the morning enjoy fellowship with the One Who likewise arose early to receive His instructions for the day from His Father.

Likewise, those who are in such deadly earnest that they are willing to pray through the night enjoy a power with God that cannot be denied. Prayer that costs nothing is worth nothing; it is simply a by-product of a cheap Christianity.

WILLIAM MACDONALD

Pray About It: The biblical principle is that God gets the firstfruits. He gets—and deserves—the best. Our money, our time, our strength should all be apportioned to Him *first*. Too often we give Him our leftover money, time, or strength.

And so what's in it for us, if we give God the first part of the day or the long hours of the night? A power with God that cannot be denied. He will not be outgiven.

> Our responsibility in prayer is not a small matter—let us therefore watch and pray.
>
> WATCHMAN NEE

June 7

> Then King David went in and sat before the LORD.
> 1 CHRONICLES 17:16

Do not be afraid of silence in your prayer time. It may be that you are meant to listen, not to speak. So wait before the Lord. Wait in stillness. Wait as David waited when he "sat before the LORD."

And in that stillness, assurance will come to you. You will know that you are heard; you will know that your Lord ponders the voice of your humble desires; you will hear quiet words spoken to you yourself, perhaps to your grateful surprise and refreshment.

Amy Carmichael

Pray About It: Miss Carmichael practiced silence before God. But she also practiced silence about her needs before people. As with George Mueller, J. Hudson Taylor, and many others, Amy Carmichael never made the needs of her orphanage known. When the temptation came to let others know of some special need, God whispered, "I know, and that is enough." Indeed it was. Her testimony is that "never once in fifteen years has a bill been left unpaid. Never once has a man or woman been told when we were in need of help. But never once have we lacked any good thing."

Today, refresh yourself in silence—both before God and man. God isn't impressed by our many words and He alone knows your need.

Speak few words, but listen as long as you wish. Wait in stillness.

Fall on your knees and grow there. There is no burden of spirit but is lighter by kneeling under it. Prayer means not always talking to Him, but waiting before Him till the dust settles and the stream runs clear.

F. B. Meyer

June 8

Go into all the world and preach the gospel to every creature.

MARK 16:15 NKJV

If Christians prayed as Christians ought, with strong commanding faith, with earnestness and sincerity; men, God-called men, God-empowered men everywhere, would be all burning to go and spread the gospel worldwide. The Word of the Lord would be glorified as never known heretofore.

The God-influenced men, the God-inspired men, the God-commissioned men, would go and kindle the flame of sacred fire for Christ, salvation, and heaven, everywhere in all nations, and soon all men would hear the glad tidings of salvation and have an opportunity to receive Jesus Christ as their personal Savior.

E. M. BOUNDS

Pray About It: In truth, there's a shortage of Christian workers in a day when the fields are white to harvest. Let's pray with commanding faith for God-called men and women to say yes when God calls. May their hearts burn with a passion for the gospel.

Today, send someone to the mission field by praying it so.

The neglect of prayer is the great reason the Church has not greater power over the masses in Christian and in heathen countries.

ANDREW MURRAY

June 9

Whom have I in heaven but you?
And earth has nothing I desire besides you.
My flesh and my heart may fail,
  but God is the strength of my heart
  and my portion forever.

PSALM 73:25–26

The essence of prayer doesn't consist in asking God for something but in opening our hearts to God, in speaking with Him, and living with Him in perpetual communion. Prayer is continual abandonment to God. Prayer doesn't mean asking God for all kinds of things we want; it is rather the desire for God Himself, the only Giver of Life,

Prayer is not asking, but union with God. Prayer is not a painful effort to gain from God help in the varying needs of our lives. Prayer is the desire to possess God Himself, the Source of all life. The true spirit of prayer does not consist in asking for blessings, but in receiving Him who is the giver of all blessings, and in living a life of fellowship with Him.

SADHU SUNDAR SINGH

Pray About It: Too often in prayer we seek the gift, when to have the Giver is to have the gifts as well. The best blessing from God is Himself. Today, let your desire for God be your prayer.

The meaning of prayer is that we get hold of God, not of the answer.

OSWALD CHAMBERS

June 10

O LORD, I call to you; come quickly to me.
Hear my voice when I call to you.
May my prayer be set before you like incense;
    may the lifting up of my hands be like the
        evening sacrifice.

PSALM 141:1–2

Prayer pulls the rope below, and the great bell rings above in the ears of God. Some scarcely stir the bell, for they pray so languidly; others give but an occasional pluck at the rope; but he who wins with heaven is the man who grasps the rope boldly and pulls continuously, with all his might.

CHARLES HADDON SPURGEON

Pray About It: This is a wonderful image of prayer. We can picture the large steeple bell and see ourselves standing below with the rope in our hands. We are commissioned to ring the bell, and what is our response? A slight tug, an occasional jerk? Or do we with both hands pull boldly with all our might?

So let our prayers be today. Ring the bell loudly.

O the boldness with which we can draw near! O the great things we have a right to ask for!

ANDREW MURRAY

June 11

My God will meet all your needs according to his glorious riches in Christ Jesus.

PHILIPPIANS 4:19

[Mary Slessor (1848–1915) was a Scottish missionary to West Africa. The people that God sent this impoverished Presbyterian woman to minister to were warring tribes ruled by witchcraft. Danger was a daily companion. She eventually won the confidence of tribal chiefs with her courage, her medical skills, and her sense of humor. But underlying all her success was her life of prayer.]

My life is one long daily, hourly, record of answered prayer. For physical health, for mental overstrain, for guidance given marvelously, for errors and dangers averted, for enmity to the Gospel subdued, for food provided at the exact hour needed, for everything that goes to make up life and my poor service.

I can testify with a full and often wonderstricken awe that I believe God answers prayer. I *know* God answers prayer. . . .

I am sitting alone here on a log among a company of natives. My children, whose very lives are a testimony that God answers prayer, are working round me. Natives are crowding past on the bush road to attend palavers, and I am at perfect peace, far from my own countrymen and conditions, because I know God answers prayer.

Food is scarce just now. We live from hand to mouth. We have not more than will be our breakfast today, but I know we shall be fed, for God answers prayer.

MARY SLESSOR

Pray About It: When it comes to the power of prayer, missionaries are among the most convinced. Daily they see God at work in the everyday routine of life. But they not only depend on their own prayers, but those of the people back home.

Today is a day to pray for missionaries around the world. If you know some by name, pray specifically for them. Their work is hard and the rewards, though great, are often delayed. But as workers on the front lines, they see God move in ways that would astonish the rest of us.

Prayer is the mighty engine that is to move the missionary work forward.

A. B. SIMPSON

Much prayer for the mission cause by those at home means much power released on the mission field. Weakness at home means weakness on the field.

ALEXANDER MACLAREN

June 12

And this is my prayer: that your love may abound more and more in knowledge and depth of insight, so that you may be able to discern what is best and may be pure and blameless until the day of Christ.

PHILIPPIANS 1:9–10

Our prayer must not be self-centered. It must arise not only because we feel our own need as a burden we must lay upon God, but also because we are so bound up in love for our fellow men that we feel their need as acutely as our own. To make intercession for men is the most powerful and practical way in which we can express our love for them.

JOHN CALVIN

Pray About It: Love must lead to prayer. Prayer must lead to action. Who have you been praying for who needs to see your love in action? What can you do to meet that person's need? Love, then pray, then *act*.

Whosoever feels the love of God and man shed abroad in his heart, feels an ardent and uninterrupted thirst after the happiness of all his fellow-creatures. His soul melts with the fervent desire which he hath continually to promote it. . . .

In his tongue is the law of kindness. The same is impressed on all his actions. The flame within is continually working itself away, and spreading abroad more and more, in every instance of goodwill to all with whom he hath to do. So that whether he thinks or speaks, or whatever he does, it all points to the same end—the advancing, by every possible way, the happiness of all his fellow-creatures.

Deceive not, therefore, your own souls: He who is not thus kind, hath not love.

JOHN WESLEY

June 13

God be merciful to me a sinner.

LUKE 18:13 KJV

One of the best prayers ever offered is this prayer from a publican which Christ Himself lauded and held up as an example. In it there is no title, no "forever and ever, Amen," but only the cry of one man's broken heart over his sins.

HENRY WARD BEECHER

Pray About It: Possibly the best prayer we can ever pray is for God's mercy. We are all in the position of the publican who went up to pray, and the only words he could come up with were those of a cry for mercy. In this story, Jesus said another man, a Pharisee, also prayed. His prayer was one of thanks that he wasn't a sinner like the publican, but was quite religious. He boasted that he tithed of his income and fasted twice a week. But he was not commended for his prayer. Jesus in fact said that the publican "went down to his house justified," rather than the religious Pharisee.

Praise God for His mercy to sinners today. Where would we be without it?

> To have pardon extended from God to we sinners fills our heart and ravishes our soul! It gives a whole heaven of joy into our thoughts of salvation from sin, and deliverance from wrath to come.
>
> JOHN BUNYAN

June 14

Therefore do not worry about tomorrow, for tomorrow will worry about itself. Each day has enough trouble of its own.

MATTHEW 6:34

Let us move on and step out boldly, even if the darkness of night means that we can scarcely see our way.

The path ahead of us will open as we press on, like the trail through the forest, or the Alpine pass that discloses but a few rods of its length.

Often, God gives work for us to do without any light or illumination at all except His own command, but those who know the way to God can find it in the dark—one step at a time.

ALEXANDER MACLAREN

Pray About It: When we move ahead with God, very often only the next step ahead of us is visible. Our nature is to want the entire pathway lit. But if it were so lit, how could we walk by faith? It's only as we trust God for the next dark step that we exercise faith.

As you pray, trust Him for today's dark step. Don't consider tomorrow. The light for tomorrow's step will only shine tomorrow.

As every day demands its bread, so every day demands its prayer. No amount of praying today will suffice for tomorrow's praying. No amount of praying for tomorrow is of any great value to us today. So leave tomorrow with its cares, its needs, its troubles in God's hands. There is no storing tomorrow's grace, neither is there any laying up of today's grace to meet tomorrow's necessities.

E. M. BOUNDS

June 15

Ho! Everyone who thirsts,
Come to the waters;
And you who have no money,
Come, buy and eat.

ISAIAH 55:1 NKJV

I had the most ardent longings after God that ever I
felt in my life. At noon in my secret time of prayer I
could do nothing but tell my Lord, in a sweet calm,
that He knew I longed for nothing but Himself,
nothing but holiness; that He had given me these
desires and He only could give me the thing desired.
I never seemed to be so unhinged from myself and
to be so wholly devoted to God. My heart was swallowed up in God most of the day.

DAVID BRAINERD

Pray About It: These words were penned as the June
15 entry in Brainerd's journal. Shortly after this,
Brainerd went to be with the Lord at age twenty-nine,
his work on earth finished. Or so his contemporaries
thought. But like so many others, Brainerd's life still
speaks nearly three centuries after his death through
the words of the diary he left.

His testimony is like that of many others who have
made prayer a priority: his heart was swallowed up
in God all day. Entries such as the one above were
common in Brainerd's book. And his ministry would
continue on after his death as William Carey, the
father of modern missions, was so moved by it that
he left all and went to India, as did missionary Henry

Martyn. Robert Murray McCheyne was also highly influenced by Brainerd's life. The result was that the consecration of this young man was as instrumental in the missionary revival of the nineteenth century as any other single force.

All because David Brainerd prayed. His powerful words give us a peek at what awaits those who pray.

> I often heard David Brainerd pray and his manner of addressing himself to God, and expressing himself before his Heavenly Father in prayer is, so far as I may judge, rarely equaled.
>
> JONATHAN EDWARDS

June 16

> Let the high praises of God be in their mouth, and a two-edged sword in their hand.
>
> PSALM 149:6 KJV

> Praising God is one of the highest and purest acts of religion. In prayer we act like men. In praise we act like angels.
>
> THOMAS WATSON

Pray About It: At this moment, God is surrounded by the angels who praise Him day and night, without end. And He is deserving of it all. Today, let's set aside our petitions, the petitions of mere men, and take on the role of the angels.

Offer the sacrifice of praise to our God. And if there's time left, then pray.

Holy, holy, holy, Lord God of hosts, Heaven and earth are full of thy glory: Glory be to thee, O Lord Most High.

THE BOOK OF COMMON PRAYER

June 17

Brothers, pray for us.

1 THESSALONIANS 5:25

Remember, your intercessions can never be mine, and my intercessions can never be yours, but the Holy Spirit makes intercession for us, without which intercession someone will be impoverished. Let us remember the depth and height and solemnity of our calling as saints.

OSWALD CHAMBERS

Pray About It: There are prayers that only you can pray. There are prayers that only I can pray. There are people for whom no one else will pray, if not you. We can't trade prayer lists and be as effective. God has put on your heart and mine those requests that only we can pray to fruition.

The word *intercession* comes from the Latin. The *inter* means "between" and *cedere* means "to go." To intercede is to go between God and the person being prayed for.

It's a solemn thing to be an intercessor. We have a responsibility to "go between" for those whom God has given us. Someday we shall see what our prayers accomplished. Until then, we intercede by faith.

It is of great consequence that our intercession for others should be personal, pointed, and definite.

ANDREW MURRAY

June 18

He went in therefore, shut the door behind the two of them, and prayed to the Lord.

2 KINGS 4:33 NKJV

There are some people, also, who claim that they can pray and commune with God just as well in one place as in another. They do their praying while they walk around and while they work. They see no use in going apart to pray.

But surely if anyone could pray well in a crowd or while engaged in work, Jesus could. No doubt He did hold communion with His Father even in His busiest hours, but this did not meet all the needs and longings of His soul.

He left the crowd, left even His own disciples, and retired into places where no eye but God's could see Him, where no human presence or voice could interrupt the quiet of His soul, and where He would be absolutely alone.

Surely if He required such conditions in praying, we do too. We need to find a place for prayer in which nothing can intrude to break the continuity of thought or devotion.

J. R. MILLER

Pray About It: Jesus didn't make public prayer a priority—He made private prayer a necessity. We must follow His example and place ourselves where no eye but God's can see us and no ear but His can hear our voice. We must be absolutely alone. Today, take time to hide from the distractions of the world and be with God.

> God sees us in secret, therefore let us seek His face in secret. Though heaven be God's palace, yet it is not His prison.
>
> THOMAS BROOKS

June 19

Amen. Come, Lord Jesus.

REVELATION 22:20

This prayer stands as the climax of Christian aspiration. It is the final prayer of the Bible. The whole revelation of the Book leads up to this. Brethren, we should pray for the coming of God's king, Jesus. How often have you prayed for this?

R. A. TORREY

Pray About It: There's coming a day that will be the last day. The Lord Jesus Christ shall return as the climax of history occurs. The early Christians watched for that day, expecting it in their lifetime. Many generations since then have also assumed theirs was the last. And one day, one of those generations will be right. Perhaps it will be ours. The book of Revelation records the prayer that that day should come soon. Even so, come, Lord Jesus.

Follow the example of previous generations and make that your prayer today, remembering the words of John Nelson Darby:

> To me the Lord's coming is not a question of prophecy, but my present hope. . . . There is no event between me and heaven.

June 20

I called him, but he gave me no answer.
SONG OF SOLOMON 5:6 KJV

No prayer is lost. There is no such thing as prayer unanswered or unnoticed by God, and some things that we count refusals or denials are simply delays.
HORATIUS BONAR

Pray About It: That prayer that you prayed weeks ago, or months ago, or even years ago, isn't lost. God heard it and it's recorded in heaven. So too the prayer you pray today will be heard and answered. No prayer from God's children is lost to God's ear. Pray today knowing that the ripple of your prayer will resound through heaven even long after you've forgotten it.

There never was, and never will be a believing prayer unanswered.
ROBERT MURRAY MCCHEYNE

June 21

But as for you, continue in what you have learned
and have become convinced of.

2 TIMOTHY 3:14

Apostasy begins in the closet. No man ever backslid
from the life and power of Christianity who continued constant and fervent in private prayer.

ADAM CLARKE

Pray About It: We've all gone through times when
our hearts seemed cold to the things of God. In such
times, God's invitation to "Come" is all the more pro-
nounced. As we come to Him, our hearts are warmed
once again. But if we ignore His call to us, we will
grow all the colder. Temptations are less easily overcome. Cynicism moves in, along with his twin companion, doubt. From them, heartache and depression
result. Don't let the apostasy begin. Stay with God.

He who prays must wage a mighty warfare against
the doubt and murmuring excited by the faintheart-
edness and unworthiness we feel with us.

MARTIN LUTHER

June 22

Brothers, my heart's desire and prayer to God for the Israelites is that they may be saved.

ROMANS 10:1

Pray for the Jews. Their return to the God of their fathers stands connected, in a way we cannot tell, with wonderful blessing to the Church, and with the coming of our Lord Jesus.

ANDREW MURRAY

Pray About It: God has not rejected the Jews. Jesus Christ was a Jew as were the first Christians. The Messiahship of Jesus is for the Jews first, then for the Gentiles. The apostle Paul made praying for his Jewish brethren a priority. The great churchman Andrew Murray understood the heart of God toward the Jewish people. Corrie ten Boom is widely known for her book *The Hiding Place*, which tells the story of the price her family paid for hiding Jews in their home during the Holocaust of World War II. But the Ten Boom family had loved the Jewish people long before Corrie was born. In fact, her story may have been an answer to a century-old prayer. In 1844, Corrie's grandfather began a prayer meeting specifically for the purpose of praying for the Jewish people. It was exactly a hundred years later that Corrie and her family were arrested.

Today, many missions organizations are dedicated to winning Jewish people to Christ. Pray for them and for the peace of Jerusalem, the city where Jesus commanded that the good news be preached first. God's directive to pray for Jerusalem has never been countermanded. And it's never been more necessary than today.

Lord Jesus, I offer myself for your people. In any way. Any time.

CORRIE TEN BOOM

Pray for the peace of Jerusalem.

PSALM 122:6

June 23

Wait on the LORD: be of good courage, and he shall strengthen thine heart: wait, I say, on the LORD.

PSALM 27:14 KJV

Frequently the richest answers are not the speediest. . . . A prayer may be all the longer on its voyage because it is bringing us a heavier freight of blessing. Delayed answers are not only trials of faith, but they give us an opportunity of honoring God by our steadfast confidence in Him under apparent repulses.

CHARLES HADDON SPURGEON

Pray About It: If your prayers are delayed in being answered, it may be because a larger blessing is coming. Don't hurry God. His long-coming answers are the sweetest when they finally arrive.

I never prayed sincerely for anything but that it came. At some time, no matter at how distant a day, somehow, in some shape—probably the last I should devise—it came.

ADONIRAM JUDSON

June 24

The man who enters by the gate is the shepherd of his sheep. The watchman opens the gate for him, and the sheep listen to his voice. He calls his own sheep by name and leads them out. When he has brought out all his own, he goes on ahead of them, and his sheep follow him because they know his voice. But they will never follow a stranger; in fact, they will run away from him because they do not recognize a stranger's voice.

JOHN 10:2-5

The prayer life calls for seasons of silent times, times when we take ourselves away from the crowd, family, loved ones, business, and get quiet before Him.

One can be too busy about his Master's work and neglect these quiet, silent times, and become lean, grow peevish, fretful, cross.

Too often we talk too much when we pray. We do not give God a chance to say one word, and not a few times, we do nothing but beg—beg—beg; there is no note of praise or thankfulness.

W. J. HARNEY

Pray About It: Why should our prayers ever consist of begging? Are we beggars before God, or sons and daughters? Do the children of kings beg their father for their necessities? No, from their father they receive all the benefits of the kingdom as their heritage as princes and princesses.

Ask confidently and quietly. Don't beg. Be silent. Offer praise and thanksgiving.

> Silence promotes the presence of God, prevents many harsh and proud words, and suppresses many dangers in the way of ridiculing or harshly judging our neighbor. Silence humbles the mind, and gradually weans it from the world; it makes a kind of solitude in the heart.
>
> FRANÇOIS FÉNELON

June 25

> If anyone would come after me, he must deny himself and take up his cross and follow me.
>
> MARK 8:34

It is helpful to start each new day with a question like the following clearly before you: "Have I surrendered this new day to God, and will I seek and obey the guidance of the Holy Spirit throughout its hours?" Wait until, with the full consent of your will, you can say, "I have; I will."

ERIC LIDDELL

Pray About It: The value of early morning prayers is that it offers the opportunity to surrender the hours ahead to God and then live confidently in the Holy Spirit throughout the day.

As you pray today, seek the guidance of the Holy Spirit and obey His lead throughout the day.

> Obedience shouldn't be hard and forced, but ready, loving and spontaneous—the daily doing of one's duty. And not merely that we do our duty, but that in doing it we become more responsive to God.
>
> PHILLIPS BROOKS

June 26

> [We] will give our attention to prayer and the ministry of the word.
>
> ACTS 6:4

Evan Roberts says he had the "call" to prayer in Newcastle Emlyn in the autumn of 1904, but unexpectedly he found himself on a tide carrying him into public ministry, and the call to prayer for the time being sunk into abeyance.

It did not return as a definite call demanding attention until sometime in the spring of 1907. He was then in Leicester, in the weakness of a breakdown in health, which had kept him aside from public work since the beginning of 1906.

Even during this time of weakness there had been many indications of his power in prayer, and some very extraordinary answers to prayer had been given.

The call to prayer came back suddenly one day in the spring of 1907. The Lord's servant had been for two hours or more, with another, dealing exhaustively in prayer with the needs of the moment. The "time of prayer" was over, and he was occupied with some other thing, when a "draw" to prayer came again, and he said to himself, "If I obey this, I shall be always 'praying.'"

He dropped the matter at hand, and followed the draw to prayer, when he discovered a spring opened, as it were, in his spirit out of which came a prayer "stream" full of unction, just as other Spirit-taught believers find God opens the Word to them for the ministry of teaching or preaching.

Evan Roberts's prayer work lasted for seven years. He said that he fell asleep each night praying and awoke in the morning with his "spirit and mind alert for dealing with God" (*The Overcomer*, December 1914).

Pray About It: The above episode from the life of Evan Roberts illustrates the way God worked in his life. Not everyone will have so dramatic an experience. But God does lead us to pray and expects that we will follow. If we don't, our hesitation may impede the work God would have for us. Listen if God calls you to more prayer.

> Give yourselves to prayer and the ministry of the Word. If you do not pray, God will probably lay you aside from your ministry as He did me, to teach you to pray.
>
> ROBERT MURRAY MCCHEYNE

When God allows one of His children to be put on the shelf, He knows where they are. Don't get off the shelf before He lifts you off. Possess your soul in patience.

Oswald Chambers

June 27

Oh, how I love your law!
I meditate on it all day long.

Psalm 119:97

[The following is a description of George Mueller's devotional hour, taken from his journal:]

The first thing I did, after having asked in a few words the Lord's blessing upon His precious Word, was to begin to meditate on the Word of God, searching as it were every verse to get a blessing out of it; not for the sake of the public ministry of the Word, nor for the sake of preaching on what I meditated upon, but for the sake of obtaining food for my own soul.

The result I have found to be almost invariably this: that after a very few minutes my soul has been led to confession, or to thanksgiving, or to intercession, or to supplication; so that, though I did not, as it were, give myself to prayer, but to meditation, yet it turned almost immediately more or less into prayer.

George Mueller

Pray About It: When prayer is hard to start, lay it aside and begin with the Word. Read a psalm and meditate on it for a moment. Then turn it into a prayer. Your spirit will soon be soaring in prayer. Fellowship with the written Word turns into fellowship with the Living Word.

> The mightiest prayers are often those drenched with the Word of God.
>
> HERBERT LOCKYER

June 28

And pray in the Spirit on all occasions with all kinds of prayers and requests.

EPHESIANS 6:18

Let *Him* pray. Give up your own prayers; give up your own desires and your own requests. Yes, you have a will; yes, you have desires and requests. Nevertheless, let Him have the will, the desire that is in the prayers *He* prays.

MADAME GUYON

Pray About It: Think for a minute. What would Jesus pray for if He were still here on earth? But He *is* still here on earth, you say. He lives in my heart. And what does Jesus in your heart pray for? When you know, you must pray for it in His name. Let Him pray for it through you. Be His prayer vessel.

> Jesus is to be always praying through His people.
>
> E. M. BOUNDS

June 29

I will walk among you and be your God, and you will be my people.

LEVITICUS 26:12

In a sense, all men may pray: it is a creature-privilege. But such prayer, sin having intervened, places God under no obligation. When, however, God enters into covenant agreement with man, prayer is the exercise of a covenant-privilege. God has obligated Himself. It is a mutual matter. God must do His part. Thus prayer becomes more than mere prayer; it is communion and fellowship.

NORMAN B. HARRISON

Pray About It: Why does God answer prayer? It's because He's instituted a new covenant with man, based on grace, not on law. Part of this new covenant is His commitment to the prayers of His people. He has given us promises regarding prayer that He *cannot* and *will not* break.

God can do anything but lie. We have His word. Prayer is a granted privilege of His children. He is bound by His integrity to hear our prayers.

Pray in confidence. He has bound Himself to hear your requests.

Covenant blessings are not meant to be looked at only, but to be appropriated. O Christian, I beseech you, do not treat God's promises as if they were curiosities for a museum, but use them as everyday sources of comfort.

CHARLES HADDON SPURGEON

June 30

Forgetting what is behind and straining toward what is ahead, I press on toward the goal to win the prize for which God has called me heavenward in Christ Jesus.

PHILIPPIANS 3:13-14

I have learned to see a need of everything God gives me, and want nothing that He denies me. Whether it be taken from or not given me, sooner or later God quiets me in Himself without it. I cast all my concerns on the Lord, and live securely on the care and wisdom of my heavenly Father.

JOSEPH ELIOT

Pray About It: The things that God has given you were given because He saw your need of them. In His role as Father, He then provided them—missing nothing.

The things you have been denied you never really needed. They are not for you. Lot's wife looked back longingly at something she couldn't have, and it meant her destruction. Those who were willing to leave Sodom behind and look ahead to God's provision, selected for them, were saved.

Look ahead.

Forget the things you don't have. You don't need them at all.

You had better be a poor person and a rich Christian, than a rich person and a poor Christian. You had better do anything and bear anything and be anything than a dwarf in grace.

THOMAS BROOKS

July 1

Again, I tell you that if two of you on earth agree about anything you ask for, it will be done for you by my Father in heaven. For where two or three come together in my name, there am I with them.

MATTHEW 18:19–20

Unite with you in prayer, one or more of the most devout disciples, especially in critical cases. One great advantage is that selfishness is apt to color our supplications, and when others are united with us, they are less affected by motives that may unduly influence us.

ARTHUR T. PIERSON

Pray About It: The value of prayer partners for special occasions can't be underestimated. Who do you have in your life that you can depend on for urgent prayer when necessary?

Prayer by oneself is indispensable, but remember that Jesus promised to be in the midst of two or three gathered in His name. Today, consider who you might ask to be an occasional or regular prayer partner. God will draw you closer to each other and to Himself.

If the prayer of one saint has power with God, then the prayer of two saints may be said to have double the moral power; and in proportion as God's people unite in asking for a specific gift, must be the certainty of its being granted.

JOHN PATON

July 2

Beyond all question, the mystery of godliness is great.

1 TIMOTHY 3:16

The reason for human intercession in the divine plan has not been wholly revealed. The repeated statements of Scripture that it is a necessary link in the chain that carries the divine energy into the impotent souls of men, in addition to its actual achievement as seen in the world, must be the sufficient evidence of the imperative need for the prayer in connection with the purpose of God. Thus in the Scriptures and in experience it is revealed that God has honored man with an exalted place of cooperation and partnership with Himself in His great projects of human transformation.

LEWIS SPERRY CHAFER

Pray About It: Face it, God could do whatever He wants, whenever He wants. Why did He even bother with creating prayer? For one important reason — He wants to use us in fulfilling His plan. We become colaborers with God as we unite with Him in prayer. This is one of the highest privileges of the believer. And yet, prayer is still a great mystery. But a mystery spawned from God's love.

Prayer is the most wonderful act in the spiritual realm as well as a most mysterious affair.

WATCHMAN NEE

July 3

Be merciful to those who doubt; snatch others from the fire and save them.

JUDE 22–23

> Some want to live within the sound
> Of church or chapel bell.
> I want to run a rescue shop
> Within a yard of hell.

C. T. STUDD

Pray About It: Nobody talks much about hell anymore. Satan has convinced most people, including many Christians, to disbelieve in hell or to minimize its importance. But Jesus warned about hell and so should we. May our prayers be as large heavenly hooks, snatching those we love from the destiny of hell. Your prayer closet can be that rescue shop within a yard of hell's gates.

Today, ask yourself: Does hell know and fear you?

If sinners be damned, at least let them leap to Hell over our bodies. If they will perish, let them perish with our arms about their knees. Let no one go there unwarned and unprayed for.

CHARLES HADDON SPURGEON

July 4

Blessed is the nation whose God is the LORD.

PSALM 33:12

I have often said it would be very desirable, and very likely to be followed with a great blessing, if there could be an agreement of all God's people in America . . . to keep a Day of Fasting and Prayer to God; wherein, we should all unite on the same day. . . .

It seems to me, it would mightily encourage and animate God's saints, in humbly and earnestly seeking God, for such blessings which concerns them all; and that it would be much for the rejoicing of all, to think, that at the same time such multitudes of God's dear children, far and near, were sending up their cries to the same common Father for the same motives.

JONATHAN EDWARDS

Pray About It: The nation that honors God is *blessed*. A nation that departs from God enters into a sad decline and ultimately falls. Today, America is well on the way to confirming that historical trend. Though founded by godly men and women who were fearless Christians, America has now become a nation of secularists who deny the influence of righteousness in exalting a nation. Many public schools have revised the history they're teaching the next generation, eliminating all mention of the true history that shaped our civilization. At the same time Hollywood openly degrades Christian morality—often with the consent (and dollars) of those who call themselves Christians—and often clearly marketed to that same younger, vulnerable generation. All the while, those who predict a strong future for America, mistakenly do so by looking to Wall Street and other economic indicators, ignoring what history has told us about such folly.

But America isn't alone in its decline. Other nations that once were in the forefront of proclaiming Christianity have also recklessly abandoned their heritage.

And yet, in spite of this gloomy news, there *is* hope. Some Christians are praying. Not content to see the destruction of their land, believers in countries all over the world are praying for revival in *their* country. Many are also interceding for America because of our historic leadership role in world affairs.

Will God answer these prayers? Will there be revival? No one knows for sure. It must surely depend on the urgency with which God's people besiege heaven for a fresh outpouring of God's Spirit. And as Jonathan Edwards notes, how encouraging it would be to know that on one singular day, millions are uniting in prayer for that one goal—God's blessing on the nation.

Some interceding Christians have set aside specific days to pray just for America. The first Friday of each month has been named by at least one group as a special day of prayer. But also on this day, the Fourth of July, Americans can surely take time to recall the rich spiritual history that led to this day of independence and *pray*. Citizens of other countries are encouraged to intercede for their native land today also.

> Let your mercy and blessing, O Lord of lords, rest upon our land and nation, upon the powers which you have ordained over us.
>
> HANDLEY C.G. MOULE
> [AS HE PRAYED FOR HIS NATIVE ENGLAND]

July 5

Then will I go to the altar of God,
to God, my joy and my delight.

PSALM 43:4

No one should give the answer that it is impossible
for a Christian occupied with worldly cares to pray
always. You can set up an altar to God in your mind
by means of prayer. And so it is fitting to pray at
your trade, on a journey, standing at a counter or
sitting at your handicraft.

JOHN CHRYSOSTOM

Pray About It: Today, at your place of work or in
your home—wherever you spend most of your days,
find a place that you can secretly consider your altar;
the counter, the desk, the workbench, the sewing
machine, the kitchen sink—wherever you spend a lot
of time. And then allow that place to be a reminder of
God's presence with you as you work.

The story is told of a farmer who stopped his plow
at the end of every tenth round of his long furrowed
field for a few moments of prayer. He said that not
only was his strength renewed but the horses had
more endurance for the day's work. What's the equivalent of the furrowed field where you work?

Find a way to regularly pray every day as you go
about your daily routine.

Prayer continues in the desire of the heart, though
the mind is employed on outward things.

JOHN WESLEY

July 6

This is the confidence that we have in him, that, if we ask any thing according to his will, he heareth us: And if we know that he hear us, whatsoever we ask, we know that we have the petitions that we desired of him.

1 JOHN 5:14–15 KJV

Many find an easy way of escape from this [verse]. They pray for whatever they think best, and then qualify it with — "if it be Thy will." This is particularly the case when it comes to prayer for the sick, and it is generally looked upon as signifying commendable submission to the unknown will of God, or perhaps by others as the best that is possible under the circumstances.

Among the many examples of Bible prayers, this kind is conspicuous by its absence. How can a hit-or-miss prayer of this spirit be in faith? And if not in faith how can it be pleasing to God?

The New Testament does not encourage us to wander on in our ignorance, it emphasizes the need of being "filled with the knowledge of His will" (Col. 1:9); it commands us to "understand what the will of the Lord is" (Eph. 5:17); it exhorts us to "prove what is the will of God" (Rom. 12:2).

Now if we are always falling back on to the safety of these "if-it-be-Thy-will prayers" we are debasing this most well-known prayer promise of the apostle John, and making it a prayer "let-out," a useful carpet under which we can sweep all our unanswered prayers. We imply that what he is really saying is this: "And this is the lack of confidence which we have in Him, that unless we are happy to ask according to His will, He will not hear us, and we shall not have our petition." So the promise that was intended to confirm our faith serves only to cover our unbelief and to confirm us in our state of weakness, in seeking to prevail with God.

ARTHUR WALLIS

Pray About It: Too often we leave God the option of not answering our prayer by tacking the words "if it be Thy will" on the end of our prayers. Of course, we want our prayers to be His will—that goes without saying. But why not make our prayers be in accordance with His will in the first place and leave off the escape clause? Through His Word and through knowing Him, learn to discern His will in a matter and pray for it to be done.

God doesn't need us to give Him an easy out if He doesn't answer as we think He should.

What God asks is a will which will no longer be divided between Him and any creature, a will pliant in His hands, which neither desires anything nor refuses anything, which wants without reservation everything which He wants, and which never, under any pretext, wants anything which He does not want.

FRANÇOIS FÉNELON

July 7

Now the end of the commandment is charity out of a pure heart, and of a good conscience, and of faith unfeigned.

1 Timothy 1:5 KJV

God doesn't look at the elegancy of your prayers to see how neat they are; nor at the geometry of your prayers to see how long they are; nor at the arithmetic of your prayers to see how many they are; nor at the music of your prayers; nor the sweetness of your voice; nor the logic of your prayers; but at the sincerity of your prayers, how hearty they are.

Thomas Brooks

Pray About It: The common denominator of all prayers honored by God is that they come from a humble heart. The proud He will not hear. Don't worry about anything except being entirely honest as you pray. God cannot be fooled. Lay it *all* before Him. Pour out your heart.

When does the building of the Spirit really begin to appear in a Christian's heart? It begins, so far as we can judge, when the believer first pours out his or her heart to God in prayer.

J. C. Ryle

July 8

Give thanks in all circumstances, for this is God's will for you in Christ Jesus.

1 THESSALONIANS 5:18

Nothing occurs by accident under the superintendence of an all-wise and perfectly just God. Nothing happens by chance in God's moral or natural government. God is a God of order, a God of law, but none-the-less a superintendent in the interest of His intelligent and redeemed creatures. Nothing can take place without the knowledge of God.

E. M. BOUNDS

Pray About It: So often we spend time telling God our woes—and that's all right, He sympathetically listens while we unload. But just remember: all that you're telling Him isn't news to Him; He's known it all. He is in utter control of this universe. There has never been one split second when something has happened of which God was unaware.

Such an awareness as we pray should add great confidence to our petitions. Pray boldly then.

Known unto God are all His ways from the beginning of the world.

GEORGE WHITEFIELD

July 9

But God has surely listened
and heard my voice in prayer.
Praise be to God,
who has not rejected my prayer
or withheld his love from me!

PSALM 66:19–20

Do we know the power of our supernatural weapon?
Do we dare to use it with the authority of a faith
that commands as well as asks? God baptizes us
with holy audacity and divine confidence! He is not
wanting great men, but He is wanting men who will
dare to prove the greatness of their God. But God!
But prayer!

A. B. SIMPSON

Pray About It: God's call to prayer is a call to wield
the most atomic weapon ever created. Our prayers
have unlimited power because our God has unlimited
power. So when we pray, it's not the might of our
prayers but the might of our God that counts. Weak
Christians become strong in prayer as they lean on the
One who is strength. "But God! But prayer!"

Unbelief says, "How can such and such things be?"
It is full of *how's;* but faith has one great answer to
the ten thousand *how's,* and that answer is—God!

C. H. MACKINTOSH

July 10

. . . the simplicity that is in Christ.

2 CORINTHIANS 11:3 KJV

Prayer has been hedged about with too many man-made rules. I am convinced that God has intended prayer to be as simple and natural and as constant a part of our spiritual life as the intercourse between a child and his parent in the home. And as a large part of that intercourse between parent and child is simply asking and receiving, just so it is with us and our heavenly Parent.

ROSALIND GOFORTH

Pray About It: Have you subconsciously allowed your prayer life to become subject to man-made rules or traditions that may seem to enhance spirituality, but which, in reality, are empty gestures toward God?

To learn prayer is to learn simplicity. We should no more complicate our communication with God with rituals than we would demand formality from our children when they want to be in our lap.

Your heavenly Father is waiting for your prayer today. Talk to Him as if He is simply the best and most wonderful daddy there ever was.

And you'll be right.

Stop! Pause! Consider! Where are we? What are we doing? . . . Praying to God! The great God, the Maker of all worlds, the Judge of all men! What reverence! What simplicity! What sincerity! What truth in the inward parts is demanded! How real we must be! How hearty! Prayer to God the noblest exercise, the loftiest effort of man, the most real thing!

E. M. BOUNDS

July 11

Do not neglect your gift.

1 TIMOTHY 4:14

Whenever we live prayerless lives we are neglecting, we are vacating, our office. What would we think if we went downtown in one of our cities, only to find desks closed and office doors locked, businessmen neglecting their office, the work they have undertaken? It is no different with Christians when they are neglectful of prayer. The work to which they have been officially called and appointed remains undone.

Moreover, we are not alone in this work. When Jesus ascended on high, it was to take upon Himself the office-work of High Priest. It is an office with a real work, an age-long task—"He ever liveth to make intercession." In appointing us to the office of priests He is privileging us to share His work. He asks us to take part of it upon ourselves. This is just what we do when we engage in prayer. How glorious the task! Surely we will not neglect it.

NORMAN B. HARRISON

Pray About It: The specific prayer life to which you are called is glorious. It is *your* assignment, *your* gift. We must not vacate our posts of prayer. The task is magnificent, the rewards—both here and in eternity—are beyond description.

Take up your office today with joy.

> Every work of God can be traced to some kneeling form.
>
> DWIGHT L. MOODY

July 12

I know how thou hast not fainted.

REVELATION 2:3

I suppose the more perfectly we live in His Presence the more quickly we shall be aware of Him, and the more clearly we shall hear Him; but I do know that at any time we may be tested by disappointment, and need to ask God to give us persistence. And He will not refuse. He understands. He has told us that He does. And in the end—oh, joy of all joys—we shall hear the Voice we love best in all the world saying to us, even to us, "I know . . . how thou hast not fainted."

AMY CARMICHAEL

Pray About It: We have all experienced disappointment in prayer. But should such disappointments discourage us? All they really do is demonstrate that we don't see the whole picture of our life as God does. We look at the bottom of the tapestry and see the loose threads. God sees the top, where the beauty resides.

In disappointment, don't faint. Grasp onto God even tighter. Don't let disappointment rob you of God. Let it drive you to Him.

> God is telling you, "You think it's all over. You see only your circumstances — failure, ruin, no results. So you say, 'This is the end.' But I say it is the beginning! I see the reward that I'm about to pour out on you. I have good things in mind for you — wonderful things. So, stop your crying!"
>
> DAVID WILKERSON

July 13

The Spirit also helpeth our infirmities [and] maketh intercession for us with groanings which cannot be uttered.

ROMANS 8:26 KJV

The soul that prays rightly must do with the help and strength of the Spirit; because it is impossible that a Christian should express himself in prayer without it. By this I mean that it is impossible that the heart, in a sincere and affectionate way, should pour out itself before God, with those groans and signs that come from a truly praying heart, without the assistance of the Spirit.

It is not the mouth that is the main thing to be looked at in prayer, but whether the heart is so full of affection and earnestness in prayer with God that it is impossible to express their sense and desire; for then a man desires indeed, when his desires are so strong, many, and mighty, that all the words, tears and groans that come from the heart cannot utter them.

That is but poor prayer which is only one of words. A man that truly prays one prayer cannot express with his mouth or pen the unutterable desires, sense, affection, and longing that went to God in his prayer. The best prayers have often more groans than words: and those words that they have are but a lean and shallow representation of the heart, life, and spirit of prayer.

JOHN BUNYAN

Pray About It: The language of the Spirit is sometimes intelligible only to God. We are wordless because our heart is simply too full or too burdened for words to suffice.

Today, allow the Spirit of God to edit your prayers to the essential words necessary. He understands all the other words you would also say, the hidden ones that have prompted that one solitary effectual groan.

Groanings which cannot be uttered are often prayers which cannot be refused.

CHARLES HADDON SPURGEON

264

July 14

So they all praised the LORD, the God of their fathers; they bowed low and fell prostrate before the LORD and the king.

I CHRONICLES 29:20

[John "Praying" Hyde (1865–1912) was a Presbyterian missionary to the Punjab area of India, where he worked in remote villages doing a largely unseen and unheralded work for the poor. Discouraged by the few conversions he saw, Hyde changed his ministry to that of prayer—intense prayer, sometimes spending forty or more hours on his knees. As a result the conversions increased dramatically; and still Hyde prayed on. And on. In 1904 he helped found the Punjab Prayer Union to emphasize prayer among missionaries and their converts in India. The following is a remembrance by one of his colleagues.]

I owe John Hyde more than I owe to any man, for showing me what a prayer-life is, and what a real consecrated life is. I shall ever praise God for bringing me into contact with him. . . . The first time I met him was in the Punjab, where he lived at the time. I had been invited to speak a few words on the Revival in the Khassia Hills to the Conference of the United States Presbyterian Mission, who had their annual session at the time there. I had traveled by night from Allahabad to Ludhiana, and reached there early in the morning. I was taken to have a cup of tea with the delegates and others, and I was introduced across the table to Mr. Hyde. All

265

that he said to me was, "I want to see you; I shall wait for you at the door." There he was waiting, and his first word was, "Come with me to the prayer room, we want you there." I do not know whether it was a command or a request. I felt I had to go. I told him that I had traveled all night, and that I was tired, and had to speak at four o'clock, but I went with him. We found half-a-dozen persons there, and Hyde went down on his face before the Lord. I knelt down, and a strange feeling crept over me. Several prayed, and then Hyde began, and I remember very little more. I knew that I was in the presence of God Himself, and had no desire to leave the place; in fact, I do not think that I thought of myself or of my surroundings, for I had entered a new world, and I wanted to remain there.

CAPTAIN E. G. CARRE

Pray About It: All who know how to pray are privileged to enter that new world into which John "Praying" Hyde ushered Captain Carre. In that world where God makes His presence known is incredible peace, joy unspeakable. We don't have to pray for forty hours to get there. We can enter in as soon as we fall on our knees. But the more we pray, the more of that world we want and the harder it is to return to this world. It's there that we want to remain. That world is open to you today, as you pray.

As you end your prayer time today, close with one of Praying Hyde's favorite expressions: *"Bol Yisu Masih, Ki Jai!"* ("Shout the Victory of Jesus Christ!")

July 15

On the last and greatest day of the Feast, Jesus stood and said in a loud voice, "If anyone is thirsty, let him come to me and drink. Whoever believes in me, as the Scripture has said, streams of living water will flow from within him."

JOHN 7:37–38

A godly man is a praying man. As soon as grace is poured in, prayer is poured out. Prayer is the soul's traffic with Heaven; God comes down to us by His Spirit, and we go up to Him by prayer.

THOMAS WATSON

Pray About It: The trouble with many Christians is that what God pours in, they *keep* in. God would have us give out all His grace, all His blessing. We do this through action and through prayer. And what happens when we give to others from the grace given to us? We get even more. We become a channel of God's presence in this world. The more grace we give out, the more God pours in.

O Lord, keep me sensitive to the grace that is round about me. May the familiar not become neglected! May I see Thy goodness in my daily bread, and may the comfort of my home take my thoughts to the mercy seat of God.

J. H. JOWETT

July 16

Thy will be done on earth as it is in heaven.

MATTHEW 6:10 KJV

Let each servant of Christ learn to know his calling. His King ever lives to pray. The Spirit of the King ever lives in us to pray. It is from heaven the blessings, which the world needs, must be called down in persevering, importunate, believing prayer. It is from heaven, in answer to prayer, the Holy Spirit will take complete possession of us to do His word through us.

ANDREW MURRAY

Pray About It: When we pray, it is from heaven that we receive our answer — from another place entirely than this earth. We forget that because our citizenship is in heaven, we have access to every spiritual blessing. It's no wonder then that Jesus told us to pray "Thy will be done on earth as it is in heaven." For God's will in heaven is forever good and right and perfect.

Can Thy will, O God, be done in earth as it is in heaven? It can be, and it must be; for a prayer wrought in the soul by the Holy Spirit is ever the shadow of a coming blessing, and He that taught us to pray after this manner did not mock us with vain words.

CHARLES SPURGEON

July 17

A longing fulfilled is sweet to the soul.

PROVERBS 13:19

Prayer is so necessary, and the source of so many blessings, that he who has discovered the treasure cannot be prevented from having recourse to it, whenever he has an opportunity.

FRANÇOIS FÉNELON

Pray About It: Those who will continue in prayer are those who have learned its secret: that prayer is the fountainhead of every blessing. Once we've discovered that, by personal experience, nothing can keep us away from praying. Today, what is the longing that God can fulfill that will be sweet to your soul?

The spirit of prayer is more precious than treasures of gold and silver.

JOHN BUNYAN

July 18

Have not I commanded thee? Be strong and of a good courage; be not afraid, neither be thou dismayed: for the LORD thy God is with thee whithersoever thou goest.

JOSHUA 1:9 KJV

The secret prayer chamber is a bloody battleground. Here violent and decisive battles are fought out. Here the fate of souls for time and eternity is determined, in quietude and solitude.

OLE HALLESBY

Pray About It: Remember that in the prayer battle, we're fighting from the high ground. God has given us the victory—we no longer need to pray for it—we need to walk in it as our blood-bought right.

The enemy seeks to rob what we have been freely given. Our battle is to simply possess that which is ours and to enforce our rights won at Calvary. We fight from the victorious side of the battle. Today, be strong and of good courage. Stand firm on the high ground in prayer.

Prayer is not preparation for work, it *is* work.
Prayer is not preparation for the battle, it *is* the battle.

OSWALD CHAMBERS

July 19

I am the bread of life. He who comes to me will never go hungry.

JOHN 6:35

When a man is born from above, the life of the Son of God is born in him, and he can either starve that life or nourish it. Prayer is the way the life of God is nourished. Our ordinary views of prayer are not found in the New Testament. We look upon prayer as a means of getting things for ourselves; the Bible idea of prayer is that we may get to know God Himself.

OSWALD CHAMBERS

Pray About It: Are you hungry today? Then eat heartily through prayer. Our Lord Jesus is our bread, our sustenance, our nourishment. When we fail to eat of Him, we grow spiritually weak. Sometimes we don't willfully neglect to feed on Him, we just get busy. But just as physical hunger pangs tell us it's time to eat food, so too does God allow spiritual hunger pangs to draw us to Him.

Eat heartily today. Be nourished by the bread of life.

My spirit is dry within me because it forgets to feed on thee.

JOHN OF THE CROSS

July 20

We, who are many, are one body, for we all partake of the one loaf.

1 CORINTHIANS 10:17

I have gone through the Book of God, and wherever I have found a man or woman of power, I have found a man or woman of prayer. I have searched through the history of the Church and have found some people who loved the liturgy and some who cared very little for the liturgy; I have some who were Calvinists and some who were Arminians; some who were rich and some who were poor; but wherever in the history of the Church I have found a man or woman of power, I have found God's children who knew how to pray.

J. C. RYLE

Pray About It: Wherever Christians are willing to pray, power results. We may differ on doctrine — some Christians reading this today are Baptists, some Pentecostals, some Methodists, Presbyterians, Lutherans, Arminians, Calvinists, Pre-Tribbers, Post-Tribbers, and just about anything else you can imagine. But beyond all those labels is the God of the Christian. The Father of all brothers and sisters who believe. And in every case, power comes when prayer is highly regarded.

Today, look around at the diversity in the body of Christ and thank God for them all — even those with whom you disagree. Christians in countries where to be a Christian is a crime are united, not divided, by their faith in Christ. Will it take such drastic steps for that to happen to us?

> I love Thy Church, O God!
> Her wall before Thee stand,
> Dear as the apple of Thine eye,
> And graven on Thy hand.
>
> TIMOTHY DWIGHT

July 21

I will save you from the hands of the wicked
  and redeem you from the grasp of the cruel.

JEREMIAH 15:21

Your child is falling from a window. By the action of a natural law he will be killed. But he cries out for help, "Father! Father!" Hearing his call, in this his day of trouble, you rush forth and catch him in your arms. Your child is saved. Natural law would have killed him, but you interposed, and, without a miracle, saved him. And cannot the great Father of all do what an earthly parent does?

NEWMAN HALL

Pray About It: When we pray, we are often asking God to intervene in natural circumstances. We, or someone we love, is falling, and we cry for help. God catches us, so to speak, and changes the natural circumstances in such a way as to effect the outcome on our behalf. Sometimes we're aware that God must do something about changing certain natural circumstances. There must be a miracle. God is not reluctant to help us either with natural means or with a miracle. Leave the choosing of the means to God, natural or miracle. If we're falling fast enough and we're caught, does it really matter how God intervenes, as long as He catches us? Then let God choose.

> They tell us of the fixed laws of nature! but who dares maintain that He who fixed these laws cannot use them for the purpose of answering His people's prayers?
>
> WILLIAM M. TAYLOR

July 22

Now the serpent was more crafty than any of the wild animals the LORD God had made. He said to the woman, "Did God really say . . . "

GENESIS 3:1

Often [when we pray] there is a wrestle. A thousand invisible enemies will seem to fill the air and crowd between you and your Lord. Each of them has a stinging or depressing word. We shall be reminded of prayers to which no answers have come yet (or what we call answers), and told that it will make no difference whether we pray or not.

We shall be shown our own dreadful nothingness so clearly that we shall hardly be able to bring ourselves to believe that such prayers as we can offer will rise to God at all. Our wrestling is with these whispering or shouting spiritual foes. We must press through, fight through, and the sword with which to fight is the blessed word of God.

AMY CARMICHAEL

Pray About It: When we pray, the accusations of the enemy are endless. Either we're not worthy to have our prayers answered, or God isn't listening or can't do what we want, or, worse yet, hears us but won't give us what we need.

It's the Word of God that we must use in such times to rout the enemy from our prayer closets. At the first hint of doubt or accusation, find a relevant Bible verse and stand unflinchingly on it. Don't let Satan respond. He has no standing when the Sword of the Spirit pierces him.

Know your Bible; learn to wield the Sword with effectiveness.

Destroy the enemy!

It is the sword of the Spirit, because He is the great Master in the use of it. Oh, that He would come and show us how He can thrust and cleave with it! In this house of prayer we have often seen Him at His work. Here the slain of the Lord have been many. We have seen this sword take off the head of many a Goliath doubt, and slay a horde of cares and unbeliefs.

CHARLES HADDON SPURGEON

July 23

Falling down on his face he will worship God, and
report that God is in you of a truth.

1 CORINTHIANS 14:25 KJV

In the afternoon "God was in me of a truth." Oh,
it was blessed company indeed! God enabled me so
to agonize in prayer that I was quite wet with sweat,
though in the shade and the cool wind. My soul was
drawn out very much for the world; I grasped for
multitudes of souls. I think I had a greater burden
for sinners than for the children of God, though I
felt as if I could spend my life in cries for both.

I enjoyed great sweetness in communion with
my dear Saviour. I think I never in my life felt such
an entire weanedness from this world and so much
resigned to God in everything. Oh, that I may
always live to God!

DAVID BRAINERD

Pray About It: David Brainerd often retreated to the
woods for times of "agonizing in prayer." This particular time was the occasion of his twenty-fifth birthday
and he had set it aside for prayer and fasting.

When a prayer warrior is so fully moved with
compassion for primarily the lost as was Brainerd, he
is most acutely identifying with the heart of God. It's
God's will that none should perish but that all should
come to everlasting life—and yet multitudes are lost.
God weeps, David Brainerd weeps, and we will weep
if we catch a glimpse of what these two see. The result

is "sweetness in communion with the dear Savior." What a reward! What a birthday present!

When his critics told William Booth he was moving too fast in his ministry to the lost, he said, "If anyone wants a reply, let him ask the lost souls in Hell whose brothers and sisters are following them there. Let him go and ask the blood-washed throng in Heaven, whose eyes are wide open at last to the value of salvation. Let him anticipate the Judgment Day, and in spirit stand before the Throne and propose, if he dares, the question to God Almighty. I think from Hell, Heaven and the Great White Throne, the answer would come back, 'More speed! Go faster! . . . Push forward! Hurry onward! Save the world!'"

July 24

Truly my soul waiteth upon God.

PSALM 62:1 KJV

[The literal translation of this verse is] "Only toward God my soul is in silence"; or, "Only for God waits my soul all hushed." The noises of contending desires, the whispers of earthly hopes, are hushed: and the soul listens.

This is the test of true waiting. Wait before God till the voices, suggestions, and energies of nature become silent. Then only can God realize his uttermost of salvation. This was the secret of Abraham's long trial. He was left waiting till nature was spent, till all expedients proving abortive were surrendered; till all that knew him pitied him for clinging to an impossible dream.

But as this great silence fell on him, the evidence of utter helplessness and despair, there arose within his soul an ever-accumulating faith in the power of God; and there was no obstacle to prevent God realizing all, and beyond all, because all the glory accrued to Himself.

This is why God keeps you waiting. All that is of self and nature must be silenced; one voice after another cease to boast; one light after another be put out; until the soul is shut up to God alone. This process prevails equally in respect to salvation from penalty, deliverance from the power of sin, and our efforts to win souls. O my soul, be silent! Hush thee! Wait thou only upon God! Surrender thy cherished plans and reliances. Only when death has done its perfect work, will He bestow the power of an endless life.

F. B. Meyer

Pray About It: We are accustomed to associating power with loudness. Silence we often see as weakness. And yet at his most crucial hour, before Pilate, Jesus was silent. There is far more power in our silence before God than in our words. Far more. And in our flesh, we make great noise when we try to accomplish God's will through natural means. Here too silence is called for. Isaac can only be born to Abraham when the great patriarch has lost hope in the natural realm. Allow every inner distracting noise and voice to be stilled. Silence even the flesh that rises up with a clamor.

Then will come the silence. God is in that silence.

How rare it is to find a soul silent enough to hear God speak.

FRANÇOIS FÉNELON

July 25

For everything God created is good, and nothing is to be rejected if it is received with thanksgiving, because it is consecrated by the word of God and prayer.

1 TIMOTHY 4:5

Wherever there is true prayer, there thanksgiving and gratitude stand hard by, ready to respond to the answer when it comes. For as prayer brings the answer, so the answer brings forth gratitude and praise. As prayer sets God to work, so answered prayer sets thanksgiving to work. Thanksgiving follows answered prayer just as day succeeds night.

True prayer and gratitude lead to full consecration, and consecration leads to more praying and better praying. A consecrated life is both a prayer life and a thanks-giving life.

E. M. BOUNDS

Pray About It: Today is a day to give thanks. Surely there have been many answers to prayer for which you can return thanks today. Even if it's your habit to thank God daily, dedicate today as a special time of gratitude.

We should never forget to return thanks for blessings already granted. If any one of us would stop and think how many of the prayers which we've offered to God have been answered, and how seldom we have gone back to God to return thanks for the answers, I'm sure we would be overwhelmed. We should be just as definite in returning thanks as we are in prayer. Often our thanks to Him is indefinite and general.

R. A. TORREY

July 26

Do not conform any longer to the pattern of this world, but be transformed by the renewing of your mind. Then you will be able to test and approve what God's will is—his good, pleasing and perfect will.

ROMANS 12:2

A servant of the Lord has well said: Prayer is the rail for God's work. Indeed, prayer is to God's will as rails are to a train. The locomotive is full of power: it is capable of running a thousand miles a day. But if there are no rails, it cannot move forward a single inch. If it dares to move without them, it will soon sink into the earth. It may be able to travel over great distances, yet it cannot go to any place where no rails have been laid. And such is the relation between prayer and God's work. I do not believe it necessary to explain in detail, for I trust everyone can recognize the meaning of this parable.

Without any doubt God is almighty and He works mightily, but He will not and cannot work if you and I do not labor together with Him in prayer, prepare the way for His will, and pray "with all prayer and supplication" to grant Him the maneuverability to so work. Many are the things which God wills to do and would like to do, but His hands are bound because His children do not sympathize with Him and have not prayed so as to prepare ways for Him. Let me say to all who have wholly given themselves to God: Do examine yourselves and see if in this respect you have limited Him day after day.

Hence our most important work is to prepare the way of the Lord. There is no other work which can be compared with this work. With God there are many "possibilities"; but these will turn into "impossibilities" if believers do not open up ways for Him.

WATCHMAN NEE

Pray About It: Today as you pray, picture yourself as laying down the rail for the locomotive of God's will. His will cannot go where no rails have been laid. This is an excellent picture of how we must pray God's will into existence.

Open up the way for the Lord to move.

Our prayers are God's opportunities.

CHARLES E. COWMAN

July 27

Thou wilt light my candle.

PSALM 18:28 KJV

God never asks for personalities. God asks for persons. He calls all kinds of people and chooses quite ordinary men and women for His great work. He somehow calls persons and makes them personalities (persons of distinctive quality). He gives power. Every kind of power comes in the Spirit: intellectual power, moral power, spiritual power, physical power. There is no higher quality of man anywhere, and he can be produced everywhere by the power of the Holy Spirit. He quickens the mind, purifies the heart, and strengthens the whole man.

SAMUEL CHADWICK

Pray About It: When we walk in the Holy Spirit, we are led by God. He makes us into the kinds of people and personalities He wants us to be. He gives Himself as the flame for the candle. In so doing we receive health in our minds, bodies, and spirits.

To pray is to be healthy in spirit. May God quicken us and strengthen us today for the work we have to do.

Prayer at its best is the expression of the whole life, for all things being equal, our prayers are only as powerful as our lives.

A. W. TOZER

July 28

Ye shall know them by their fruits.

MATTHEW 7:16 KJV

For my part, and I have been long at it, I desire no other gift of prayer than that which ends in making me a better and better woman. By its fruits your prayer will be known to yourselves and others.

TERESA OF ÁVILA

Pray About It: If the changes that occur to us as active pray-ers aren't seen by others as making us better men and women — better Christians — then something is amiss in our prayers. Our lives bear the outward fruit of the inward work of God that occurs in prayer. It will be seen by ourselves and others. The fruit of prayer is a better life. Today, allow the fruit of the Spirit to be seen by those who know you. To see the fruit is to see the Spirit.

Walking down the avenue of prayer, we acquire something of His likeness, and unconsciously we become witnesses to others of His beauty and His grace.

E. M. BOUNDS

July 29

And he arose.

MARK 4:39 KJV

Our Saviour hears the prayers of His children. The roar of the storm He did not hear in His sound sleep; but the moment there was a cry from His disciples for help He instantly awoke. What a revelation of heart have we here! He is never asleep to His people when they call upon Him. Amid the wildest tumults of this world He ever hears the faintest cry of prayer. Nor is He ever too weary to listen to His children in distress.

J. R. MILLER

Pray About It: Through the constant din, God hears that faint prayer. He awakes, not from the clamor of the storm, but from the words of fear in His children. He then rebukes the storm.

Praise God. He is awake to our cries. Always listening. Today He will hear your cry.

[God's] honor is at stake when we pray—and he will not be mocked for not answering! The Bible says of him: "He will not suffer thy foot to be moved . . . he that keepeth Israel shall neither slumber nor sleep" (Psalm 121:3–4). Our God is awake at all times. And he is attentive to our every need.

DAVID WILKERSON

July 30

Then the LORD said, "There is a place near me where you may stand on a rock. When my glory passes by, I will put you in a cleft in the rock and cover you with my hand until I have passed by. Then I will remove my hand and you will see my back; but my face must not be seen."

EXODUS 33:21–23

Once as I rode out into the woods for my health, in 1737, having alighted from my horse in a retired place, as my manner commonly had been to walk for divine contemplation and prayer, I had a view that for me was extraordinary, of the glory of the Son of God.

As near as I can judge, this continued about an hour; and kept me the greater part of the time in a flood of tears and weeping aloud. I felt an ardency of soul to be what I know not otherwise how to express, emptied and annihilated; to love Him with a holy and pure love; to serve and follow Him; to be perfectly sanctified and made pure with a divine and heavenly purity.

JONATHAN EDWARDS

Pray About It: It sounds so casual—Jonathan Edwards simply took a ride into the woods for his health. And then, finding a quiet place, he dismounted and took a walk to think and to pray. And then—all of sudden he had a view of the glory of the Son of God. For an hour the result was continuous weeping. But those weren't tears of sadness. How can one behold such purity and love and be sad? His desire was then to be emptied, annihilated. And then to be sanctified and pure.

If we would yearn for God Himself, we too might have such times of refreshing. But it's important to remember that Edwards frequently visited the woods to pray. As a boy, Edwards says, "I, with some of my schoolmates joined together and built a booth in a swamp, in a very retired spot, for a place of prayers."

God is often pleased to reveal Himself to those who seek Him in natural surroundings. It's as if we join a chorus of worshippers as the very rocks and trees cry out in adoration of Him whom most men ignore.

Consider the similar experience of the great nineteenth century evangelist, Charles Finney who also often sought God surrounded by nature:

> Mr. Gale, my minister, was standing at the door of the meeting house, and as I came up, all at once the glory of God shone upon and around me, in a manner most marvelous. The day was just beginning to dawn. But all at once a light perfectly ineffable shone in my soul, that almost prostrated me to the ground. In this light is seemed as if I could see that all nature praised and worshipped God except man. This light seemed to be like the brightness of the sun in every direction. It was too intense for the eyes. I remember casting my eyes down and breaking into a flood of tears, in view of the fact that mankind did not praise God. I think I knew something then, by actual experience, of that light

that prostrated Paul on his way to Damascus. It was surely a light such as I could not have endured long.

When I burst out into such loud weeping, Mr. Gale asked, "What is the matter, brother Finney?" I could not tell him. I found that he had seen no light; and that he was reason why I should be in such a state of mind. I therefore said but little. I believe I merely replied that I saw the glory of God; and that I could not endure to think of the manner in which He was treated by men. Indeed, it did not seem to me at the time that the vision of His glory which I had, was to be described in words. I wept it out; and the vision, if it may be so called, passed away and left my mind calm.

July 31

Simon, Simon, Satan has asked to sift you as wheat. But I have prayed for you, Simon, that your faith may not fail. And when you have turned back, strengthen your brothers.

LUKE 22:31–32

How encouraging is the thought of the Redeemer's never-ceasing intercession for us. When we pray, He pleads for us; and when we are not praying, He is advocating our cause, and by His supplications shielding us from unseen dangers. We little know what we owe to our Saviour's prayers. When we reach the hilltops of heaven, and look back upon all the way whereby the Lord our God hath led us, how we shall praise Him who, before the eternal throne, has pleaded our cause against our unseen enemies.

Charles Haddon Spurgeon

Pray About It: Because we're only human, it's normal for us to think of God's presence as something we cultivate in prayer. Like a water faucet that we turn on when we need its use and turn off when finished, so we often go to our time of prayer and turn on God and then turn Him off till next time as we leave our prayer time. But God isn't that way. He neither sleeps nor slumbers. Nor does Jesus ever stop interceding for us. All last night as you slept, Christ was interceding on your behalf. All of today, long after you've left your place of prayer, He will still be thinking of you.

Today, let's thank God for His ceaseless love and attention to us, even when our thoughts are far from Him.

Whenever God encourages your heart with the promise that in Satan's sifting your faith will not fail, then take that encouragement and double your joy by using it to strengthen your brothers and sisters.

John Piper

August 1

The fruit of the Spirit is . . . temperance.

GALATIANS 5:22−23 KJV

Christians of strong faith are Christians of much prayer. It is in the dying to self which much prayer implies, in closer union to Jesus, that the spirit of faith will come in power. Faith needs prayer for its full growth.

It is only in a life of temperance and self-denial that there will be the heart or the strength to pray much.

Without voluntary separation even from what is lawful, no one will attain power in prayer.

ANDREW MURRAY

Pray About It: Anyone can shoot small arrowlike prayers to heaven without much fuss. But to be a faithful pray-er requires death to self—a voluntary separation from what is lawful to us. That TV program that is so enticing or the craft project or the chatty phone call or the business appointment all compete with time for prayer.

Pray first, just as you give the first of your income to the Lord, and then if there's time left over, pursue your leisure activities. Many good, noble, even profitable things must give way to make time for prayer. The good is always the enemy of the best.

Here again, if we would pray aright, we must look to the Spirit of God to teach us to pray.

R. A. TORREY

August 2

These are the words of the Amen, the faithful and true witness, the ruler of God's creation. I know your deeds, that you are neither cold nor hot. I wish you were either one or the other! So, because you are lukewarm—neither hot nor cold—I am about to spit you out of my mouth.

REVELATION 3:14–16

Cold prayers shall never have any warm answers. God will suit His returns to our requests. Lifeless services shall have lifeless answers. When men are dull, God will be dumb.

THOMAS BROOKS

Pray About It: Many of us were taught to pray by rote as a child. As a result, sometimes we still rattle off our requests in an almost detached manner. If you would have the living God answer, your prayers must be *living* prayers.

Today, speak living prayers to God, from a heart that's alive to Him.

When thou prayest, rather let thy heart be without words than thy words without heart.

JOHN BUNYAN

August 3

But you, dear friends, build yourselves up in your most holy faith and pray in the Holy Spirit.

JUDE 20

You must pray with all your might. That does not mean saying your prayers, or sitting gazing about in church or chapel with eyes wide open while someone else says them for you. It means fervent, effectual, untiring wrestling with God. . . . This kind of prayer be sure the devil and the world and your own indolent, unbelieving nature will oppose. They will pour water on this flame.

WILLIAM BOOTH

Pray About It: Non-Christians and religious folk won't understand your commitment to prayer. To most people prayer is a nicety of the religious life, not a necessity as dear as breathing itself for the Christian. Be fervent. Be effectual. And don't be surprised at scoffers.

The Christian on his knees sees more than the philosopher on tiptoe.

DWIGHT L. MOODY

August 4

The king's heart is in the hand of the LORD;
he directs it like a watercourse wherever he pleases.

PROVERBS 21:1

Men may spurn our appeals, reject our message,
oppose our arguments, despise our person—but
they are helpless against our prayer. Fellow Christians who love the cause of Christ—to prayer! To
prayer! The times are calling us to it. We must press
on.

J. SIDLOW BAXTER

Pray About It: Don't worry about the reaction of
those for whom you pray. They may resist you and
your message, and your arguments, but they can't prevail against God. Many are the testimonies of those
who were saved, much to their own amazement,
through the prayers of others. Keep on praying for
that one who is hard of heart. He or she will come
around. God will soften their hearts.

During this year I was informed about the conversion of one of the very greatest sinners, that I ever
heard of in all my service for the Lord. Repeatedly I
fell on my knees with his wife, and asked the Lord
for his conversion. She often came to me in the
deepest distress of soul, due to the barbarous and
cruel treatment that she received from him, in his
bitter enmity against her for the Lord's sake, and
because he could not provoke her to be in a passion.
And now this awful persecutor is converted.

GEORGE MUELLER

August 5

When he had received the drink, Jesus said, "It is finished."

JOHN 19:30

We try to explain why God answers prayer on the ground of reason; it is nonsense. God answers prayer on the ground of redemption and on no other ground.

Let us never forget that our prayers are heard, not because we are in earnest, not because we suffer, but because Jesus suffered.

OSWALD CHAMBERS

Pray About It: When Jesus breathed the words "It is finished" from the cross, He made it possible for every believer to come to enter the holiest of holies with *boldness*.

There is no way to understand our access to God through natural reason. The cross is foolishness to those who don't know Christ. But to us, we see and appreciate the goodness of God to sinners. Today, reflect on the cross and His words, "It is finished."

"It is finished." The implication of the Greek word is "This is complete." This is redemption complete. You can't add to it. You can't subtract from it. It doesn't need something the priest says added to it. Jesus made a perfect redemption for men.

LEONARD RAVENHILL

August 6

To keep me from becoming conceited because of these surpassingly great revelations, there was given me a thorn in my flesh, a messenger of Satan, to torment me. Three times I pleaded with the Lord to take it away from me. But he said to me, "My grace is sufficient for you, for my power is made perfect in weakness." Therefore I will boast all the more gladly about my weaknesses, so that Christ's power may rest on me.

2 CORINTHIANS 12:7–9

We too have our thorns in the flesh, apparent obstructions to the progress of the Kingdom of God. We pray that the hindrance might be taken away, yet it remains. Apparently God wishes to give grace in order that these seemingly adverse circumstances may be converted into our slaves, and made to minister to our own highest interests, to the welfare of others and the glory of God.

[Hymn writer] Frances Ridley Havergal was as frail as the most delicate porcelain. She prayed for greater strength, but the thorn remained. But who will say that her prayer was unanswered? Think of the tender songs that were sung from her frail tent! Her very weaknesses endowed her with delicacies of intuition, discernments in sacred exploration which have made her the precious guide and teacher of tens of thousands. Her power was made perfect in weakness. . . .

J. H. JOWETT

Pray About It: Frances Havergal (1836–1879) was a poet and a hymn writer. In her hymns you can sense her love of God. And she, like Paul, and no doubt like each of us, prayed for a thorn in the flesh to be removed, but to no avail.

God would give the strength to bear was the answer. And often it's our answer too. If you've prayed and the thorn remains, then consider that God means it as a vehicle of His strength. Out of your pain can come beauty as was the case with Frances Havergal.

Here is one of her hymns. Sing it if you know it. If you don't know it, just read her words. God's grace will suffice for your thorn.

> *Take my life, and let it be consecrated, Lord, to Thee.*
> *Take my moments and my days; let them flow in*
> *   ceaseless praise.*
> *Take my hands, and let them move at the impulse*
> *   of Thy love.*
> *Take my feet, and let them be swift and beautiful*
> *   for Thee.*
> *Take my voice, and let me sing always, only,*
> *   for my King.*
> *Take my lips, and let them be filled with messages*
> *   from Thee.*
> *Take my silver and my gold; not a mite would*
> *   I withhold.*
> *Take my intellect, and use every power as Thou*
> *   shalt choose.*

Take my will, and make it Thine; it shall be no longer mine.

Take my heart, it is Thine own; it shall be Thy royal throne.

Take my love, my Lord, I pour at Thy feet its treasure store.

Take myself, and I will be ever, only, all for Thee.

Here's the story of how Frances came to write this hymn:

I went for a little visit of five days (to Areley House). There were ten persons in the house, some unconverted and long prayed for, some converted, but not rejoicing Christians. He gave me the prayer, "Lord, give me all in this house!" And He just did. Before I left the house every one had got a blessing. The last night of my visit after I had retired, the governess asked me to go to the two daughters. They were crying, but then and there both of them trusted and rejoiced; it was nearly midnight. I was too happy to sleep, and passed most of the night in praise and renewal of my own consecration; and these little couplets formed themselves, and chimed in my heart one after another till they finished with "Ever, Only, ALL for Thee!"

August 7

The righteous will flourish like a palm tree,
they will grow like a cedar of Lebanon.

PSALM 92:12

Strength will not come to us without our going deep to find it. A few hasty and lazy prayers will never bring it into us. We need *deep* communion with Christ if we are to get it at all. There is no part of a tree so invisible as its roots: but none more essential to its growth and fruitfulness: and just as the visible condition of the tree is an unfailing index of what the unseen roots are doing, our visible lives will soon tell whether or not our invisible roots are going deep: for dryness below ground soon means deadness above ground.

G. H. KNIGHT

Pray About It: When you are at prayer, you're sending down roots. If your prayer is shallow, your roots will be shallow and during the storm, you will be uprooted. But if, as you pray, you allow your roots to sink deep, you will have the strength of an oak during the storm.

As you pray today, may your roots penetrate the soil deeply.

God is telling us, "Try to measure the growth of the cedar tree. Camp under it for a month, and tell me how far you see it grow. Even after six months, you probably won't notice any growth. Yet that tree is putting down deep roots! You see, I water the tree with my rain. And any tree that's watered properly is going to grow. Yet such growth is not discernible to the human eye. It grows, but in secret!"

DAVID WILKERSON

August 8

Enlarge the place of your tent,
    stretch your tent curtains wide,
      do not hold back;
lengthen your cords,
    strengthen your stakes.

ISAIAH 54:2

Pray the largest prayers. You cannot think a prayer so large that God, in answering it, will not wish you had made it larger. Pray not for crutches but for wings!

PHILLIPS BROOKS

Pray About It: Spread the pegs of your tent wider. God is a big God. He specializes in large answers to large prayers. He will give you wings, not crutches. You can never ask too much. But as high as your requests are, so high shall your praises be.

Prayer plumes the wings of God's young eaglets so that they may learn to mount above the clouds. Prayer brings inner strength to God's warriors and sends them forth to spiritual battle with their muscles firm and their armor in place.

CHARLES HADDON SPURGEON

August 9

The righteous will live by faith.

ROMANS 1:17

Do you believe when you have come from prayer that is dry, that it was because of poor preparation and that the time you spent before Him has done you no good? If you do, then your belief is fallacious. Genuine prayer does not consist in enjoying the Lord, nor enjoying His light. Nor is it in having gained knowledge of spiritual things. . . .

The consistency of true prayer is in faith, and in waiting on Him. First you believe that you are in His presence. You believe that you are turning to Him with your heart. And you wait there before Him, tranquilly. These are the only preparations that you need. The final results contain a great deal of fruit.

MICHAEL MOLINOS

Pray About It: There is no dryness when faith is at work. This is true because faith is based on the objective truth which isn't affected by dryness or abundance. God hears, no matter how dry you may *feel*. Just wait before Him in faith. Ignore feelings. Follow the steps that Michael Molinos proposes:

1. Believe you are in His presence.
2. Turn to Him with your heart.
3. Wait tranquilly.

Prayer is not given to us as a burden to be borne or an irksome duty to fulfill, but to be a joy and power to which there is no limit.

A. E. RICHARDSON

August 10

God chose the weak things of the world to shame
the strong.

1 CORINTHIANS 1:27

All God's giants have been weak men who did
great things for God because they reckoned on God
being with them.

J. HUDSON TAYLOR

Pray About It: There's a misconception that the great
men and women of the past were spiritual giants, not
given to the same faults we have. And yet many of
them had their moodiness, their pride, their feelings
of abandonment.

Even David experienced all of this, and more. You
can enter your prayer time knowing that you serve the
same God as these weak believers we now recognize
as normal men and women who simply relied on God
being with them.

Forget your weakness. God is with you.

My faith consisted of a high notion and esteem of
God, and I had no other care at first but to faith-
fully reject every other thought.

BROTHER LAWRENCE

August 11

The Spirit of the Lord is upon me, because he hath anointed me to preach the gospel to the poor; he hath sent me to heal the brokenhearted, to preach deliverance to the captives, and recovering of sight to the blind, to set at liberty them that are bruised.

LUKE 4:18 KJV

A true prayer is an inventory of needs, a catalog of necessities, an exposure of secret wounds, a revelation of hidden poverty.

CHARLES HADDON SPURGEON

Pray About It: Today, let God have a list of your needs and necessities. Open your secret wounds to Him for cleansing and binding up. Surrender your hidden poverty for His riches. When Jesus read from Isaiah in the synagogue, all eyes were on Him. As He sat down, He said to those present, "This day is this scripture fulfilled in your ears."

On that basis, we can ask Him to heal us, to deliver us, to set us at liberty.

The best prayer comes from a strong inward need of necessity. When our lives are serene and placid, our prayers are apt to be dull and listless. When we reach a crisis, a moment of danger, a serious illness, or a heavy bereavement, then our prayers are fervent and vital. Someone has wisely said, "The arrow that is to enter heaven must be launched from a bow fully bent." A sense of urgency, of helplessness, of conscious need is the womb from which the best prayers are born.

WILLIAM MACDONALD

August 12

[This was Elijah's plea:] "Hear me, O LORD, hear me, that this people may know that thou art the LORD God."

1 KINGS 18:37 KJV

The answer to prayer is the part of prayer which glorifies God. Unanswered prayers are dumb oracles which leave the praying ones in darkness, doubt, and bewilderment and which carry no conviction to the unbeliever. It is not the act or the attitude of praying which gives efficacy to prayer. It is not abject prostration of the body before God, the vehement or quiet utterance to God, the exquisite beauty and poetry of the diction of our prayers, which do the deed. It is not the marvelous array of argument and eloquence in praying which makes prayer effectual. Not one or all of these are the things which glorify God. It is the *answer* which brings glory to His name.

E. M. BOUNDS

Pray About It: Why pray if we don't expect an answer? God is glorified when we see His faithfulness made real through answered prayer. Thank God for the answers that are already on their way, and then watch for them. He will glorify Himself through your prayers.

Let our prayer be that God may advance His work, not for our glory—not for our sake—but for the sake of His beloved Son whom He hath sent.

DWIGHT MOODY

August 13

Therefore rejoice, you heavens
  and you who dwell in them!
But woe to the earth and the sea,
  because the devil has gone down to you!
He is filled with fury,
  because he knows that his time is short.

REVELATION 12:12

We are living in an unprecedented age of satanic activity. It appears that the enemy, knowing that his time is short, has come with great wrath even as the Apostle St. John said it would be. He seems to be "throwing in," as we say, everything he has. It is the "battle of the bulge" for the powers of darkness. Many Christian workers have capitulated before the unseen spirit forces from the pit that are charging the atmosphere of the world with poisonous fumes which, if taken without the gas-mask of faith and the victory of the Son of God, are proving fatal. . . .

F. J. HUEGEL

Pray About It: Make no mistake: as the return of the Lord approaches, the enemy will unleash even greater evils in our direction. Christians today face more blatant wickedness than did our ancestors. And our descendants are likely to face even more. With such oppression afoot, the Christian pray-er must be militant in standing *against* evil and *for* good. This will likely cost you some friendships, as the trend of the world is to call evil "good" and good "evil."

But do the right thing. Pray the right way. Stand fast against evil. Put on your spiritual gas mask and get to work.

> You should not turn your back on Satan, for this will mean *you* are running away instead of *him* running away from you! You should face him and let him turn his back. . . . . If you are afraid of him, you are finished!
>
> WATCHMAN NEE

August 14

A Canaanite woman from that vicinity came to him, crying out, "Lord, Son of David, have mercy on me! My daughter is suffering terribly from demon-possession."

Jesus did not answer a word. So his disciples came to him and urged him, "Send her away, for she keeps crying out after us."

He answered, "I was sent only to the lost sheep of Israel."

The woman came and knelt before him. "Lord, help me!" she said.

He replied, "It is not right to take the children's bread and toss it to their dogs."

"Yes, Lord," she said, "but even the dogs eat the crumbs that fall from their masters' table."

Then Jesus answered, "Woman, you have great faith! Your request is granted." And her daughter was healed from that very hour.

MATTHEW 15:22–28

While we recognize the doctrine of divine sovereignty, this should no more keep us from asking in faith for the healing of our bodies than the doctrine of election should prevent our asking with the fullest assurance for the salvation of our souls. We must not bear so hard upon divine sovereignty as practically to deny man's freedom to ask or expect miraculous healing.

Some even push God almost into an iron fixedness where even the Almighty is not at liberty to work miracles any longer—as though God was under bonds to restrain this office of His omnipotence since the apostolic age. We must keep these two great elements of prayer in equilibrium: believing strongly but asking submissively. We should present our request with one hand holding up "Thus saith the Lord," and the other hand holding up "The will of the Lord be done."

A. J. GORDON

Pray About It: In recent decades the subject of divine healing has largely been preached in Pentecostal churches. It wasn't always that way. Many men and women of God believed strongly in the power of God to heal the sick: Andrew Murray, A. B. Simpson, R. A. Torrey, and A. J. Gordon to name just a few. Study the Word, read books by men and women of faith, and apply the Word to your situation. Divine healing is the children's bread. You're one of the children.

O! Be not hopeless, be not despondent. There is a balm in Gilead, there is a Physician there, there is healing for our sickness. What is impossible with man is possible with God. What you see no possibility of doing, grace will do. Confess the disease, trust the Physician, claim the healing, pray the prayer of faith.

ANDREW MURRAY

August 15

Do not store up for yourselves treasures on earth, where moth and rust destroy, and where thieves break in and steal. But store up for yourselves treasures in heaven, where moth and rust do not destroy, and where thieves do not break in and steal. For where your treasure is, there your heart will be also.

MATTHEW 6:19–21

Prayer is God's business to which men and women can attend. Prayer is God's *necessary* business, which only Christians can do, and that Christians must do. Men and women who belong to God are obliged to pray. They are not obliged to have success in business. Material success is incidental, occasional, and merely nominal, as far as integrity to heaven and loyalty to God are concerned.

In the light of eternity, we are neither better nor worse with or without earthly success. Achievement in the eyes of the world is never to be considered a sign of great reputation or sterling character in the eyes of God. Our obligation to God is that of prayer. Prayer is loyalty to God. Nonpraying is to reject Christ and to abandon heaven. A life of prayer is the only life which heaven counts.

E. M. BOUNDS

Pray About It: You have one goal in life. Just one. Knowing God is the one pursuit around which all else pales in comparison.

Life is short. Your communion with God is all that really matters; your money will gain you no eternal advantages.

Today, face God and place all that you have on the altar. Consign your material goods to His keeping or His disposal. Sever your emotional ties to this world's wealth. Give Him all. He must come first.

If your heart is still attached to the world's goods, your prayers will be weak.

Only one life 'twill soon be passed.
Only what's done for Christ will last.

AUTHOR UNKNOWN

For all the promises of God in him are yea, and in him Amen, unto the glory of God by us.

2 CORINTHIANS 1:20 KJV

August 16

You hear, O LORD, the desire of the afflicted;
  you encourage them, and you listen to their cry.

PSALM 10:17

God will fill the hungry because He Himself has stirred up the hunger. As in the case of prayer, when God prepares the heart to pray, He prepares His ear to hear. So in the case of spiritual hunger, when God prepares the heart to hunger, He will prepare His hand to fill.

THOMAS WATSON

Pray About It: We often think that prayer begins with us. True prayer has its origin in God. He prepares our heart to pray and His ear to hear that His will may be done. To be a part of His work is a wonder.

Today, as you pray, think about God creating that hunger to pray in your heart. Then surely He must answer the very prayers He originates.

Every Christian will become at last what his desires have made him. We are all the sum total of our hungers. The great saints have all had thirsting hearts.

MILES STANFORD

August 17

He gave them their request; but sent leanness into their soul.

PSALM 106:15 KJV

When we learn to pray in the Holy Spirit, we find there are some things for which we cannot pray, we sense a need for restraint. Never push and say, "I know it is God's will and I am going to stick to it." Beware.

Remember the children of Israel: "He gave them their request; but sent leanness into their soul." Let the Spirit of God teach you what He is driving at and learn not to grieve Him. If we are abiding in Jesus Christ we shall ask what He wants us to ask, whether we are conscious of doing so or not.

OSWALD CHAMBERS

Pray About It: We pray amiss because we have selfishly assumed that what we want must be the will of God. We prod on in our praying, trying to convince God of our case. But if God isn't in it, better let it go. Or would you rather He grant the request and send leanness into your soul? Never push. Be willing to back down from a prayer when you sense His restraint.

Quiet waiting before God would save from many a mistake and from many a sorrow.

J. HUDSON TAYLOR

August 18

Likewise reckon ye also yourselves to be dead indeed unto sin, but alive unto God through Jesus Christ our Lord.

ROMANS 6:11 KJV

God never ceases to speak to us; but the noise of the world without, and the tumult of our passions within, bewilder us, and prevent us from listening to Him.

FRANÇOIS FÉNELON

Pray About It: It's hard to know which is more distracting to our prayers — the pull of the world with its distractions or the tug of our own passions to fulfill their every desire.

But in the middle of it all is the voice of God speaking to us, quite loudly actually. Listen to Him today — reckon yourself alive to God and dead to the world and to your flesh.

The first and last stages of holy living are crowned with praying.

E. M. BOUNDS

August 19

Praise the LORD, for the LORD is good: sing praises unto his name; for it is pleasant.

PSALM 135:3 KJV

Have you ever noticed how much we are urged in the Bible to praise the Lord? It seemed to be almost the principal part of the worship of the Israelites. This is the continual refrain all through the Bible. I believe that if we counted we would find there are more commands given and more examples set for the giving of thanks than for the doing or the leaving undone of anything else.

From the teaching of Scripture it is evident that the Lord loves to be thanked and praised just as much as we like it. I am sure that it gives Him real pleasure just as it does us and that our failure to thank Him for His good and perfect gifts wounds His loving heart just as our hearts are wounded when our loved ones fail to appreciate the benefits we have so enjoyed bestowing on them. What a joy it is to us to receive from our friends an acknowledgment of their thanksgiving for our gifts, and it is a joy to the Lord to receive thanks and praise from us.

HANNAH WHITALL SMITH

Pray About It: The book of Psalms is full of admonitions to praise the Lord. And in the New Testament we're told to give God thanks in all circumstances. The foundation for prayer is a humble, thankful spirit. Today, as you enter God's presence, do so with thanksgiving and praise. He never tires of hearing it and we can never tire of offering it. It's what we're most commanded to do in the Bible—and it's the most rewarding to obey.

This is not a time for trifling or joking or silliness or superficiality. Worship comes from roots that are too deep in God, and is meant to take root too deep in the human heart, and focuses so relentlessly on God himself that it has to be a seriously joyful (or joyfully serious) affair.

JOHN PIPER

August 20

After this manner therefore pray ye . . .

MATTHEW 6:9 KJV

Jesus would always find time for prayer, or make time for it. If his days were full of excitement and toil, he would take time out of his nights for communing with God. At least he never allowed himself to be robbed of his hours of devotion.

There are some Christians who think they are excused from prayer and meditation in secret because they are so busy. Their work presses them so in the morning that they cannot possibly get time to pray. Their cares occupy them so all day that they do not find one quiet moment to go apart with God.

In the evening there are so many social or other engagements — meetings, societies, parties — or they are so tired, that prayer is crowded out. The example of Christ speaks its solemn rebuke of all such trifling. We must find time for communion with God, or God will not find time to bless us.

J. R. Miller

Pray About It: When Jesus instructed His disciples to "pray after this manner," He gave them an example of how to pray. So too did He give an example of the place prayer ought to occupy in our life as He separated Himself to commune with the Father.

Today, emulate Jesus. Pray as He prayed. Separate yourself for time alone with Him. If you're too busy to pray, you're too busy.

> We are too busy to pray, and so we're too busy to have power. We have a great deal of activity, but we accomplish little . . . we have much machinery, but few results.

R. A. Torrey

August 21

For this reason I kneel before the Father.

EPHESIANS 3:14

Pray distinctly. Pray upon your knees. One grows tired sometimes of the free thought which is yet perfectly true, that a man can pray anywhere and anyhow. But men have found it good to make the whole system pray. Kneel down, and the very bending of these obstinate and unused knees of yours will make the soul kneel down in the humility in which it can be exalted in the sight of God.

PHILLIPS BROOKS

Pray About It: Kneeling has become the traditional pose for prayer. The prophet Daniel knelt as he prayed, as did many other great pray-ers of the faith. William Newell said that kneeling is a good way to pray, precisely because it's uncomfortable (it's hard to fall asleep on one's knees). Of course we can pray in any position, but today we will kneel, if physically possible. The bending of the knees to God is a picture of our broken strength. It signifies surrender, as do uplifted hands. Pray distinctly to God today. And do so with surrender in your heart and in your knees. Then drink from the great fountain of God.

Is there any place in any of our rooms where there is a little bit of carpet worn white from our knees?

ALEXANDER MACLAREN

A Christian who kneels before God will stand before men.

LEONARD RAVENHILL

August 22

You ought to say, "If it is the Lord's will, we will live and do this or that."

James 4:15

Be slow to take new steps in the Lord's service, or in your business, or in your families. Weigh everything well; weigh all in the light of the Holy Scriptures, and in the fear of God. Seek to have no will of your own, in order to ascertain the mind of God, regarding any steps you propose to take, so that you can honestly say, you are willing to do the will of God, if He will only please to instruct you. But when you have found out what the will of God is, seek for His help, and seek it earnestly, perseveringly, patiently, believingly, and expectingly: and you will surely, in His own time and way, obtain it.

George Mueller

Pray About It: Today is a day for taking inventory. What is our work? Is it God's choice for us, or our own choosing? Has it been fruitful? Is it time to move on? Or are we indeed exactly where God wants us? Far too often we don't move forward because we don't take time to reflect on our lives. Then when we are old we wonder how we missed God's call to something better. And make no mistake, if God's calling you to move on, it's to something better. But don't move hastily—that's as big a mistake as staying too long. Simply pray and ask God to reveal His will. He will make it plain.

The saint who advances on his knees never retreats.

Jim Elliot

August 23

The LORD Almighty, wonderful in counsel and magnificent in wisdom.

ISAIAH 28:29

The magnificence of all true prayer—its nobility, its royalty, its absolute divinity—all stand in this: that it is the greatest act and office that man or angel can ever enter on or perform. Earth is at its very best, and heaven is at its highest, when men and angels magnify their duty of prayer and of praise before the throne of God. The magnificence of God is the source and the measure of the magnificence of prayer.

ALEXANDER WHYTE

Pray About It: Prayer is magnificent first, because it's the highest calling for man. There's nothing else we can do that surpasses prayer. It's our ultimate activity.

Secondly, prayer is magnificent because the God to whom we pray is Magnificent. As Paternus, a fifth-century Christian, told his son, "Think magnificently of God."

Make that your motto today.

O, believing brethren! What an instrument is this which God hath put into your hands! Prayer moves Him that moves the universe.

ROBERT MURRAY MCCHEYNE

August 24

For we which have believed do enter into rest.

HEBREWS 4:3 KJV

Do not pray yourself out of faith. You may tell Him that you are waiting and that you are still believing Him and therefore praise Him for the answer. There is nothing that so fully clinches faith as to be so sure of the answer that you can thank God for it. Prayers that pray us out of faith deny both God's promise in His Word and also His whisper "Yes," that He gave us in our hearts. Such prayers are but the expression of the unrest of one's heart, and unrest implies unbelief in reference to the answer to prayer. This prayer that prays ourselves out of faith frequently arises from centering our thoughts on the difficulty rather than on God's promise. Abraham "considered not his own body," "he staggered not at the promise of God" (Rom. 4:19–20). May we watch and pray that we enter not into temptation of praying ourselves out of faith.

B. H. P.

Pray About It: When we have prayed and received assurance that God will answer, we can from there on out praise God for the yet unseen answer until it comes. When we know that He has granted our request, there's no use in continuing to ask. Just praise and offer thanksgiving. The approaching answer will soon manifest itself. Don't pray your faith away.

The time for the blessing is when you begin to praise God for it. For, brethren, you may be sure that when you put up a thanksgiving on the ground that God has answered your prayer, you really have prevailed with God.

CHARLES HADDON SPURGEON

August 25

But do not forget this one thing, dear friends: With the Lord a day is like a thousand years, and a thousand years are like a day. The Lord is not slow in keeping his promise, as some understand slowness. He is patient with you, not wanting anyone to perish, but everyone to come to repentance.

2 PETER 3:8–9

God's movement seems so slow to us. His march through history, the coming of justice to the weak and oppressed, the shining of light in the dark places—all this has so often been called slow. God is so big, so great. He is moving steadily on. The apparent slowness only spells out the greatness of His size and of His plans. It takes time to swing great things forward. Time is but a hyphen between two eternities. God lives and moves in eternity. He breathes in the atmosphere of greatness.

S. D. GORDON

Let God engineer.

OSWALD CHAMBERS

Pray About It: Time flows forward at God's command. We weigh our prayer list against the fast-moving calendar and wonder at God's slow movement. But to God a thousand years is but a day. He's never slow—we are simply too fast. His apparent slowness is a measure of His greatness. This is the one to whom we pray—the Ancient of Days. Thank Him for His slowness, because it shows itself also in His slowness to anger.

Oswald Chambers had a motto when it came to waiting for God: "Let God engineer." When God is slow according to our timetable, we get restless and want God to hurry up. Sometimes our impatience prompts us to try and take matters into our own hands.

But relax. God knows your need. And in only the twinkling of an eye this life shall all be behind us and eternity with God stretched out in an endless line of glory. Until then, let God engineer.

August 26

His master replied, "Well done, good and faithful servant! You have been faithful with a few things; I will put you in charge of many things. Come and share your master's happiness!"

MATTHEW 25:23

Prayer is simply God's appointed means of accomplishing His work in the world. If He chose, He could act arbitrarily without regard to prayer or lack of it.

All power originates in God and belongs to Him alone. He ordained prayer not primarily as a means of getting things done for himself, but as part of the apprenticeship program for training the Church for her royal duties which will follow the Marriage Supper of the Lamb. Unless she understands this and enters into sincere cooperation with God's plan of prayer, the power needed to overcome and bind Satan on earth will not be released.

God has the power to overcome Satan without the cooperation of His Church through prayer and faith, but if He did it without her it would deprive her of enforcement practice and rob her of the strength she would gain in overcoming. This is God's primary reason for inaugurating the system of prayer and unequivocally binding himself to answer. Therefore, there is no authority apart from persistent believing prayer.

PAUL BILLHEIMER

Pray About It: Most Christians know that this life is training for the next. The lessons we learn about patience and goodness and authority will be useful as we undertake our duties in eternity. God gives prayer as one of the tools of training. As we practice prayer, we become better at it. We sharpen our spiritual senses in preparation for our real work. As you pray today, consider that you're an apprentice to a higher calling.

Lord! To us You have entrusted Your work, on our prayer the coming of Your kingdom depends, in our prayer too You can glorify Your name; "Lord, teach us to pray." Yes, us, Lord; we offer ourselves as learners; we would indeed be taught of You. "Lord, teach *us* to pray."

ANDREW MURRAY

August 27

With my whole heart have I sought thee: O let me not wander from thy commandments.

PSALM 119:10 KJV

Now, O Christian, cease for awhile from your work, withdraw yourself from your stormy thoughts, forget your weary and burdensome struggling, give yourself for a time to God, and rest calmly in Him.

Leave all around you where God is not, and where you wilt find no help from Him; go into the inner chamber of your heart, and shut the door behind you.

ANSELM

Pray About It: Entering into prayer is a leaving behind of our earthly duties for a while. And when we return to them, we come to them refreshed and prepared.

Jesus prayed and fulfilled His mission on earth. We too have a mission and it can only be discovered in our times of prayer. And there too we gain the strength to complete our mission.

> All earthly things
>> With earth will fade away;
> Prayer grasps eternity.
>> Then pray, always pray!

E. H. BICKERSTETH

August 28

Now you are the body of Christ, and each one of you is a part of it.

1 CORINTHIANS 12:27

The life-blood of the Church is prayer for one another, and the adoration of the Lord is its vital breath.

ALEXEI KHOMIAKOV

All are one in Christ—Christians on earth and saints in heaven.

T. DEWITT TALMADGE

Pray About It: Most Christians understand that the body of Christ is to be unified. We are one body with one head, Christ Jesus. But not only are we one with each other here on earth, but we are all part of the complete church, comprising of all Christians past, present, and future. We are the bride of Christ. We learn from those who have come ahead of us; we pass on what we know of God to those who will follow—always united with every believer in every age. Pray for the body of Christ today. Ask for boldness, purity, wisdom, love, compassion, and a heart for evangelism.

August 29

He who goes out weeping,
    carrying seed to sow,
will return with songs of joy,
    carrying sheaves with him.

PSALM 126:6

Prayer is striking the winning blow . . . service is gathering up the results.

S. D. GORDON

Pray About It: Make the following prayer from Charles Haddon Spurgeon your prayer today. Commit all you have to God—your time, your talents, your thoughts. Take His love as yours. Ask for clarity for your life purpose. Ask for singleness of eye. Ask how you may gather up the results of your prayers.

Lord, help me to glorify thee. I am poor, help me to glorify thee by contentment. I am sick, help me to give thee honour by patience. I have talents, help me to extol thee by spending them for thee. I have time, Lord, help me to redeem it, that I may serve thee. I have a heart to feel, Lord, let that heart feel no love but thine, and glow with no flame but affection for thee. I have a head to think, Lord, help me to think of thee and for thee. Thou hast put me in this world for something, Lord; show me what that is, and help me to work out my life-purpose.

CHARLES HADDON SPURGEON

August 30

May the righteous be glad
   and rejoice before God;
   may they be happy and joyful.

PSALM 68:3

He who has learned to pray has learned the greatest
secret of a holy and happy life.

WILLIAM LAW

Pray About It: With all our current material prosperity, there are still people with serious problems and no solution in sight. It won't take long today until you pass someone who has been robbed of happiness by the troubles they face. Maybe you're such a person.

And yet, is there really such a thing as an unhappy prayer warrior? Prayer, rightly defined, brings victory.

Happiness is built into prayer, and a by-product of personal holiness, but it's elusive to those who are caught up in the pursuit of riches or who try to solve their problems with worldly wisdom.

Today, share the secret of happiness through prayer with someone who needs to know. Some people near you today are seeking the very answer you possess.

This is a secret that is best unkept.

How much needless care would we save ourselves if we but believed in prayer as the means of relieving those cares, and would learn the happy art of casting all our cares in prayer upon God.

E. M. BOUNDS

August 31

And ye shall observe this thing [the sprinkling of the blood] for an ordinance to thee and to thy sons for ever.

EXODUS 12:24 KJV

The Israelites sprinkled blood in Egypt and it brought deliverance!

Rahab used the blood-line token and it brought deliverance!

The High Priests of the Old Testament sprinkled blood and it brought forgiveness!

Jesus sprinkled His own Blood and purchased salvation for all mankind!

We, the New Testament sons and daughters of the High Priest Jesus, may now sprinkle Blood for forgiveness, salvation, redemption, healing, protection and victory!

Lest anyone should think that the sprinkling of the blood was for the Old Testament saints only, and that the practice ceased when Jesus sprinkled His own precious Blood on our behalf, I would remind you of God's command in Exodus that the sprinkling of the blood is God's ordinance *forever*. If Blood must be sprinkled today, then it must be the New Testament priests who do it — and we are those priests if we believe in the Son of God.

H. A. MAXWELL WHYTE

Pray About It: There's an old-time hymn, "There's Power in the Blood," that is rich in meaning for the prayer warrior. The blood of Christ is the basis for success in prayer. Throughout the Bible, the scarlet thread of salvation is present, from the Passover blood of the lamb to Rahab's scarlet cord in the window, to Christ's sacrifice at Calvary. Learning to plead the blood of Christ in prayer is a vital lesson every Christian must learn.

As you pray, look to the blood of Christ and all that it has accomplished. As another fine Christian song says, "The blood will never lose its power." It's there for you and me today.

Would you be free from the burden of sin?
There's power in the blood, power in the blood;
Would you over evil a victory win?
There's wonderful power in the blood.

There is power, power, wonder working power
   In the blood of the Lamb;
There is power, power, wonder working power
   In the precious blood of the Lamb.

LEWIS ELLIS JONES

September 1

It was now about the sixth hour, and darkness came over the whole land until the ninth hour, for the sun stopped shining. And the curtain of the temple was torn in two.

LUKE 23:44–45

In praying do not think of yourself as knocking at a closed door. Christ's dying cry rent the veil in two, and opened up both to vision and entrance the holy of holies with the mercy seat.

Let us come boldly to a throne of grace. God is not a reluctant God, needing to be besieged like a walled city, which must be compelled to capitulate.

ARTHUR T. PIERSON

Pray About It: The gates to heaven are always open to the one who prays. There's no need to beg or besiege. Through Christ we have open access to God. Must a child beg a parent for his needs? Never!

God is not reluctant to answer our prayers.

Our prayers must never grovel, they must soar and mount. We need a heavenly frame of mind.

CHARLES HADDON SPURGEON

September 2

Jesus said, "Father, forgive them, for they do not know what they are doing."

LUKE 23:34

In praying for His enemies not only did Christ set before us a perfect example of how we should treat those who wrong and hate us, but He also taught us never to regard any as beyond the reach of prayer.

If Christ prayed for His murderers then surely we have encouragement to pray now for the very chief of sinners! Christian reader, never lose hope. Does it seem a waste of time for you to continue praying for that man, that woman, that wayward child of yours? Does their case seem to become more hopeless every day? Does it look as though they had gotten beyond the reach of Divine mercy?

Perhaps that one you have prayed for so long has been ensnared by one of the Satanic cults of the day, or he may now be an avowed and blatant infidel, in a word, an open enemy of Christ. Remember then the Cross. Christ prayed for His enemies. Learn then not to look on any as beyond the reach of prayer.

ARTHUR PINK

Pray About It: I don't know a single Christian who doesn't have some "hard case" for whom he's praying. Sometimes it's a grown child who shows no interest in Christ. Maybe it's an aged parent approaching death. Or an unbelieving spouse. Or perhaps a neighbor for whom we have compassion and would like to see come to Christ. It may even be an enemy, such as the enemies of Christ who put Him to death. And yet Christ prayed for them. He wouldn't have done so if He thought there was no hope for them. I'd like to believe that some of the disciples we read about in the book of Acts, gathered in the Upper Room, were those very ones Christ had prayed for.

Who is your hard case? Who is your enemy? Don't lose heart. Keep praying. Though it may take *years*, keep praying.

> More than a century ago George Mueller, that prince of intercessors, began to pray for five personal friends. After five years one of them came to Christ. In ten years two more were born again. Mueller prayed on for 25 years and the fourth man was saved. For the fifth, Mueller prayed until the time of his death, and this friend came also to Christ a few months afterward. For the latter friend, Mueller had prayed for almost 52 years.
>
> JAMES MCCONKEY

September 3

He departed again into a mountain himself alone.
JOHN 6:15 KJV

Man needs to be alone with God. Without this, God cannot have the opportunity to shine into his heart, to transform his nature by His divine working, to take possession and to fill him with the fullness of God. Man needs to be alone with God, to yield to the presence and the power of His holiness, of His life and of His love. Christ on earth needed it; He could not live the life of a Son here in the flesh, without at times separating Himself entirely from His surroundings and being alone with God. How much more must this be indispensable to us!

When our Lord Jesus gave us the blessed command to enter our inner chamber, shut the door, pray to our Father in secret, all alone, He gave us the promise that the Father would hear such prayers, and mightily answer them in our life before men. What a great privilege is the opportunity of daily prayer to begin each morning. Let it be the one thing our hearts are set on, seeking and finding, discovering and meeting God.

ANDREW MURRAY

I love the lonely creative hours with God.

MADAME GUYON

Pray About It: If we think about it, we realize it's true: It's not possible for us to give our attention to God unless we're alone. We're too easily distracted by life. We may, of course, pray anytime, anywhere—but for our deep communion with God we must be shut away.

We must come to the place of loving those lonely hours with God. We can do so when we think about the beauty of being alone with God.

At the age of eighty-one the great Christian preacher, John Nelson Darby, wrote: "Do not reckon yourself lonely: it is a good thing to be alone with God. I have always been alone but I bless God for it."

September 4

"Come now, let us reason together,"
says the LORD.

ISAIAH 1:18

Plead with God: plead with God: plead with God! That praying is poor shift that is not made up of pleading. "Bring forth your reasons," saith the Lord. Bring forth your strong arguments. O, what prayers were those of John Knox, when he seemed to say to God, "Save Scotland for this reason—for that reason—for another reason—for yet one more reason"—the number of his motives still multiplying with the fervor of his heart. So did he labor with God as though he pleaded for his life, and would not let Him go until he had gained his suit for Scotland.

CHARLES HADDON SPURGEON

Pray About It: John Knox had one burden: the people of Scotland. It was his prayer to God, "Give me Scotland or I die," that caused Queen Mary to say she feared the prayers of John Knox more than an army of soldiers.

Can you be passionate about your desires? Passionate enough to plead with God unrelentingly?

O God of all power, who has called from death the great Pastor of the sheep, our Lord Jesus; comfort and defend the flock which He has redeemed by the blood of the eternal testament. Increase the number of true preachers, lighten the heart of the ignorant, relieve the pains of the afflicted, especially those who suffer for their Christian faith, by the power of our Lord Jesus Christ.

JOHN KNOX

September 5

Quench not the Spirit.

1 THESSALONIANS 5:19 KJV

When the Holy Spirit is urging you to pray, you should do so. If you do not pray, you will feel suffocated within as if there is something left undone. In the event you still do not pray, you will feel even more weighed down. Finally, if you do not pray at all, the spirit of prayer as well as the burden of prayer will be so dulled that it will be difficult for you to regain such feeling and to pray the prayer according to God's will afterwards.

Each time God puts a prayer thought into us His Holy Spirit first moves us into having a burden to pray for that particular matter. As soon as we receive such feeling we should immediately give ourselves to prayer. We should pay the cost of praying well for this matter. For when we are moved by the Holy Spirit, our own spirit instantly senses a burden as though something were laid upon our heart. After we pray it out we feel relieved as though having a heavy stone removed from off us. But in case we do not pour it out in prayer, we will get the feeling of something not yet done. Were we to be faithful in prayer, that is to say, were we to pray as soon as the burden comes upon us, prayer would not become a weight, it would instead be light and pleasant.

What a pity that so many people quench the Holy Spirit here. They quench the sensation which the Holy Spirit gives to move them to pray. Hereafter, few of such sensations will ever come upon them. Thus they are no longer useful vessels before the Lord. The Lord can achieve nothing through them since they are no longer able to breathe out in prayer the will of God.

Watchman Nee

Pray About It: When a Christian has become an experienced pray-er, God can use that person to pray His will into effect. He does this by placing a prayer burden on the heart of the pray-er that can only be discharged through prevailing prayer.

Sometimes we receive these burdens and are unaware of what they are. All we know is that we feel a certain heaviness about a particular matter. If we would pray fully, we would sense a lightening of our prayer burden because we allow the Holy Spirit to pray through us.

Has God given you such burdens? Is there a heaviness you've been feeling lately about a person, a situation, or perhaps a foreign land? Then pray for it until the burden is fully discharged. And be willing to receive new burdens from the Lord.

Burden is the secret of prayer.

Watchman Nee

September 6

After removing Saul, he made David their king. He testified concerning him: "I have found David son of Jesse a man after my own heart; he will do everything I want him to do."

ACTS 13:22

God is looking for a man, or woman, whose heart will always be set on Him, and who will trust Him for all He desires to do. God is eager to work more mightily now than He ever has through any soul. The clock of the centuries points to the eleventh hour.

The world is waiting yet to see what God can do through a consecrated soul. Not the world alone, but God Himself is waiting for one who will be more fully devoted to Him than any who have ever lived; who will be willing to be nothing that Christ may be all; who will grasp God's own purposes; and taking His humility and His faith, His love and His power, will, without hindering, continue to let God do exploits.

There is no limit to what God can do with a man, providing he does not touch the glory.

CHARLES E. COWMAN

Pray About It: In our humanity, we are still prone to pride. God seeks to find men and women who will work with Him without any thought to personal gain or glory. When God finds such a person, miracles happen.

The wonderful thing about being an intercessor is that all our work is done in secret. There is no cause for glory. As for what we pray for, our lips are sealed to the outside world. When God answers, inwardly we beam with the knowledge that God has allowed us to participate in His work. But all the glory goes to Him. We must not touch it in any manner.

> I have committed myself and my all into God's hands and He has accepted the offering. Life henceforth can never be the same.
>
> CHARLES E. COWMAN

September 7

> For Christ did not send me to baptize, but to preach the gospel — not with words of human wisdom, lest the cross of Christ be emptied of its power.
>
> 1 CORINTHIANS 1:17

No advance in the spiritual life can be realized without the foundation of the Cross. Before the Holy Spirit's intercession prayer-life can be truly known, we must be shown by Him how to stand in the position of Christ's death, and by His working let the death of Christ be applied experientially.

> JESSIE PENN-LEWIS

Pray About It: We pray because of the work of the Cross. First, the fact that in history, Christ died for the sins of humankind gives us access to God. But secondly, the Cross must also work experientially in our own lives.

The Cross is the ground from which we pray.

> God answers prayer on the ground of Redemption and on no other ground.
>
> OSWALD CHAMBERS

September 8

He went up into a mountain apart to pray.

MATTHEW 14:23 KJV

Neglect of prayer is at once a source and sign of weakness. Surely we need to remind ourselves constantly of this fact as demonstrated in the life of our Lord. Having become our Saviour and Lord, He is our pattern. If then He found the necessity for such times of communion with His Father, alone, how can we hope to live our lives, or render our service acceptably to Him, if we neglect them?

There can be no question, moreover, that in His case these seasons were not merely occasions when He asked gifts from His Father. In all probability petition occupied a very important place in such seasons, but by no means the principal place.

They were times of communion in which He poured out the joy of His Spirit in adoring praise; and in which He remained in silence, and heard the speech of God in His own soul. And so it must ever be with us, if our lives are to be strong in themselves, and victorious in their service.

GEORGE CAMPBELL MORGAN

Pray About It: Neglect of prayer is a sign of weakness in a Christian. In the same way that neglect of food will render a body weak and prone to illness, so too prayerlessness will cause a believer to suffer weakness of spirit, opening him or her to the spiritual diseases common to those who are spiritually weak. If Christ knew the importance of prayer and practiced it often, how can we then neglect it and expect to be strong?

Feebleness in prayer is the mark of disease.

ANDREW MURRAY

September 9

On him we have set our hope that he will continue to deliver us, as you help us by your prayers. Then many will give thanks on our behalf for the gracious favor granted us in answer to the prayers of many.

2 CORINTHIANS 1:10–11

We must not yield to the idea that, because we are feeble members, doing no great work, our prayers won't make much difference. It may be that this is the very reason why the Lord keeps us in the shade, because he hath need of us for the work of intercession. . . .

See how wonderfully Paul valued the prayer of others. He distinctly expresses this to every church but one to whom he wrote. Would he have asked their prayers so fervently if he thought it would not make much difference?

FRANCES RIDLEY HAVERGAL

Pray About It: When we look around at the ministries that God has truly blessed, they all have one thing in common: They were born and sustained through the prayers of supporters. And for some ministries, when the prayers ceased and human efforts began, God removed His blessing.

If God has called us to work for Him in the shadows of the prayer closet and has given the higher profile work to others, let's receive our prayer work with joy. If the truth be known, the work of the intercessor is the most important work of all. It's a high calling, not a second-class assignment.

Today, thank God for calling you to the ministry of intercession. And intercede robustly for your prayer list.

Blessed Lord! I come now to accept this my calling. For this I would forsake all and follow Thee. Into Thy hands I would believingly yield my whole being: form, train, inspire me to be the one of Thy prayer-legion, wrestlers who watch and strive in prayer, Israels, God's princes, who have power and prevail.

Take possession of my heart, and fill it with the one desire for the glory of God in the ingathering, and sanctification, and union of those whom the Father hath given Thee.

Take my mind and let this be my study and my wisdom, to know when prayer can bring a blessing.

Take me wholly and fit me as a priest ever to stand before God and to bless in His Name.

ANDREW MURRAY

September 10

May my prayer be set before you like incense.

PSALM 141:2

Each one had a harp and they were holding golden bowls full of incense, which are the prayers of the saints.

REVELATION 5:8

When God hungers for some special satisfaction, he seeks out a prayer to answer. Our prayer is the sweet aroma from the kitchen ascending up into the King's chambers making him hungry for the meal. But the actual enjoyment of the meal is his own glorious work in answering our prayer. The food of God is to answer our prayer. The most wonderful thing about the Bible is that it reveals a God who satisfies his appetite for joy by answering prayers. He has no deficiency in himself that he needs to fill up, so he gets his satisfaction by magnifying the glory of his riches by filling up the deficiencies of people who pray.

JOHN PIPER

Pray About It: God is looking for prayers to answer. When He does so, it satisfies a part of His Fatherly nature. It allows Him to express His love as nothing else can do.

Your every prayer wafts like incense to heaven and elicits a response from a God who is hungry to move on your behalf.

When you pray, think about the incense that you're offering God. It will make a difference.

That which ascends as prayer descends as blessing, like the vapor that is drawn up by the kiss of the sun to fall in the freshening rain.

ALEXANDER MACLAREN

September 11

Then King David went in and sat before the LORD.

1 CHRONICLES 17:16

Time spent in quiet prostration of soul before the Lord is most invigorating. David "sat before the Lord"; it is a great thing to hold these sacred sittings; the mind being receptive, like an open flower drinking in the sunbeams, or the sensitive photographic plate accepting the image before it. Quietude, which some men cannot abide, because it reveals their inward poverty, is as a palace of cedar to the wise, for along its hallowed courts the King in his beauty deigns to walk.

CHARLES HADDON SPURGEON

Pray About It: Being quiet seems impossible for some people, revealing "their inward poverty," but to prayers, silence is the palace wherein we behold the King.

Today, remain quiet before the King of Glory. Meditate on Him. Worship the King.

Our intercourse with God resembles that with a friend; at first, there are a thousand things to be told, and as many to be asked; but after a time, these diminish, while the pleasure of being together does not. Everything has been said, but the satisfaction of seeing each other, of feeling that one is near the other, or reposing in the enjoyment of a pure and sweet friendship, can be felt without conversation; the silence is eloquent and mutually understood. Each feels that the other is in perfect sympathy with him, and that their two hearts are incessantly poured one into the other, and constitute but one.

FRANÇOIS FÉNELON

September 12

For the word of God is living and active.

HEBREWS 4:12

In the true prayer of faith the intercessor must spend time with the Father to appropriate the promises of His Word, and must permit himself to be taught by the Holy Spirit, whether the promises can be applied to this particular case.

ANDREW MURRAY

Pray About It: Don't assume you can choose a verse of Scripture and randomly apply it to your situation in a way that suits you. God, through the ministry of the Holy Spirit, may quicken a verse for a given situation and give you the faith to stand on it in prayer, but don't use God's Word to try and maneuver God into doing what you want.

[Through prayer] we cannot make God do what He does not want to do, but we can hinder Him from doing what He does wish to do.

WATCHMAN NEE

September 13

If you have any encouragement from being united with Christ, if any comfort from his love, if any fellowship with the Spirit, if any tenderness and compassion, then make my joy complete by being like-minded, having the same love, being one in spirit and purpose.

PHILIPPIANS 2:1–2

It is when we realize our oneness with Christ in death, and in resurrection, that prayer becomes the marvelous force that we find it was in the life of the Savior; the invincible dynamic that it reveals itself to be in the book of Acts; and the ineffable experience of the great saints of the ages.

F. J. HUEGEL

Pray About It: We don't pray alone. We are one with Christ and it's through Him and by Him that we pray. Watchman Nee once declared that the secret of victory was never to see oneself outside of Christ. This is particularly true as we pray. We are empowered by the One who lives in us. We are one with Christ, bone of His bone, flesh of His flesh.

In prayer today, see yourself united with Christ and then pray from that place of security.

> Wilt thou say, "*Yes!*" to all His longing for union with thee, and with a glad and eager abandonment, hand thyself and all that concerns thee over into His hands? If though wilt, then shall thy soul begin to know something of the joy of union with Christ.
>
> HANNAH WHITALL SMITH

September 14

> But Moses' hands became heavy; so they took a stone and put it under him, and he sat on it. And Aaron and Hur supported his hands, one on one side, and the other on the other side; and his hands were steady until the going down of the sun.
>
> EXODUS 17:12 KJV

Moses' hands became heavy. So do ours often, and we are very apt to lean on Aaron and Hur to hold them up, in other words, to depend on others to help us by their earnestness and steadfastness.

There is something kindling to prayer in being with others who are praying, and all through the Bible this is recognized—even in Gethsemane our dear Lord seems to have wanted human companionship in prayer. But He pressed through that sense of need as He must have done often before, and He can give it to us to press through. He can teach us more than we have yet learned of "access with confidence"; He can draw us deep into His own blessed Presence, even as He drew many a man of old—and among them was Moses—and He can strengthen our hands so that they shall be steady until the going down of the sun.

AMY CARMICHAEL

Pray About It: It's not uncommon to want fellowship with other human beings as we pray. Moses needed Aaron, Jesus wanted His disciples to stay awake with Him while He prayed. But there is a way to be alone with God and still have a sense of companionship. That way is to realize that at any given moment, Christians are at prayer all around the world. There is, in reality, a 24-hour-a-day, 365-day-a-year prayer chain going on that will continue until the return of Christ. Our sense of camaraderie comes from knowing that as we pray, others are praying too. We are joined with them in the same magnificent work for God.

Today, pray with a sense of oneness with the others who are now praying, this very minute, perhaps even some who have read these words today. You will experience that "kindling" with them of which Amy Carmichael spoke.

> The spirit of the Church of God is the spirit of the divine movement. Is she idle, barren, or unfruitful? No; she acts, but her activity is in dependence upon the Spirit of God, who moves and governs her. Just so should it be in her members; that they may be spiritual children of the Church, they must be moved by the Spirit [in prayer].

MADAME GUYON

September 15

. . . and will watch to see what he will say unto me.

HABAKKUK 2:1 KJV

I do not think we have enough of the wondering spirit that the Holy Spirit gives. It is the child-spirit. A child is always wide awake with wonder. But as we get older we forget that a child's wonder is nearer the truth than our older knowledge. When through Jesus Christ we are rightly related to God, we learn to watch and wait, and wait wonderingly. "I wonder how God will answer this prayer." "I wonder how God will answer the prayer the Holy Spirit is praying in me." "I wonder what glory God will bring to Himself out of the strange perplexities I am in." "I wonder what new turn His providence will take in manifesting Himself in my ways."

The child-like wondering mind of the Holy Spirit, if I may so say reverently, was exhibited in the Lord Jesus Christ as everlasting wonder and expectancy at His Father's working. "I speak not of myself," and, "the Father that dwelleth in me, he doeth the works" (John 14:10). Our Lord said that when the Holy Spirit is come, "He shall not speak of himself; but whatsoever he shall hear, that shall he speak." The Lord Jesus spoke and worked from the great big child-heart of God. God almighty became incarnate as a little child, and Jesus Christ's message in us must become that of little children. God always keeps the minds of His children open with wonder, with open-eyed expectancy for Him to come in where He likes.

OSWALD CHAMBERS

Pray About It: The kingdom of God is childlike, Jesus told us. Not childish, but childlike. Have you lost your sense of wonder at the world God made or at the mysteries of redemption? Or the magnificent things He has prepared for us in eternity? Today, come to God with a renewed childlike spirit. Be wide awake with wonder and let that wonder show up in the way you pray.

> Be free, gay, simple, a child. But be a sturdy child, who fears nothing, who speaks out frankly, who lets himself be led, who is carried in the arms; in a word, one who knows nothing, can do nothing, can anticipate and change nothing, but who has a freedom and a strength forbidden to the great. This childhood baffles the wise, and God Himself speaks by the mouth of such children.
>
> FRANÇOIS FÉNELON

September 16

Many, O LORD my God,
    are the wonders you have done.
The things you planned for us
    no one can recount to you;
were I to speak and tell of them,
    they would be too many to declare.

PSALM 40:5

Get on two or three good promises. Press down hard on them. Anchor to them. Things will break up. Things will break loose. Things will break over.

God hears you, and His thoughts toward you are good. He will answer. Dare to trust Him anywhere. God always hears and answers prayer.

W. J. HARNEY

Pray About It: Have you remembered to anchor your prayers to the promises of God? Today, take time to find a promise on which to anchor your requests. Get a word from the Lord for your situation and stay on it. Make sure it's God's word for your situation though, and not an attempt on your part to maneuver God.

> The Word of God is the fulcrum upon which the lever of prayer is placed and by which things are mightily moved.

E. M. BOUNDS

September 17

LORD, you have assigned me my portion and
  my cup;
  you have made my lot secure.
The boundary lines have fallen for me in pleasant
  places;
  surely I have a delightful inheritance.

PSALM 16:5–6

God does not show us the whole plan of our life at a burst, but unfolds it to us bit by bit. Each day He gives us the opportunity of weaving a curtain, carving a peg, fashioning the metal. We know not what we do, but at the end of our life the disjointed pieces will suddenly come together, and we shall see the symmetry and beauty of the divine thought. Then we shall be satisfied. In the meantime let us believe that God's love and wisdom are doing the very best for us.

In the morning ask God to show you His plan for the day in the unfolding of its events, and to give you grace to do or bear all that He may have prepared. In the midst of the day's engagements, often look up and say, "Father, is this in the plan?"

At night, be still, and match your actual with God's ideal, confessing your sins and shortcomings, and asking that His will may be more perfectly done with you, even as in heaven.

F. B. Meyer

Pray About It: If we make prayer a vital part of each day, we will one day look back at the unfolding of the events in our life and see how God worked out all He had in mind for us. Even today, our life will unfold a bit more; the carving of the peg, the weave of the curtain, the fashioning of the metal. Ask today, "Father, is this in the plan?"

> Happy the soul which by a sincere self-renunciation, holds itself ceaselessly in the hands of its Creator, ready to do everything which He wishes; which never stops saying to itself a hundred times a day, "Lord, what would you have me do?"
>
> François Fénelon

September 18

I pray for them. I am not praying for the world, but for those you have given me, for they are yours.

JOHN 17:9

Christ's prayer took in all believers in all ages. Our sympathies, and consequently our prayers, should take in the whole Church of Christ. It is astounding how narrow is the circle taken in by the prayers of the average Christian. Every child of God is my brother and remembered in my prayer. Let us give our prayers a wider sweep.

R. A. TORREY

Pray About It: Today, broaden the scope of your prayers for the body of Christ. Pray for denominations or fellowships that are different from yours. Pray for the body of Christ worldwide — and for the body of Christ of future years. Lay a groundwork of prayer for the church that will protect it from harm and allow it to flourish, winning many to the Lord.

The true church lives and moves and has its being in prayer.

LEONARD RAVENHILL

September 19

And when you pray, do not keep on babbling like pagans, for they think they will be heard because of their many words.

MATTHEW 6:7

Some men will spin out a long prayer telling God who and what he is, or they pray out a whole system of divinity. Some people preach, others exhort the people, till everybody wishes they would stop, and God wishes so, too, most undoubtedly.

CHARLES G. FINNEY

Pray About It: Learn to edit your prayers before you speak them. By that I mean, cut out the unnecessary preaching and detailing of situations that God already knows. This is especially true in public praying. Make your prayers solidly to the point. Never use prayer as a means of preaching, exhorting, or filling the air with words. Neither God nor man are impressed.

[Almost all of the prayers recorded in the Bible] are exceedingly short ones. The prayers which brought such remarkable responses from Heaven were . . . brief and to the point, fervent but definite. No soul is heard because of the multitude of his words, but only when his petitions come from the heart, are prompted by a longing for God's glory, and are presented in childlike faith.

A. W. PINK

September 20

The secret of the LORD is with them that fear him;
and He will show them His covenant.

PSALM 25:14 KJV

Then Daniel praised the God of heaven and said:

"Praise be to the name of God for ever and ever;
    wisdom and power are his.
He changes times and seasons;
    he sets up kings and deposes them.
He gives wisdom to the wise
    and knowledge to the discerning.
He reveals deep and hidden things;
    he knows what lies in darkness,
    and light dwells with him.
I thank and praise you, O God of my fathers:
    You have given me wisdom and power,
you have made known to me what we asked of you,
    you have made known to us the dream of
        the king."

DANIEL 2:19–23

Daniel's was a life of utmost devotion to his God.
It centered wholly in Him. In intimate communion with the Lord he sought to know His mind
and with equal fidelity to do His will. Resolutely
determining at the outset, in the midst of adverse
circumstances, to be separated from his God and
well-pleasing unto Him, he grew in favor with God
and in esteem with men.

Daniel's prayer-life was seemingly its dominant characteristic, its ruling passion. When he had risen to the premiership of the realm, his political enemies plotted against him. They found but one vulnerable point—his habit of prayer. They acted upon the conviction that he would continue in it at all costs, even to death itself. And he did. But God's answer to such devotion was his deliverance from the lions and his enemies' destruction by them, much to the glorification of His name and worship under the king's edict.

Daniel's whole life, with the marvelous book that bears his name, is a remarkable testimony, not to the fact that God answers prayer, but to the manner in which He responds to such a life in the revealing of His mind and will. "The secret of the Lord is with them that fear him; and He will show them His covenant" (Ps. 25:14). The word for "secret" means counsel, the intimate converse of confidants or familiar friends. Doubtless this very scripture was Daniel's frequent inspiration in prayer. It was thus he came to know the secret of the king's dream and its interpretation. It was thus that the Lord entrusted him with the revealing of His prophetic program down to the end.

NORMAN B. HARRISON

Pray About It: God's secrets are open to those who pray. The prayer closet is the chamber of revelation to the child of God. What was available to Daniel is ours as well.

Schedule time soon to read the book of Daniel, the story of one of God's great pray-ers. His commitment will inspire you and add backbone to your prayer life.

Daniel wasn't the only one to whom God revealed secrets; there were many others. And today, God continues to reveal secrets to those who know Him. But these secrets are shared in the silent times of prayer, not the hurried rote prayers we too often pray.

Settle into God today. Become the kind of person God can entrust with His secrets.

> [It is here, in prayer] that the deep secrets are revealed, not by a momentary illumination, but in God Himself, where they are all hidden.
>
> MADAME GUYON

September 21

Hope thou in God.

PSALM 42:5 KJV

Remember this: There is never a time when we may not hope in God. Whatever our necessities, however great our difficulties, and though to all appearance help is impossible, yet our business is to *hope in God*, and in the Lord's own time help will come.

Oh the hundreds, yea, the thousands of times that I have found it thus within the past seventy years and four months!

When it seemed impossible that help could come, help *did* come; for God has His own resources.

He is not confined. In ten thousand different ways, and at ten thousand different times God may help us.

Our business is to spread our cases before the Lord, in childlike simplicity to pour out all our heart before God, saying,

"I do not deserve that Thou shouldst hear me and answer my requests, but for the sake of my precious Lord Jesus; for *His* sake answer my prayer, and give me grace quietly to wait till it please Thee to answer my prayer. For I believe Thou wilt do it on Thine own time and way."

More prayer, more exercise of faith, more patient waiting, and the result will be abundant blessing. Thus I have found it many hundreds of times, and therefore I continually say to myself, *"Hope thou in God."*

GEORGE MUELLER

Pray About It: After a long, long life of serving God, George Mueller's testimony was still strong. He was one of the church's most magnificent pray-ers. He never gave up. At age seventy, Mueller left on a worldwide mission that lasted for seventeen years. He lived to age ninety-three, still praying, still believing until his last breath.

Today is a day of hope. "Hope thou in God" today. Make hope your anchor. Never give up.

May thy grace, O Lord, make that possible to me which seems impossible to me by nature.

AMY CARMICHAEL

September 22

And the LORD said to Moses, "I will do the very thing you have asked, because I am pleased with you and I know you by name."

Then Moses said, "Now show me your glory."

And the LORD said, "I will cause all my goodness to pass in front of you, and I will proclaim my name, the LORD, in your presence. I will have mercy on whom I will have mercy, and I will have compassion on whom I will have compassion. But," he said, "you cannot see my face, for no one may see me and live."

Then the LORD said, "There is a place near me where you may stand on a rock. When my glory passes by, I will put you in a cleft in the rock and cover you with my hand until I have passed by. Then I will remove my hand and you will see my back; but my face must not be seen."

EXODUS 33:17–23

I had an overwhelming experience of the Lord's presence. I felt so powerfully overcome by the nearness of the Holy Spirit that I had to ask the Lord to draw back lest He kill me. It was so glorious that I couldn't stand more than a small portion of it.

MORDECAI HAM

Pray About It: The testimonies of those who have known God in secret all have this in common: When God comes near, the pray-er can never be the same. Yes, we can experience God in such a way that we are filled with awe at Him and yet terror at our own sinfulness. And if in this life, we can stand only a small portion of God, what shall it be like to see Him face-to-face someday? Glorious indeed!

Today, bow low before God. Seek Him alone and worship. Recite aloud Psalm 150 in its entirety.

Praise the LORD.
Praise God in his sanctuary;
  praise him in his mighty heavens.
Praise him for his acts of power;
  praise him for his surpassing greatness.
Praise him with the sounding of the trumpet,
  praise him with the harp and lyre,
praise him with tambourine and dancing,
  praise him with the strings and flute,
praise him with the clash of cymbals,
  praise him with resounding cymbals.
Let everything that has breath praise the LORD.
Praise the LORD.

PSALM 150

Count upon your God to do for you everything that you can desire of Him. Honour God as a God who gives liberally. Honour God and believe that He asks nothing from you but what He is going first to give. And then come praise and surrender and consecration.

ANDREW MURRAY

September 23

> . . . and after the fire a still small voice.
>
> 1 KINGS 19:12 KJV

Often the Spirit will prompt us to prayer, when, judging from external circumstances, we shall be inclined to conclude that no real danger exists, or any special necessity for prayer. But how often have we afterwards discovered, it may be to our cost, that through disregarding the Divine call we were betrayed into a snare or overcome by a temptation!

EVAN HOPKINS

Pray About It: Sometimes we sense a need to pray for something that seems to come out of the blue and we want to dismiss it. And yet God does speak to us at times this way. He seeks reliable men and women on whom He can place special burdens for prayer at certain times. Learn to obey His promptings.

Today, if God leads you, follow Him in prayer.

It is God's way to do the unexpected. Were we to put it to a vote as to which they thought the more likely, for the Lord to have spoken to Elijah through the mighty wind and earthquake or the still small voice, we suppose the great majority would say the former. And it is not much the same in our own spiritual experience? We earnestly beg Him to grant us a more definite and settled assurance of our acceptance in Christ, and then look for His answer in a sort of electric shock imparted to our souls or in an extraordinary vision; when instead, it is by the still small voice of the Spirit bearing witness with our spirit that we are the children of God. Again, we beseech the Lord that we may grow in grace, and then expect His answer in the form of more conscious enjoyment of His presence; whereas He quietly gives us to see more of the hidden depravity of our hearts. Yes, God often does the unexpected in His dealings with us.

A. W. PINK

September 24

I will arise and go to my father, and will say unto him, Father, I have sinned against heaven, and before thee, And am no more worthy to be called thy son: make me as one of thy hired servants. And he arose, and came to his father. But when he was yet a great way off, his father saw him, and had compassion, and ran, and fell on his neck, and kissed him.

LUKE 15:18–20 KJV

You can at will close your eyes and, in vision, call up before you the men and women whom you love yet know to be lost. Friend after friend has wrought with and entreated them: you yourself would almost be willing to be anathema for them, if so they might be saved: but all has been in vain. Suppose now there came some day a message from the Lord

Jesus Christ promising that if you would but ask, He himself would go to these unsaved ones and deal directly with them. What an unheard of privilege would you count it to have Jesus Christ himself deal in person with a soul you loved!

To have Jesus Christ work—not indeed in the body but in the Spirit—in your home, your church, your community; to have Jesus Christ give secret messages to your lost loved ones: to have Jesus Christ speak, woo, and win, as none else could: to have Jesus Christ with all His tact, wisdom, winsomeness, patience, gentleness, and compassion following on with unwearied zeal and tenderest love to bring back to God that soul for whom He had died—what a promise! And yet this is exactly what prayer will accomplish, for He explicitly says, "If ye *ask* I will *do*."

Think a moment of that unsaved loved one for whom all these years *you* have been doing. You have pleaded, argued, and expostulated in vain. You have preached Christ, you have tried to live Christ. You have exhausted every device and means that love, faith, or hope could conceive. Now that all *your* doing has failed, how wondrous it would be into that life to bring *His* doing through your *asking*.

Hear Him speak: "My child, *you* know not how to convict of sin, but *I*, who work as you pray, can bow down that soul in a very agony of conviction. *You* know not when to woo, and when to reprove, but *I*, who work as you ask, know just when to pour in the balm of love, and when to let fall the sharp, quick blow of needed judgment. *You* cannot follow a soul in daily, unbroken pursuit, for you are finite and must eat, rest, and sleep, but *I*, who do as you ask, follow that soul day and night, with sleepless vigilance, through every second of his existence. Now comforting, now troubling; now giving darkness, now light; now sending prosperity, now adversity, now using the knife, now the healing balm; chastening, troubling; bereaving, blessing; bending, breaking, making, yea, *I* can do all things needful to be done to bring that wanderer to himself and cause him to cry I will arise and go unto my Father."

JAMES A. MCCONKEY

Pray About It: Today, invite the Lord Jesus Christ Himself to deal with that unsaved friend, relative, coworker, acquaintance. You can be more effective in prayer than in all the words you've used to try and convince him or her to accept Christ. Cease speaking directly to the person about Christ until you have seen the Lord move in his or her heart in response to your prayer.

It's possible to move men through God by prayer alone.

J. OSWALD SANDERS

September 25

But you are a chosen people, a royal priesthood, a holy nation, a people belonging to God, that you may declare the praises of him who called you out of darkness into his wonderful light.

1 PETER 2:9

Consider how great a privilege it is, when angels are present, and archangels throng around, when cherubim and seraphim encircle with their blaze the throne, that a mortal man or woman may approach with unrestrained confidence, and converse with Almighty God Himself. Wherever else and whenever else has such an honor as this ever been conferred?

JOHN CHRYSOSTOM

Pray About It: There's no question about it: that sinful man now has access to God Himself is awesome. Christ was our great High Priest, who having accomplished His work of redemption, sat down at the right hand of the Father. We now have access that, prior to Christ, would have caused the death of the interloper.

We need no priest or intermediary—we have all the access to our heavenly Father as a child has to his own loving earthly father.

Pray today as close to the throne as you can come. You have a right as His child to do so.

We talk about heaven being so far away. It is within speaking distance to those who belong there.

DWIGHT L. MOODY

September 26

Thy word is very pure: therefore thy servant loveth it.

PSALM 119:140 KJV

Turn to the Scripture: choose some passage that is simple and fairly practical. Next, come to the Lord. Come quietly and humbly.

There, before Him, read a small portion of the passage of Scripture you have opened to. . . . But in coming to the Lord by means of "praying the Scripture," you do not read quickly; you read very slowly. You do not move from one passage to another, not until you have sensed the very heart of what you have read. . . . If you read quickly, it will benefit you little. You will be like a bee that merely skims the surface of the flower.

Instead, in this new way of reading with prayer, you must become as the bee who penetrates into the depths of the flower. You plunge deeply within to remove its deepest nectar.

MADAME GUYON

Pray About It: Choose a psalm and pray it back to God. Read slowly and absorb the spirit of the psalm. This practice should become a frequent part of your time with God. It should act as a perfect segue to prayer. It will also enrich your understanding of God's Word.

Turn the Bible into prayer.

ROBERT MURRAY McCHEYNE

September 27

When you ask, you do not receive, because you ask
with wrong motives, that you may spend what you
get on your pleasures.

JAMES 4:3

A great many people get discouraged because they
are praying with wrong motives—for temporal blessings; for what is not good for them. God
doesn't answer such prayers; and they ought to
thank Him for it.

The men who are taken up most prominently in
Scripture, perhaps the most eminent men who ever
lived, don't get their prayers answered.

Thus, it's no sign that God doesn't love us, if
we don't get our prayers answered as we want them
answered.

Consider Moses, whom God favors more than
any man in the Old Testament. He prayed as no
one else prayed. He was a man of prayer, and we
can hear him praying to God to allow him to take
His people into the promised land. But God didn't
answer his prayer—not because He didn't love
him, but because He had something else in store
for him.

We can imagine Him talking to Moses as a
mother to a child, who is asking for something she
does not wish him to have. God says: "That will
do, Moses! I hear you; I know you want to go over
there pretty bad; but I am not going to let you go.
It's no use." But God did for him that which was

much greater than any answer to his prayer could have been. He did for him what He never did for any other man. He conferred upon him the greatest, the most sublime distinction He could give to any mortal. *God buried him.* . . .

God does not answer our prayers, sometimes, because we ask for things that would be harmful to us. We would get a good many things we asked for, if God did not love us too well to answer our prayers.

Dwight L. Moody

Pray About It: Not only did Moses' prayer not get answered, but even Jesus prayed a prayer which God didn't answer. In the garden at Gethsemane, Jesus prayed for "this cup to pass from me, if it's possible." And then Jesus added, "Nevertheless, not my will but yours be done."

Can you imagine our fate if God had answered Jesus' prayer and let that cup of suffering that lay ahead pass from Him? We would still be in our sins.

God knows best—for Moses, for Jesus, and for us. And twenty centuries later, that's still the determining factor in how God answers prayer.

His love decides. And it will always be that way.

Faith in God will not get for you everything you may want, but it will get for you what God wants you to have.

Vance Havner

September 28

And being in anguish, he prayed more earnestly, and his sweat was like drops of blood falling to the ground.

LUKE 22:44

There is no power like that of prevailing prayer—of Abraham pleading for Sodom, Jacob wrestling in the stillness of the night, Moses standing in the breach, Hannah intoxicated with sorrow, David heartbroken with remorse and grief, Jesus in sweat of blood.

Add to this list from the records of the church your personal observation and experience, and always there is the cost of passion unto blood. Such prayer prevails. It turns ordinary mortals into men of power. It brings power. It brings fire. It brings rain. It brings life. It brings God.

SAMUEL CHADWICK

Pray About It: Passion in prayer equals prevailing prayer. If you would be passionate, remember those who have prayed in victory before you. If you were to ask them, "Was it worth the cost?" every one of them would answer, "Yes! A thousand times yes!"

Today, be passionate with God about your prayers. Spread them fervently before Him with all your heart.

Prevailing prayer is that prayer which attains the blessing it seeks.

CHARLES G. FINNEY

September 29

In this you greatly rejoice, though now for a little while you may have had to suffer grief in all kinds of trials. These have come so that your faith—of greater worth than gold, which perishes even though refined by fire—may be proved genuine and may result in praise, glory and honor when Jesus Christ is revealed.

1 PETER 1:6–7

In one thousand trials, it is not five hundred of them that work for the believer's good, but nine hundred and ninety-nine of them, and one beside.

GEORGE MUELLER

Pray About It: Great pray-ers are often men and women of great trials. The two seem to go hand in hand. But there's a third partner to the triangle of prayer—and that's great victory. Those who would enjoy the latter must also have the other two. George Mueller was once asked how to have strong faith. The old prayer warrior replied, "The only way to learn strong faith is to endure great trials. I have learned my faith by standing firm amid severe testings."

If severe testing is your lot in life, that means God has designed great victories to accompany those trials. Rejoice that God has allowed you the same pathway that He's chosen for His choicest saints.

All one thousand of your trials are meant for good. Such knowledge should provide you great courage and speed your prayers to the Father's throne.

Our difficulties, our trials, and our worries about tomorrow all vanish when we look to God.

OSWALD CHAMBERS

September 30

For no one can lay any foundation other than the one already laid, which is Jesus Christ.

1 CORINTHIANS 3:11

Prayer must be based upon promise, but thank God, his promises are always broader than our prayers! No fear of building inverted pyramids here, for Jesus Christ is the foundation.

FRANCES RIDLEY HAVERGAL

Pray About It: Today, picture your prayers as buildings under construction. Under each prayer — each building — is the promise of God as the foundation. And the foundation, the promise of God, is broader than the prayer. There is thus no chance of the building collapsing. No chance of the prayer that rests upon the promise of God failing.

Build with God today, through your prayers.

The story of every great Christian achievement is the history of answered prayer.

E. M. BOUNDS

October 1

Thy prayers and thine alms are come up for a memorial before God.

ACTS 10:4 KJV

What a beautiful expression the angel used to Cornelius, "Thy prayers are come up for a memorial." It would almost seem as if his years of supplications had accumulated before the Throne of God, and at last the answer broke in blessings on the head of Cornelius.

So God is represented as treasuring the prayers of His saints. They are sent up as memorials before Him. They are kept in sweet remembrance before Him. We are called "the Lord's remembrancers," in Isaiah 62:6 and are commanded to give Him no rest, day nor night, but crowd the heavens with our petitions and in due time the answer will come with its accumulated blessings.

A. B. SIMPSON

Pray About It: What does God think of the prayers of His people? It is all detailed here. Our prayers aren't bothersome to God; they are *precious*. And as we pray, we are the Lord's remembrancers, remembering all that He is and has done.

Today, remember His goodness and offer up your prayers with the knowledge that they are a perpetual delight, a sweet smelling incense. And like those of Cornelius, they, along with our alms, "come up as a memorial before God."

We are to be God's remembrancers on the earth. We are to be men of prayer, and especially of intercessory prayer. We are to be, for a time, in this world, that which our Lord is everlastingly in heaven.

ALEXANDER WHYTE

October 2

He rained down manna for the people to eat,
  he gave them the grain of heaven.

PSALM 78:24

I am persuaded that I ought never to do anything without prayer, and, if possible, special secret prayer. . . . I ought to pray far more for our church, for our ministers by name, and for my own clear guidance in the right way, that I may not be led aside, or driven aside from following Christ. . . . I should pray much more in peaceful days, that I may be guided rightly when days of trial come. I ought to spend the best hours of the day in communion with God. It is my noblest and most fruitful employment, and is not to be thrust into any corner. For me, the morning hours from six to eight are the most uninterrupted, and should be thus employed, if I can prevent drowsiness. A little time after breakfast might be given to intercession. After tea is my best hour, and that should be solemnly dedicated to God, if possible.

ROBERT MURRAY MCCHEYNE

Pray About It: It's nice to read that great pray-ers of the past had to fight drowsiness, even those who counted prayer as the most important activity of their day. It's also nice to hear that "after tea" was a good hour for this eighteenth-century Christian. What is your equivalent of "after tea"?

Remember that your hour of prayer may not be the same as another Christian's. Do try to get with Him in the morning, however, as it sets the tone for the day. The manna must be gathered early or it is spoiled. But prayer in the evening is also suitable, as we think back on the goodness of God during the day, and we look ahead to tomorrow.

> Wake up, man, wake up when you pray, for it is insulting to God to give him sleepy worship.
>
> Charles Haddon Spurgeon

October 3

Is any one of you sick? He should call the elders of the church to pray over him and anoint him with oil in the name of the Lord. And the prayer offered in faith will make the sick person well; the Lord will raise him up.

James 5:14–15

[Jonathan and Rosalind Goforth were missionaries to China in the early twentieth century. In her journal, she records the following event, one with which many pray-ers can identify.]

We were stationed temporarily at Weihuifu, in the southern part of the Honan Field. When holding a women's study class at a distant outstation, I stayed in the home of Dr. Fan, the chief elder of the church there.

Just as the class was closing, Mrs. Fan asked me to visit a very sick boy, who had been sent home from the Weihuifu Boys' School, far gone with tuberculosis of the lungs. It was late afternoon when we reached the boy's home. We found the lad on a stool outside the door. My heart sank as I watched how he almost doubled up with every effort to get breath. Foam fell from his mouth, and his face had an ashen, deathly look. His mother and others gathered around as I prayed. But it seemed hypocrisy for me to pray that he might be healed, for I simply had not the faith for such a miracle. So I prayed for the mother and finally ended by praying that the boy might be given *dying grace*.

Then, as we started back across the fields, these words kept ringing in my ears, "Call for the elders of the church and let them pray over him." Over and over again these words came, till on reaching the Fans' home I determined just to obey, though I could not work up any faith that the boy would live. I would *blindly obey*.

But when I told Dr. Fan what I wanted to do, he at first refused to join me, saying, "Why, the boy

371

is dying!" But I persisted, and he gave way as I said, "Dr. Fan, I honestly have not the faith to believe for the boy's healing, but if I return home without at least obeying what seems like God's voice, I will be utterly miserable and conscience stricken."

The boy was brought. Elders and friends gathered about, and the boy was placed in the midst. We all knelt on the earthen floor. The elders prayed. Then I closed, praying much as I had before. The boy was taken home, and the following morning I left for Changte.

A year later, when attending presbytery at Weihuifu, I met Mrs. Fan and inquired, "Did that boy die?" (Oh, the sadness of no faith!)

The reply came, "Why, no, the lad is quite well and helping his father!"

Two years passed, and I was again at Weihuifu helping another missionary with special meetings for women. One day, as we sat at dinner and I was telling her this story, a knock came on the door, and in walked a tall, strong, fine looking young man, the photographer who had taken several pictures for us the previous day. He handed my colleague the photos with a few words; then turning to me, he said (of course in Chinese), "I see you do not know me, Mrs. Goforth."

I replied, "No, I have no remembrance of having seen you before."

At this he smiled and, coming forwards, gave me a bow, saying, "I am the boy you prayed for almost three years ago. I have never forgotten you."

Words could never describe my feelings at this moment. Glad, yes, but oh, so sad and humbled! Then came a glimpse of God's infinite love and patience in using such a faithless channel to work His miracle. Truly as the heavens are high above the earth, so are His ways higher than our ways!

ROSALIND GOFORTH

Pray About It: Mrs. Goforth isn't alone. How many of us have prayed for the healing of someone, all the while our minds full of doubt? But even when we are weak, He is still strong and He still reigns.

When you can't believe that God will hear your prayers, at least obey when He prompts action. Here, Mrs. Goforth, though she could not pray in faith, at least sent for the elders in obedience to God's Word. And God restored a boy who was at death's door. God remains faithful to our obedience, even when our faith is weak.

He who does not cover and supply the wants of the body by prayer will never cover and supply the wants of his soul. Both body and soul are dependent on God, and prayer is but the crying expression of that dependence.

E. M. BOUNDS

October 4

They all joined together constantly in prayer, along with the women and Mary the mother of Jesus, and with his brothers.

ACTS 1:14

The early church was without doubt a praying church, and what tremendous things they accomplished through prayer alone: prison doors were opened, fanatical opponents were struck down and converted to Christ, signs and wonders were done. But the open secret was that the early church knew the presence and power of the Holy Spirit, not theoretically but experientially. Those first believers were mighty in prayers because they were mighty in the Spirit.

ARTHUR WALLIS

Pray About It: Most Christians are pretty knowledgeable about God the Father and Jesus Christ. But the Holy Spirit? Most believers actually know less about the third person of the Trinity. And yet it is the Holy Spirit who holds the key to prayer. It's through Him that we pray, that we groan before God. He's the one who knows how to pray the will of God through us. He convicts us of sin, He comforts us, and He teaches us all things.

Today, do not pray to the Holy Spirit, but pray with the aid of the Holy Spirit. Ask Him to use you as a vessel to accomplish the will of God.

On Pentecost, the Holy Spirit filled both the men and the women. They began to speak as the Holy Spirit gave them words. The Holy Spirit still comes.

CATHERINE BOOTH

October 5

You will not fear the terror of night,
    nor the arrow that flies by day,
nor the pestilence that stalks in the darkness,
    nor the plague that destroys at midday.
A thousand may fall at your side,
    ten thousand at your right hand,
    but it will not come near you.

PSALM 91:5–7

On the coast of Scotland, one stormy night, a woman came to the house of her pastor, and said to the minister, "Rise, and pray for my husband, for he is on the sea in a storm." The Christian wife and her pastor knelt down and prayed for the salvation of the sea-captain. Sure enough, at that very hour the vessel was tossed upon the angry seas. The ship plunged in the wave, and it seemed as if it would never come up again; but it righted, and came to the top of the wave. It plunged again, and for a long while the captain thought it would never rise; but it began to shake itself from the wave, and again bounded the sea. The third time it went down, and all hands on board gave up the last hope. But again it mounted. As it came out of the foaming billows, the captain said to his crew, "Lads, surely there was some God's soul on the land praying for us tonight, or we would never have come up out of that." Prayer is a mighty influence. It is a strong and sure sickle. Let us all lay hold of it.

T. DEWITT TALMADGE

Pray About It: God protects His people in times of danger — especially in response to prayer. Have you prayed a hedge of protection around your loved ones? The rough seas they face are no less dangerous than a ship caught in a tempest. Pray for them with the same urgency. Your prayer today can calm their rough sea.

George Benfield, a driver on the Midland Railway, living at Derby, was standing on the footplate oiling his engine, the train being stationary, when his foot slipped; he fell on the space between the lines. He heard the express coming on, and had only time enough to lie full length on the "six-foot" when it rushed by, and he escaped unhurt. He returned to his home in the middle of the night and as he was going up-stairs he heard one of his children, a girl about eight years old, crying and sobbing. "Oh, father," she said, "I thought somebody came and told me that you were going to be killed, and I got out of bed and prayed that God would not let you die."

Was it only a dream, a coincidence? George Benfield and others believed that he owed his life to that prayer.

DEAN HOLE

October 6

Therefore I tell you, whatever you ask for in prayer, believe that you have received it, and it will be yours.

MARK 11:24

Let us not allow our prayer to jump about like a grasshopper, hopping to another matter before the first one is thoroughly prayed through, and before this second matter is thoroughly prayed for, we are found skipping back to the very first matter.

WATCHMAN NEE

Pray About It: In our praying, let's be thorough in our asking. Our minds are too often like grasshoppers or butterflies, flitting from here to there and back again. God would have us pray through a matter before we move on to the next request. Be thorough in your prayers today. Know why you're praying. Make your case before God.

Only begin prayers that you're prepared to pray through to their end.

To what end, O my soul, art thou retired to this place?

JOHN BUNYAN

October 7

Night and day we pray most earnestly. . . .

1 THESSALONIANS 3:10

Why is it that God does not give to us the very first time we ask Him, the things that we ask of Him? The answer is plain: God would do more for us, and better for us, than to merely give us that thing. He would do us the far greater good of training us into persistent faith.

The things that we get by our other forms of effort than prayer to God, do not always become ours the first time we make an effort to get them. For our own good God compels us to be persistent in our effort, and just so God does not always give us what we ask in prayer the first time we pray.

Just as He would train us to be strong men and women along the other lines of effort, so also He would train us to be and make us to be strong men and women of prayer by compelling us to pray hard for the best things. He compels us to "Pray through."

R. A. TORREY

Pray About It: Prayer builds our faith. If God dispensed answers the first time we prayed, where would faith come in? His seeming delay to answering our prayers requires us to remain faithful. He would have us be strong.

The less I pray, the harder it gets. The more I pray, the better it goes.

MARTIN LUTHER

October 8

And the LORD said unto David my father, Whereas it was in thine heart to build an house unto my name, thou didst well that it was in thine heart. Nevertheless thou shalt not build the house; but thy son that shall come forth out of thy loins, he shall build the house unto my name. And the LORD hath performed his word that he spake.

1 KINGS 8:18–20 KJV

God never says "No" coldly; He whispers into the heart that is attentive to His word, "It was well that it was in thine heart."

Encouraged by this, David gave himself wholeheartedly to the task of gathering the materials. In 1 Chronicles 29:2–3, where David spoke to his people concerning Solomon and the temple, he said, "Now I have prepared with all my might for the house of God the gold . . . the silver . . . the brass . . . the iron . . . and wood; onyx stones . . . and all manner of precious stones . . . because I have set my affection to the house of God, I have of mine own proper good, of gold and silver, which I have given to the house of my God, over and above all that I have prepared for the holy house."

This man, who had been denied the fulfillment of his vision, instead of sulking about it, gave himself completely to the task in the best way he knew how, preparing that which he himself would never be able to complete.

If you cannot build, you can gather the materials; if you cannot go, you can send somebody else. If

God has said "No" to you, you can make it possible for someone else to fill that place on which you had set your heart.

The vision need never have been in vain, even though it remains unfulfilled, for God's refusals in life are loaded with immeasurable possibilities of blessing.

It all depends, however, on whether at the moment when God has said "no" you sulk or you seek—if you seek, you will find that God is right there with blessing such as you have never experienced before.

ALAN REDPATH

Pray About It: Moses never saw the Promised Land. David didn't see the temple. But both men were responsible for bringing the vision to pass in the next generation.

Do you ever feel like God has passed you by? That you've not done the great work you once thought you would? Is it that for which you still pray?

Have no regrets. Your vision may still come to pass in those who follow. Paul knew that some planted, some watered, and some harvested. He knew that all three were important. You may not have harvested, but if you have prayed, you are as vital a part of the work of God as the one who harvests.

Give thanks. Your work has not been in vain. Others will do their part and God's work will be complete.

Although God refused David's request, He said to him, "It was well that it was in thine heart." Wasn't it good of God to tell him that? Surely it left a permanent glow in David's life.

ALAN REDPATH

October 9

Test everything. Hold on to the good. Avoid every kind of evil.

1 Thessalonians 5:21–22

What some call providential openings, are often powerful temptations. Our wandering heart may cry, "At last, here is a pathway opened before me." But perhaps that path is one not to be taken, but to be rejected.

John Newton

Pray About It: Many of us have made drastic choices because we based a decision on what we thought was God's leading. Later, to our regret, we learned otherwise. As you pray, watch for providential openings, but don't assume any opening is providential. Such openings must be consistent with God's Word and they will usually bear the scrutiny of more mature brothers and sisters who can be more objective. There's safety in a multitude of counselors. Ask others, read the Word, and wait, before you walk that seemingly right path. It may be one to be rejected.

Here's the counsel of one of the great pray-ers of all time, George Mueller:

How to Ascertain the Will of God

1. I seek at the beginning to get my heart into such a state that it has no will of its own in regard to a given matter. Nine-tenths of the trouble with people is just here. Nine-tenths of the difficul-

ties are overcome when our hearts are ready to do the Lord's will, whatever it may be. When one is truly in this state, it is usually but a little way to the knowledge of what his will is.

2. Having done this, I do not leave the result to feeling or simple impression. If so, I make myself liable to great delusions.

3. I seek the will of the Spirit of God through, or in connection with, the Word of God. The Spirit and the Word must be combined. If I look to the Spirit alone without the Word, I lay myself open to great delusions also. If the Holy Ghost guides us at all, He will do it according to the Scriptures and never contrary to them.

4. Next I take into account providential circumstances. These often plainly indicate God's Will in connection with His Word and Spirit.

5. I ask God in prayer to reveal His will to me aright.

6. Thus, through prayer to God, the study of the Word, and reflection, I come to a deliberate judgment according to the best of my ability and knowledge, and if my mind is thus at peace, and continues so after two or three more petitions, I proceed accordingly. In trivial matters, and in transactions involving the most important issues, I have found this method always effective.

October 10

They devoted themselves to the apostles' teaching and to the fellowship, to the breaking of bread and to prayer.

ACTS 2:42

Of this I am fully persuaded: With a once-a-week prayer meeting, no church (here or in any other place, at this or any time) is going to get us a heaven-born, Spirit-operated revival. Before "Pentecost was fully come," the disciples prayed; and as they were praying, the Spirit fell upon them; after Pentecost we discover that twenty-eight chapters in Acts mention prayer, for they "continued in prayer," says the record.

We need prayer to obtain victory and then prayer to maintain victory. We need to pray about our praying; we must pray unction upon others as they are praying. We must pray alone; we must pray together; we must pray in the night and not cease in the day.

LEONARD RAVENHILL

Pray About It: In times of prosperity, we tend to pray less. We aren't as needy as we are when times are rough. Will it take the onset of hard times to get the church of God to praying? Will it take hardship in our own life to persuade us to pray? If times are good, continue in prayer, thanking God and gaining strength. *There may be lean times ahead. Don't be caught short in that day.*

When Dwight Moody was aboard a ship that was in turbulent waters, he was asked to join others in prayer for deliverance. His simple reply was, "I'm prayed-up already."

October 11

Finally, brothers, pray for us that the message of the Lord may spread rapidly and be honored, just as it was with you. And pray that we may be delivered from wicked and evil men, for not everyone has faith.

2 THESSALONIANS 3:1–2

I see churches and schemes and missionary enterprises, and holiness movements, all tagged with His Name, and how little of Himself! I wish every breath I drew, all speech I made, could make Him come and seem more real to men. Nothing is worth living for but just Himself.

OSWALD CHAMBERS

Pray About It: The focus of prayer is that Christ might be made known. When the body of Christ is functioning as it should, men are drawn to the Savior. But when we fritter our days away caught up with empty movements bearing His name, we don't meet God's standard. There have been many such movements in recent years, but very little real depth of movement toward God Himself.

Be careful of schemes that bear the name of Christ but are devoid of His Spirit.

Surely God will have a people in this place.

J. HUDSON TAYLOR

October 12

Others went out on the sea in ships;
   they were merchants on the mighty waters.
They saw the works of the LORD,
   his wonderful deeds in the deep.

PSALM 107:23–24

Too few Christians live radiantly, beautifully, abundantly. We do not rise to the level of the joys that are fitting of God's heirs.

We do not know the love of Christ in the sense that we are conscious ourselves of being loved by Christ with all infinite tenderness.

There are far deeper joys within our reach than we have experienced. The beauty of the Lord does not shine always in our faces and glow in our characters and appear in our dispositions and tempers.

We are like the Galilean fishermen, toiling and taking nothing. Is it any wonder some of us are discouraged and almost ready at times to give up?

But listen to the Master's voice as it breaks on our ears: "Launch out into the deep and let down your nets for a draught." The trouble with us is, we have been trying only the shallows of God's love. Half consecration knows nothing of the best things of divine grace. We must cut the last chain that binds us back to the shore of this world, and like Columbus, put out to sea to discover new worlds of blessing. We can best hasten the coming of the Kingdom of Christ in its full glory by letting love have its victories in us—the love that bears all things and endures all things — and by doing ever the gentle deeds that comfort lonely hearts and relieve suffering and distress.

J. R. MILLER

Pray About It: Without a deep prayer life, we live in the shallows of God's presence. There are deeper waters of His love that God calls us to in prayer. To see them we must not be afraid of the deep, we must venture out.

Don't be afraid to leave the shallows near the shore; God will show you wonders. Step out.

As seamen in the life of faith, let us launch out into the deep and find that all things are possible to the Christian that believes.

A. B. SIMPSON

October 13

But when it pleased God . . .

GALATIANS 1:15 KJV

It takes God time to answer prayer. We often fail to give God a chance in that respect. It takes time for God to paint a rose. It takes time for God to grow an oak. It takes time for God to make bread from wheat fields. He takes the earth. He pulverizes. He softens. He enriches. He wets with showers and dews. He warms with life. He gives the blade, the stock, the amber grain, and then at last the bread for the hungry.

All this takes time. Therefore we sow, and till, and wait, and trust, until all God's purpose has been wrought out. We give God a chance in this matter of time. We need to learn this same lesson in our prayer life. It takes God time to answer prayer.

J. H. M.

Pray About It: It's our nature to want things to happen quickly. With God, a day is as a thousand years. He takes His time in creating oaks, and in answering the acorns of prayers that we pray.

Don't rush God. Today, by faith, tell God that you will lay down your timetable in favor of His. Then wait expectantly, *as long as it takes.*

The prayer that begins with trustfulness and passes on to waiting will always end in thankfulness, triumph, and praise.

ALEXANDER MACLAREN

October 14

When a man's ways are pleasing to the LORD,
   he makes even his enemies live at peace with him.
PROVERBS 16:7

A Confederate soldier was on sentry duty on the edge of a wood. It was a dark night and very cold, and he was a little frightened because the enemy was supposed to be near at hand. He felt very homesick and miserable, and about midnight, when everything was very still, he was beginning to feel very weary and thought that he would comfort himself by praying and singing a hymn. He remembered singing this hymn —

"All my trust on Thee is stayed,
All my help from Thee I bring,
Cover my defenseless head
With the shadow of Thy wing."

After he had sung those words a strange peace came down upon him, and through the long night he remembered having felt no more fear.

"Now," said another man, "listen to my story. I was a Union soldier, and was in the wood that night with a party of scouts. I saw you standing up, although I didn't see your face, and my men had their rifles focused upon you waiting the word to fire, but when you sang out —

'Cover my defenseless head
With the shadow of Thy wing,'

I said, 'Boys, put down your rifles; we will go home.' I couldn't kill you after that."

DWIGHT L. MOODY

Pray About It: You have prayed for your enemies, but are you aware that God will make even your enemies to be at peace with you? Continue to pray for them today. Don't pray that they come around to your way of thinking. Pray for God to bless them. You'll get a blessing too.

If we could only read the secret history of our enemies, we would find in each man's life sorrow and suffering enough to disarm all hostility.

HENRY WADSWORTH LONGFELLOW

October 15

And I will pour out on the house of David and the inhabitants of Jerusalem a spirit of grace and supplication. They will look on me, the one they have pierced, and they will mourn for him as one mourns for an only child, and grieve bitterly for him as one grieves for a firstborn son.

ZECHARIAH 12:10

When God has something very great to accomplish for His church, it is His will that there should precede it, the extraordinary prayers of His people. And it is revealed that when God is about to accomplish great things for His Church, He will begin by remarkably pouring out the spirit of grace and supplication.

JONATHAN EDWARDS

Pray About It: The sign that God wants to do something great in a nation is that He first gets His church on its knees. God is doing that. People are praying across America and around the world. We must also be watching and *expecting* Him to do great things in our homes, churches, and nation.

When God intends great mercy for His people, the first thing He does is to set them a-praying.

MATTHEW HENRY

October 16

I will send down showers in season; there will be showers of blessing.

EZEKIEL 34:26

It isn't raining afflictions for you. It is raining tenderness, love, compassion, patience, and a thousand other flowers and fruits of the blessed Spirit, which are bringing into your life such a spiritual enrichment as all the fullness of worldly prosperity and ease was ever able to beget in your innermost soul.

JAMES McCONKEY

Pray About It: Although affliction seems to bring us more quickly to prayer, God's purpose in affliction is for our good. The storms that are falling in your life right now are bringing showers of blessing, but you must pray.

The good that these showers will bring to you could have come in no other way.

The Lord gets His best soldiers out of the highlands of affliction.

CHARLES HADDON SPURGEON

October 17

Then I set my face toward the Lord God to make request by prayer and supplications with fasting, sackcloth and ashes.

DANIEL 9:3

From the first moment of human history even to the last— *God's will shall be done!*

Even though it may come through a seeming catastrophe or a crime—there may indeed be secondary causes and the action of human evil—but behind every event remains the great first cause.

If we could imagine that one human action in history has eluded the predestination or knowledge of God, we could suppose then that all human actions might also do so—that all things may drift rudderless to sea, at the whim of every wave, a victim of every tempest and hurricane.

One leak in the ship of Providence would sink her, one hour in which Omnipotence relaxed its grasp and she would fall to atoms.

CHARLES HADDON SPURGEON

Pray About It: Make no mistake—we can never thwart God's will though our prayers. Instead, our prayers validate and usher God's will into existence. Prayer is God's chosen method of directing human events in the way that He wills.

This is, to the human mind, a great mystery. One that will never be fully grasped this side of heaven. To try to figure it out is counterproductive. A child never tries to figure out why a parent blesses him so, he just trusts that parent. Consider Isaac who traveled with his father, Abraham, unaware that, unless God intervened, he would be sacrificed to God. Isaac trusted his father Abraham. Abraham trusted his Father God.

And He is trustworthy. Nothing happens without His knowledge or outside of His will. Ever.

So as we pray, we can trust that God is weaving the perfect tapestry of our lives through the threads of our prayers. We will pray His will and it shall be done. No exceptions. Our prayers become the vehicle through which God accomplishes that which He wants to do—His perfect will.

> That our prayers for the execution of the very things God has decreed to happen are not meaningless, is clearly taught in the Scriptures. Elijah knew that God was about to give rain, but that did not prevent him from praying for the promised rain.
>
> Daniel understood by the writings of the prophets that the captivity was to last but seventy years, yet when these seventy years were almost ended, we are told that he "set his face unto the Lord God, to seek by prayer and supplications, with fasting and sackcloth and ashes" (Daniel 9:2–3).
>
> God told the prophet Jeremiah, "For I know the thoughts that I think toward you, saith the Lord, thoughts of peace, and not of evil, to give you an expected end"; but instead of adding, "there is, therefore, no need for you to supplicate me for these things," He said, "Then shall ye call upon me, and ye shall go and pray unto me, and I will hearken unto you" (Jeremiah 29:12).

Here then is the design of prayer: not that God's will may be altered but it may be accomplished in His own good time and way. It is because God has promised certain things, that we can ask for them with the full assurance of faith. It is God's purpose that His will shall be brought about by His own appointed means, and that He may do His People good upon His own terms, and that is, by the "means" and "terms" of prayer and supplication.

A. W. PINK

October 18

But Jesus often withdrew to lonely places and prayed.

LUKE 5:16

Almost anything associated with the ministry may be learned with an average amount of intelligent application. It is not hard to preach or manage church affairs or pay a social call. . . .

But prayer—that is another matter. . . . There the lonely man of God must wrestle it out alone, sometimes in fasting and tears and weariness untold. There every man must be an original, for true prayer cannot be imitated.

A. W. TOZER

Pray About It: One problem many of us face in private prayer is the loneliness of the practice. There, shut up in our prayer closets, we can do nothing but pray. We see no one, we speak to no other human being, nor do we hear another human voice. Maybe that's why we're so quick to be finished with our devotions. We want the companionship of another human being. We want to begin our day, see our friends, get about our work.

And yet the promise of prayer is a companionship unachievable by any other earthly endeavor. Jesus knew the joy to be found only in the "lonely places." When we're finally finished with our restlessness before God and settle down, it's then and only then that we're able to know Him intimately and individually.

It's then that prayer becomes its own reward.

God makes all His best people in loneliness.

LEONARD RAVENHILL

October 19

Believe in the Lord Jesus, and you will be saved—you and your household.

ACTS 16:31

If you have a son or daughter that you are anxious about don't be ashamed to present them for prayer; it shows your love for them. What better could we do for our children and our friends than to pray God to bless them; and any one that would get angry because we prayed for them must show they are under the power of the devil; they must have their hearts hardened, and be very blind. . . .

Our God is able to break the hardest hearts. Let us make our requests known unto God; and let us expect he will give us an answer. He is constantly answering prayer for the sons and daughters that have been presented here and in other places, sons and daughters who have been presented for prayers have been saved. . . . God is answering prayer. My dear friends, let us keep on praying. God is able to save these people, and there is none but God who does answer prayer.

Don't let infidelity come in and make us believe that God has got a deaf ear and cannot answer: or that his arm is shortened and cannot deliver. Our God is a prayer-answering God. How many mothers have had their sons and daughters saved, not through some sermon, but by the mighty power of God converting them.

DWIGHT L. MOODY

Pray About It: Today we pray for our sons and daughters. If you have none, then pray for someone else's children. We're thinking primarily of those children who have not yet accepted Christ or who have wandered very far from Him. God knows the heartbreak of a parent whose child is rebellious.

We are His children who were once far from Him, in rebellion. And God was grieved. Yet through His mercy He saved us.

It was for a good reason that Jesus told the parable of the prodigal son. It was to show the Father-heart of God aching for a child who has turned his back on what he knows is right. So God sees, knows, and understands fully about that wayward child.

He even knows about your *obedient* child. Our children are loved greatly by God. For them we must keep praying.

And as we look through the Bible, time and time again we see that God's plan is for *families* to be saved. Noah's family was on the ark. The Hebrew family was saved in their homes by the blood of the Passover lamb. Rahab's family was saved by the scarlet cord in her window. When Jesus healed the son of a nobleman (John 4:53), the whole household was saved. Peter's word to Cornelius was that all his household would be saved. Paul and Silas told their jailers that if they believed on the Lord Jesus Christ, they and their household would be saved. God believes in "household salvation."

Keep praying. Keep praying. Keep praying.

Once while traveling, William Booth's rail car was detained. He took advantage of the opportunity and exhorted some idle factory workers. He said, "Some of you men never pray, you gave up praying long ago. But I'm going to say to you, won't you pray for your children that they may be different?" Within minutes 700 men knelt in silent prayer.

Stand firm before God that your household may all be transformed.

WATCHMAN NEE

October 20

I . . . have need of nothing.

THE LAODICEAN CHURCH, REVELATION 3:17 KJV

Those who use prayer as a mere form have no real sense of want. They pray by habit or ritual. Why should God hear them? They do not feel that they need him. They are not so burdened with their wants as to be driven to prayer for them.

We must reflect upon our condition and circumstances until we realize our need, and fall on our knees in earnest prayer, as having something really to ask.

JOHN PATON

Pray About It: In what areas do you feel no need for God to move? Are you financially secure? Is there always food on the table? Is your health good? Job secure? Marriage strong?

If there's any area that you take for granted, God wants you to reflect again. He must be your source for all. Not just the areas where the need is obvious, but perhaps more especially in the places where there is no perceivable lack.

Thank God today for the areas where He has blessed. Refuse to take them for granted. Surrender them back to Him. And then ask God to reveal your true needs today. Finally, thank God for the privilege of prayer. Never take *that* for granted.

Oh Lord, when I pray, let me feel it to be a privilege, not an exercise or duty.

HANNAH WHITALL SMITH

October 21

I am the true vine, and my Father is the gardener.

JOHN 15:1

Open wide every avenue of your being to receive
the blessed influences your Divine Husbandman
may bring to bear upon you. Bask in the sunshine
of His love. Drink in the waters of His goodness.
Keep your face upturned to Him. You need make
no efforts to grow. But let your efforts instead be
all concentrated on this, that you abide in the Vine.

HANNAH WHITALL SMITH

Pray About It: One of the conditions that Jesus put
on prayer was that we abide in Him and His words
abide in us.

Today, turn your face toward Him. Be planted
in Him. Make no effort to grow. Growing happens
naturally, not by effort. This is especially true in the
spiritual life. Simply abide and pray with confidence.
God will take care of the rest.

The Holy Spirit reveals our needs to us. This is
always the first element in prayer: a painful consciousness of failure and necessity. The Spirit of
prayer is the spirit of dependence and conscious
need.

A. B. SIMPSON

October 22

Lord, all my desire is before thee.

PSALM 38:9 KJV

Oh let us see that prayer in sympathy with God is more vital than any other thing! For God can only work in matters for which His children have shown sympathy. He refuses to work in areas where there are no prayers and where His people's will is not united with His will. Prayer with joined wills is real prayer. The highest motive of prayer is not in having it answered. It is to join man's will with God's so that He may be able to work.

WATCHMAN NEE

Pray About It: The benefit of prayer is that it puts us in sympathy with God Himself. We come to love what He loves and hate what He hates. In so doing, we understand how to pray according to His will.

As you pray, ask yourself: Is this in sympathy with the mind of God? Or is this at odds with what God wants to do?

To pray is to desire. But it is to desire what God would have us desire. He who desires not from the bottom of his heart, offers a deceitful prayer.

FRANÇOIS FÉNELON

October 23

God is not a man, that he should lie,
  nor a son of man, that he should change
    his mind.
Does he speak and then not act?
  Does he promise and not fulfill?

NUMBERS 23:19

Remember that faith is not a strange sensation that comes over you in rare moments, a magic thrill from something in the minister's voice, a mystic trance to be reached once in a while, then lost for weeks or years. It is a sturdy confidence that God will keep His promises, confidence enough to walk out on them and live there, although the world expects them to crack and crumble under you any day.

VANCE HAVNER

Pray About It: Refuse to allow your feelings to measure the effectiveness of your prayers. God does not put you in a trance nor give you outward signs that you've been heard. Further, such dependencies are the enemy of faith. Faith is the sturdy confidence that you've been heard, based on God's promise in His Word.

Satan is a master when it comes to orchestrating feelings in Christians. He loves it when we get those goose-bump sensations, because he knows that when they leave, we'll assume we're no longer connected to God.

This doesn't mean that we're to leave our emotions outside the prayer-room door, rather it means that emotions such as joy, tears, love, or excitement may follow our prayers—but they may never lead our prayers or offer us proof that we've been heard.

Stop considering your emotions and simply regard your will, which is the real king in your being. Is your will open to God? Does your will decide to believe? Does your will choose to obey? If this is the case, then you are in the Lord's hands.

HANNAH WHITALL SMITH

October 24

"Woe to me!" I cried. "I am ruined! For I am a man of unclean lips, and I live among a people of unclean lips, and my eyes have seen the King, the LORD Almighty."

ISAIAH 6:5

That which brings the praying soul near to God is humility of heart. That which gives wings to prayer is lowliness of mind. That which gives ready access to the throne of grace is self-depreciation.

Pride, self-esteem, and self-praise effectually shut the door of prayer. He who would come to God must approach Him with self hid from his eyes. He must not be puffed-up with self-conceit, nor be possessed with an over-estimate of his virtues and good works.

E. M. BOUNDS

Pray About It: To be humble is to know two things: The holiness of God and the sinfulness of man. When we really understand the full grace of God toward fallen man, we have no other option but humility. When Isaiah finally "got it," his response was "woe unto me, for I am a man of unclean lips."

Today, reflect on the grace of God and see at its core the basis for our humility before God. We are nothing; He is all.

> What a man is on his knees before God, that he is—no more, no less.
>
> ROBERT MURRAY MCCHEYNE

October 25

> Ask and you will receive, and your joy will be complete.
> JOHN 16:24

A man must have some definite object before his mind. He cannot pray effectively for a variety of objects at once. The mind of man is so constituted that it cannot fasten its desires intensely upon many things at the same time. All the instances of effectual prayer recorded in the Bible were of this kind. Wherever you see that the blessing sought for in prayer was attained, you will find that the prayer which was offered was prayer for that definite object.

CHARLES G. FINNEY

Pray About It: Order your requests so that when you pray for something, it's foremost on your mind. Be definite with God. Tell Him the need exactly. Let Him answer in His own way, but He wants you to articulate the definite need. This causes us to be exacting in our prayers—and in other areas of our life. Learn to say only in prayer exactly what you mean. God doesn't want us to be scatterbrained or offer religious platitudes when we pray.

> The prayer that prevails is strikingly specific. It narrows itself right down to one object, which presses itself on the attention, and on the heart, and fills the vision, and becomes for the time the supreme object to be sought, and obtained, if need be, by the supreme act of the life of the petitioner.
>
> W. J. HARNEY

October 26

I am the Almighty God—El Shaddai—walk before me, and be thou perfect.

GENESIS 17:1 KJV

We must never make the blunder of trying to forecast the way God is going to answer our prayer. When God made a tremendous promise to Abraham, Abraham thought of the best way to help God fulfill His promise and did the wisest thing he knew according to flesh and blood common sense reasoning. But God refused to speak to him for thirteen years, until every possibility of his relying on his own intelligent understanding was at an end. Then God came to him and said, "I am the Almighty God" — El Shaddai — "walk before me, and be thou perfect."

Oswald Chambers

Pray About It: At all costs, we must resist the urge to help God answer our prayers. Abraham suffered terribly trying to help God fulfill His promise. What we're really saying is "God, I really don't think You can do it unless I prime the pump for You and get things started." Nor should we try to guess what God's going to do. Let Him do it in His way and in His time.

El Shaddai means "the all-sufficient one." The imagery actually conveyed is "the double-breasted one," as in a mother's bosom. Today, be nourished and let Him be El Shaddai — let Him be all-sufficient.

Thou hast El Shaddai to be thine. Thy power to be holy will much depend upon thy grasping with all the intensity of thy faith the cheering fact that this God is thy God for ever and ever, thy daily portion, thine all-sufficient consolation. Thou dares not, canst not, wilt not, wander into the ways of sin when thou knowest that such a God is thy shepherd and guide.

Charles Haddon Spurgeon

October 27

Fear ye not therefore, ye are of more value than many sparrows.

MATTHEW 10:31 KJV

Fear not. Don't be too cast down at the deceitfulness of your hearts. Do not fear devils; you shall have the victory even over them. The Lord Jesus has made you more than conquerors over all. Plead with your Savior, plead: plead His promises. Wrestle, wrestle with God in prayer. . . . Do not be terrified by your adversaries; the king of the church has them all in a chain: be kind to them, pray for them; but fear them not.

GEORGE WHITEFIELD

Pray About It: Often we pray when confronted with a crisis. We panic, and so we pray. Yet time after time in the Bible God's people are told to "fear not." *Fear not!* Would it be repeated so many times unless God wanted us to get the message that we don't need to be afraid? We are highly valued in God's eyes, more than any of His other creations, including sparrows.

The best way to meet any crisis is to be prayed up ahead of time, to always be walking in absolute victory. The worst course of action is to panic.

Today, be strong in God's love as you pray. And *fear not!*

Be strong in God's love. Never get into panics.

OSWALD CHAMBERS

October 28

You do not have, because you do not ask God.

JAMES 4:2

Prayer is the easiest and hardest of all things, the simplest and the sublimest; the weakest and the most powerful. Its results lie outside the range of human possibilities — they are limited only by the omnipotence of God. Few Christians have anything but a vague idea of the power of prayer. Fewer still have any experience of that power.

The Church seems almost wholly unaware of the power God has given her. This spiritual blank check on the infinite resources of God's wisdom and power is rarely, if ever, used, and *never* used to the full measure of honoring God.

Prayer is our most formidable weapon, and yet the one in which we are the least skilled and the most reluctant to use.

E. M. BOUNDS

Pray About It: The most remarkable thing about prayer is that we human beings have been *invited* into God's presence to fellowship with Him. Further, we've been told to ask freely of our heavenly Father for all our needs.

We have been given an incredible, truly unbelievable, magnificent gift in prayer. That's what makes it so amazing that so many Christians live and die without knowing about and using this gift. How do they do it? To live without communion with God is like living in a loveless marriage.

Don't let this happen to you. You have all the resources of God available to you. Use them frequently and wisely. Today thank God for His unspeakable gift of prayer.

> Prayer, when we think of it, and perform it aright,—prayer is a magnificent thing—and a venturesome,—for any man to do. For prayer builds, and fits out, and mans, and launches a frail vessel of faith on the deep and wide sea of God's sovereignty: and sets her sails for a harbour nothing short of heaven.
>
> ALEXANDER WHYTE

October 29

> God is love. Whoever lives in love lives in God, and God in him.
>
> 1 JOHN 4:16

> Lord, help me to keep my *love!* Whatever else I lose, may I never lose *that!* Though all the lights go out from my life, let not *this* torch be extinguished!
>
> GEORGE MATHESON

Pray About It: What George Matheson was referring to about the "lights going out" of his life was the loss of his sight. The great man of God and hymn writer suffered from blindness for a large portion of his later life. He was willing to lose his sight, but not the torch of his love.

How can we spend time with God, who is love, and not be great lovers ourselves? We can't. As Augustine says, if we love little, we'll pray little. If we love much, we'll pray much.

Let love guide your praying today.

> He that loveth little prayeth little; he that loveth much prayeth much.
>
> AUGUSTINE

October 30

> God is our refuge and strength,
>   an ever-present help in trouble.
>
> PSALM 46:1

> Never keep a trouble half an hour on your own mind before you tell it to God. As soon as the trouble comes, quick, the first thing, tell it to your Father.
>
> CHARLES HADDON SPURGEON

Pray About It: We are not often in the habit of going first to God when trouble comes. We usually allow a new arrival of a problem to fester a bit in our minds. We try to figure our way out of it—and then if nothing is apparent, we take it to God. But God would have us get in the habit of fleeing to Him in prayer at the very onset of a problem.

Watch today. If trouble arises, go first and quickly to Him.

We ought to act with God in the greatest simplicity, speaking to Him frankly and plainly, and imploring His assistance in our affairs, just as they happen.

BROTHER LAWRENCE

October 31

The elders who direct the affairs of the church well are worthy of double honor, especially those whose work is preaching and teaching.

1 TIMOTHY 5:17

If Christians who have been complaining about their ministers had said and acted less before men and had taken the trouble to cry to God for their ministers, if they had risen and stormed heaven with their humble, fervent, and incessant prayers for their pastors, they would have much more in the way of success.

JONATHAN EDWARDS

Pray About It: Are you critical of church leadership? Have you expressed your concern to God? To God *alone?* If you've been complaining openly to others, then you may actually be hindering God from moving in your pastor's life.

If you can't respect and honor your church leadership, then you should move to another church. Both you and that pastor will benefit from the change. Men who are called to shepherd God's flock need the support of their congregations. All pastors, without exception, have faults—because they're still human beings, prone to error. What they need are people who will daily undergird them in prayer and uphold them before others in the local body.

Today, make a point of praying for your pastor and other local church leaders. Honor them as they obey God's call on their life.

> Do you want a new minister? I can tell you how to get one. Pray for the one you have till God makes him over.
>
> R. A. Torrey

November 1

Fear thou not; for I am with thee: be not dismayed; for I am thy God: I will strengthen thee; yea, I will help thee; yea, I will uphold thee with the right hand of my righteousness.

ISAIAH 41:10 KJV

The Christian who is ready to risk all for God can count upon God to do all for him. It is as Christians live that they pray. It is the life that prays. It is the life that, with whole-hearted devotion, gives up all for God and to God, that can claim all from God. Our God longs exceedingly to prove Himself the Faithful God and Mighty Helper of His people. He only waits for hearts wholly turned from the world to Himself, and open to receive His gifts.

ANDREW MURRAY

Pray About It: When we're children, we slowly learn to do the things that we must as adults. We learn to walk, talk, eat properly, assume responsibility, and all the other duties of adulthood. In our Christian life, we should grow as pray-ers, and yet never lose our childlike spirit. The responsibilities adults have in prayer are different from those when we were children and prayed at our bedsides.

Now, when we understand the realities of the spiritual life, we have taken on duties and burdens that we must discharge.

"It is the life that prays," Murray says. And with wholehearted devotion, let's assume the mantle of responsibility for our prayer tasks.

To be little with God is to be little for God.

E. M. Bounds

November 2

See thou tell no man.

Matthew 8:4 KJV

When I was a young Christian, I had many seasons of communing with God which cannot be described in words. Not infrequently those seasons would end in an impression on my mind like this: *See that thou tell no man.* I did not understand at the time. Several times I paid no attention to this injunction, but tried to tell my Christian brethren what communications the Lord had made to me, or rather, what seasons of communion I had with Him.

But I soon found it would not do to tell my brethren what was passing between the Lord and my soul. They could not understand it. They would look surprised, and sometimes, I thought, incredulous. I soon learned to keep quiet in regard to those divine manifestations, and say but little about them.

Charles G. Finney

Pray About It: Time alone with God is very personal. It should never be paraded in front of others for any reason. Sometimes we share with others as God leads, but for the most part, our secret sessions with God are too personal to reveal to others. The injunction from God to us is, "Tell no man."

You cannot tell in public—even to them that fear God—all that God has done for your soul.

ALEXANDER WHYTE

November 5

Whatsoever ye shall ask in my name, that will I do, that the Father may be glorified in the Son.

JOHN 14:13 KJV

What is it to pray in Christ's name? There is nothing mystical or mysterious about this expression. If one will go through the Bible and examine all passages in which the expression "in My name" or "in His name" or synonymous expressions are used, he will find that it means just about what it does in modern usage. If I go to a bank and hand in a check with my name signed to it, I ask of that bank *in my own name*. If I have money deposited in that bank, the check will be cashed; if not, it will not be.

If, however, I go to the bank with somebody else's name signed to the check, I am asking *in his name*, and it does not matter whether I have money in that bank or any other if the person whose name is signed to the check has money there, the check will be cashed. . . . So it is when I go to the bank of heaven, when I go to God in prayer. I have nothing deposited there, I have absolutely no credit there, and if I go in my own name I will get absolutely nothing; but Jesus has unlimited credit in heaven, and He has granted to me the privilege of going to the bank with His name on my checks; and when I thus go, my prayers will be honored to any extent.

R. A. TORREY

Prayer takes the people to the Bank of Faith, and obtains the golden blessing. Mind how you pray! Pray! Make real business of it! Never let it be a dead formality! People pray a long time, but do not get what they are supposed to ask for, *because they do not plead the promise in a truthful business-like way.* If you were to go into a bank and stand an hour talking to the clerk, and then come out again without your cash, what would be the good of it?

CHARLES HADDON SPURGEON

Pray About It: Our access to God is founded upon the principle of covenant, which is simply another word for "testament." When we believed, we entered into God's covenant wherein we secure certain "legal" rights God established, one of which is prayer. We pray in Christ's name because that's part of the covenant. The words themselves aren't magic, but they represent our standing before God on the basis of (or in the name of) Christ.

Today, enter into the Bank of Faith and withdraw what is rightfully yours in the name of Christ. When we do, we are, in a very real sense, about our Father's business.

November 4

For thus saith the high and lofty One that inhabiteth eternity, whose name is Holy; I dwell in the
high and holy place, with him also that is of a contrite and humble spirit, to revive the spirit of the
humble, and to revive the heart of the contrite ones.

ISAIAH 57:15 KJV

Why has God appointed that we should pray? The
vast majority of people would reply, In order that
we may obtain from God the things which we need.
While this is one of the purposes of prayer, it is
by no means the chief one. Moreover, it considers
prayer only from the *human* side, and prayer sadly
needs to be viewed from the *Divine* side. Let us
look, then, at some of the reasons why God has
bidden us to pray.

First and foremost, prayer has been appointed
that the Lord God Himself should be honoured.
God requires us to recognize that He is, indeed,
"the high and lofty One that inhabiteth eternity."
God requires that we shall own His universal
dominion: in petitioning God for rain, Elijah did
but confess His control over the elements; in praying to God to deliver a poor sinner from the wrath
to come, we acknowledge that "salvation is of the
Lord" (Jonah 2:9); in supplicating His blessing on
the Gospel unto the uttermost parts of the earth, we
declare His rulership over the whole world.

Again, God requires that we shall *worship* Him
and prayer, real prayer, is an act of worship. Prayer
is an act of worship inasmuch as it is the prostrating

of the soul before Him; inasmuch as it is a calling upon His great and holy name; inasmuch as it is the owning of His goodness, His power, His immutability, His grace; and inasmuch as it is the recognition of His sovereignty, owned by a submission to His will. It is highly significant to notice in this connection that the Temple was not termed by Christ the House of Sacrifice, but instead, the House of Prayer.

Again; prayer redounds to God's glory, for in prayer we do but acknowledge our dependency upon Him. When we humbly supplicate the Divine Being we cast ourselves upon His power and mercy. In seeking blessings from God we own that He is the Author and Fountain of every good and perfect gift. That prayer brings glory to God is further seen from the fact that prayer calls faith into exercise, and nothing from us is so honouring and pleasing to Him as the confidence of our hearts.

A. W. Pink

Pray About It: From the human side, prayer strengthens us and makes us more Christlike. But let's consider prayer from the divine side in that it glorifies God. Prayer acknowledges God as Sovereign, as Lord. Prayer gives God an avenue to be honored as He meets our needs, supplies our daily bread, and in every other way, affirms our dependency upon Him. Regard your prayers today as vehicles for honoring God and acknowledging His lordship.

Glory to God for all things!

John Chrysostom

November 5

Give attention to your servant's prayer and his plea for mercy, O Lord my God. Hear the cry and the prayer that your servant is praying in your presence.

2 CHRONICLES 5:19

No one can believe how powerful prayer is, and what it is able to effect, but those who have learned it by experience. It is a great matter when in extreme need to take hold on prayer. I know whenever I have prayed earnestly that I have been amply heard, and have obtained more than I prayed for. God indeed sometimes delayed, but at last he came.

MARTIN LUTHER

Pray About It: That prayer works doesn't need to be proven to those who have made prayer a priority. Powerful prayer brings a Powerful God into action, prompting Powerful Answers. He hears amply and gives more than we ask. Though sometimes delayed according to our timetable, God's timing is unquestionable.

All great pray-ers, Martin Luther included, learn their craft by experience. There are no shortcuts.

God doesn't answer prayer. He answers *desperate* prayer!

LEONARD RAVENHILL

November 6

I provide water in the desert
  and streams in the wasteland,
to give drink to my people, my chosen,
  the people I formed for myself
  that they may proclaim my praise.

ISAIAH 43:20−21

Dear Lord, it seems that you are so madly in love with your creatures that you could not live without us. So you created us; and then, when we turned away from you, you redeemed us. Yet you are God, and so have no need of us.

Your greatness is made no greater by our creation; your power is made no stronger by our redemption. You have no duty to care for us, no debt to repay us. It is love, and love alone, which moves you.

CATHERINE OF SIENNA

Pray About It: God is love. In His love, He lives with us and in us. In His love, He listens to our prayers. He is committed to us as to nothing else in this entire universe.

The great violin-maker, Stradivari, marked every one of his carefully made instruments with the name of Jesus. For that reason, these treasured masterpieces of creation are still called Stradivarius del Gesu to this day.

In His creation of us, His human instruments, God has also marked each of us by the death of His Son for us. God so loves us—it is truly as if God could not live without us.

Think about this as you pray: A God who wants companionship with you.

Make God's day. Talk to Him.

Beloved, what manner of love is this wherewith God hath loved us; so as to give his *only Son*, in glory equal with the Father, in Majesty co-eternal?

What manner of love is this wherewith the only-begotten Son of God hath loved us so as to *empty himself*, as far as possible, of his eternal God-head; as to divest himself of that glory which he had with the Father before the world began; as to take upon him the form of a servant, being found in fashion as a man; and then, to humble himself still further, "being obedient unto death, even the death of the cross!"

JOHN WESLEY

November 7

The great dragon was hurled down—that ancient serpent called the devil, or Satan, who leads the whole world astray.

REVELATION 12:9

Let's say that two men quarrel over a certain point. We'll call them Christian and Apollyon. Apollyon notices that Christian has a certain weapon which would give him a sure victory. They meet in a deadly battle, and Apollyon resolves to take away the lethal weapon from his opponent, and destroy it.

For the moment the main cause of the quarrel has become subordinate. The great point now is: Who shall get possession of this powerful weapon on which everything depends?

So it is in the conflict between Satan and the believer. God's child can conquer everything by prayer. Is it any wonder that Satan does his utmost to snatch the weapon from the Christian, or to hinder him in the use of it?

Andrew Murray

Pray About It: Satan's tactics are many. But they all have one goal in common: deactivate the Christian's atomic weapon of prayer. Nullify it. Disarm the church of God.

In this scheme, Satan has been largely successful. Prayer has become a P.S. in our relationship to God, if it's present at all.

Make sure your divine weapon is fully operational. And use it—for God's purposes and to thwart Satan's. Let us disarm *him*.

Effectual, fervent prayer has been the mightiest weapon of God's mightiest soldiers.

E. M. Bounds

November 8

During the days of Jesus' life on earth, he offered up prayers and petitions with loud cries and tears to the one who could save him from death, and he was heard because of his reverent submission.

HEBREWS 5:7

It is delightful to hear a Christian wrestle with God, and say, "I will not let thee go except thou bless me," but that must be said softly, and not in a hectoring spirit, as though we could command and exact blessings from the Lord of all.

Remember, it is still a human being wrestling, even though permitted to wrestle with the eternal I AM.

We may have a certain familiarity with God, but it is a *holy* familiarity. There is boldness, but the boldness which springs from grace and is the work of the Spirit; not the boldness of the haughty rebel who struts in the presence of his offended king. It's the boldness of the child who fears because he loves, and loves because he fears.

Never fall into a prideful style of impertinent address to God, He is not to be assailed as an antagonist, but entreated as our Lord and God. Let us be humble and lowly in spirit, and so let us pray.

CHARLES HADDON SPURGEON

Pray About It: One of the paradoxes of the Christian life is that we are to be meek and also bold. We beseech God, but we also secure the answers to our prayers, without doubting. The Christian learns through practice how to differentiate between meekness, which has best been defined as "strength under control," and the ungodly brashness that is an insult to God.

Wrestle as a man or woman who would not be denied. But all the while, bear in mind that we are the clay. He is the potter.

> Sons of God cannot live without prayer. They are wrestling Jacobs. They are men in whom the Holy Ghost so works, that they can no more live without prayer than I can live without breathing. They must pray.
>
> CHARLES HADDON SPURGEON

November 9

I love you, O LORD, my strength.
The LORD is my rock, my fortress and my deliverer;
　my God is my rock, in whom I take refuge.
He is my shield and the horn of my salvation,
　my stronghold.

PSALM 18:1–2

A dear friend of mine who was an avid deer hunter, told me the following story: "Rising early one morning," he said, "I heard the baying of my deerhounds in pursuit of their quarry.

"Looking away to a broad, open field in front of me, I saw a young fawn making its way across the meadow, looking as if its strength was nearly spent. Reaching the rails of the field, it leaped over and crouched within ten feet from where I stood.

"A moment later, two of the hounds advanced, and the fawn ran in my direction and pushed its head between my legs. I lifted the little thing to my breast, and, swinging round and round, fought off the dogs. I felt, just then, that all the dogs in the world could not, and should not capture that fawn after its weakness had appealed to my strength."

So is it, when human helplessness appeals to Almighty God. Well do I remember when the hounds of sin were after my soul, until, at last, I ran into the arms of Almighty God.

A. C. DIXON

Pray About It: It seems amazing that a wild fawn would run to a man for protection from the pursuing hounds. But then, maybe it sensed the truth: *that it had no other place to go.*

We're very much like that fawn, chased by the enemy, by crushing circumstances, or by our own failures. From all of these baying hounds, God stands ready to fend off all of our pursuers. In our weakness, we must appeal to His strength.

> Jesus Christ looks out for the weak ones whom the world shoves to the wall. He puts His back to the wall and receives them into His arms.
>
> OSWALD CHAMBERS

November 10

Who then is the faithful and wise servant?

MATTHEW 24:45

The battle of prayer is against two things in the earth-lies: wandering thoughts, and lack of intimacy with God's character as revealed in His word. Neither can be cured at once, but they can be cured by discipline.

OSWALD CHAMBERS

Pray About It: The word *discipline* bothers us when applied to certain activities — like prayer. We want to think of ourselves as such sensitive pray-ers that we will pray often enough if we just wait until the Spirit moves us. The truth is, sometimes we need to move ourselves into our prayer closets — by the napes of our necks if necessary — and get down to business. If we don't like the word *discipline*, we can substitute the word *faithfulness.*

Are we going to be faithful servants? Will we determine to win the battle against both the wandering thoughts that plague us in prayer and also the lack of intimacy with God that prayerlessness begets?

Be disciplined in prayer today. Be faithful.

You are not the only one troubled by wandering thoughts. Our mind constantly wanders, but our will is the mistress of our faculties and must recall the mind and bring it back to God as often as necessary.

BROTHER LAWRENCE

November 11

Behold, I go forward, but he is not there; and backward, but I cannot perceive him: on the left hand, where he doth work, but I cannot behold him: he hideth himself on the right hand, that I cannot see him.

JOB 23:8–9 KJV

The Lord Jesus is looking about everywhere for that Christian who will remain faithful and loving even when He has withdrawn Himself. If the Lord finds such a faithful soul, when He does return, He rewards the faithfulness of His child. He pours out upon that faithful one abundant goodness and tender caresses of love.

Here, then, is something you must understand.

You *will* have times of spiritual dryness. It is part of the Lord's way.

MADAME GUYON

Pray About It: We have all experienced the lonely feeling that for some reason God has withdrawn from our lives. This season of dryness, as Madame Guyon calls it, can last for days, weeks, months, or even years. For Moses, the trip to the desert was forty years.

When God seems far away, remember to trust in His promise to never leave or forsake us. It's our feelings that have judged Him missing—and feelings can never override the Word of God.

Be patient and lean hard on God's Word. And don't feel like the dryness is a result of something you've done. It's not. His presence is there and you will again know that He's there. In due time.

> The God of Israel, the Saviour, is sometimes a God that hideth Himself, but never a God that absenteth Himself, sometimes in the dark, but never at a distance.
>
> MATTHEW HENRY

November 12

I am the LORD;
in its time I will do this swiftly.

ISAIAH 60:22

God's delays are not denials, nor are they neglectful or unkind. He is waiting with watchful eye and intent for the precise moment to strike, when He can give a blessing which will be without alloy, and which will flood our life with blessings so royal, so plenteous, so divine, that eternity will be too short to utter all our praise.

F. B. MEYER

Pray About It: God's answers to prayer are always *precisely on time*. He's never late, not even a second. The blessing to come to you will be "so royal, so plenteous, so divine that eternity will be too short" to praise Him.

Repeat, or sing if you can, the familiar lines:

When we've been there ten thousand years,
   Bright shining as the sun,
We've no less days to sing God's praise,
   Than when we'd first begun.

JOHN NEWTON

November 13

Make the most of every opportunity.

COLOSSIANS 4:5

While Helen Hunt Jackson [author of the nine-teenth-century classic novel *Ramona*] lay upon her sickbed, she wrote a poem of penitent regret and petition for opportunity to retrieve the past with purposeful service.

It came too late, for in four days after she had written these lines, she was dead. The shuttle of time runs swiftly back and forth for us, let us busy ourselves weaving a life-fabric whose warp and woof are Love and Service for Him "who loved us and gave Himself for us."

There is no time to waste in prayerless idleness or aimlessness.

NORMAN B. HARRISON

Pray About It: We all want to live a life with as few regrets as possible. When we come to our last day, we want to know that we've finished our race well. Read Miss Jackson's poem and offer yourself to God today and ask Him to keep reminding you of "the brevity of our opportunity."

The Brevity of Our Opportunity

Father, I scarcely dare to pray,
So clear I see, now it is done,
That I have wasted half my day,
And left my work but just begun.
So clear I see that things I thought
Were right or harmless were a sin;
So clear I see that I have sought,
Unconscious, selfish aims to win.
So clear I see that I have hurt
The souls I might have help'd to save,
That I have slothful been, inert,
Deaf to the class Thy leaders gave.
In outskirts of Thy Kingdom vast,
Father, the humblest spot give me;
Set me the lowliest task Thou hast,
Let me repentant, work for Thee.

HELEN HUNT JACKSON

November 14

One generation will commend your works to another;
    they will tell of your mighty acts.
They will speak of the glorious splendor of your
      majesty,
    and I will meditate on your wonderful works.
They will tell of the power of your awesome works,
    and I will proclaim your great deeds.
They will celebrate your abundant goodness
    and joyfully sing of your righteousness.

PSALM 145:4–7

All our life is like a day of celebration for us; we are convinced, in fact, that God is always everywhere. We work while singing, we sail while reciting hymns, we accomplish all other occupations of life while praying.

CLEMENT OF ALEXANDRIA

Pray About It: Clement can speak to us with some authority. As a second-century Christian, and one of the church fathers, he no doubt knew how the earliest Christians lived.

Today, imitate those early Christians by making a day of celebration. Work and sing, sail (with or without a boat!), and recite hymns. Pray and do all else besides.

Enjoy your faith today.

I am ever playing in God's presence as well as praying in it.

OSWALD CHAMBERS

November 15

Pray that I may be rescued from the unbelievers in Judea and that my service in Jerusalem may be acceptable to the saints there, so that by God's will I may come to you with joy and together with you be refreshed.

ROMANS 15:31–32

For our prayer to be truly effective, we must spread out our prayer like a net. What does this mean? It means we must pray so that nothing is left out which should be prayed for. We will not allow anything to slip away. Without such a "prayer net" we will not be able to obtain good results.

A person who knows how to pray knows how to pour out his heart desire completely before God. He will use all kinds of prayers to surround as with a net the thing he prays for so that the adversary can do absolutely nothing.

Nowadays our prayers are too loose, they are not tight enough. Though we may use many words, our prayers are not well-rounded, thus providing the enemy loopholes through which to make his attack. But if our prayers are like spreading nets, the enemy will have no opening by which to get in. And thus shall our petitions before God be realized.

WATCHMAN NEE

Pray About It: How loose or tight is your net of prayers? This analogy tells us how to envision our prayers. If we're vague, the net is loose and the answer may slip away. If the net is tight, the adversary can do no harm.

Pray a net around your situation today. And keep the net tight.

Nothing is too great and nothing is too small to be subject of prayer. Prayer reaches down to the least things of life and includes the greatest things which concern us.

E. M. BOUNDS

November 16

We love because he first loved us.

1 JOHN 4:19

Prayer is an earnest and familiar talking with God.

JOHN KNOX

Pray About It: Bottom line: prayer is talking to God. But to expand on that bottom line, consider that prayer is talking and listening to the One Person in the universe who loves you beyond your wildest imagination. He loves not just by virtue of His having created you, He genuinely loves you for who you are. He accepts you, He understands what others misunderstand, and He *supports* you. He is firmly committed to you and your future. His ways of hearing and fulfilling your prayers are centered around what's best for you.

Today, let your talk with God reflect your appreciation for Him. He has blessed you, as you know only too well.

God is the only person I can talk to.

ROBERT MURRAY MCCHEYNE

November 17

When Solomon finished praying, fire came down from heaven and consumed the burnt offering and the sacrifices, and the glory of the LORD filled the temple. The priests could not enter the temple of the LORD because the glory of the LORD filled it. When all the Israelites saw the fire coming down and the glory of the LORD above the temple, they knelt on the pavement with their faces to the ground, and they worshiped and gave thanks to the LORD, saying,

"He is good; his love endures forever."

Then the king and all the people offered sacrifices before the LORD.

2 CHRONICLES 7:1–4

After the prayer, the fire!

When Solomon finished praying the fire came down from heaven. That fire is the symbol of the Holy God. When Solomon had prayed, the holy Flame was in their midst.

But not only is the flame the symbol of the Holy; it also typifies the power which can make us holy. Nothing can cleanse as effectively as fire can. Where water fails, fire succeeds. After an epidemic water is comparatively impotent, so we commit disease infected garments to the flames. It was the great fire of London which delivered London from the tyranny of the bubonic plague.

And so it is with my soul. God, who is holy flame, will burn out the germs of my sin. Our God is a consuming fire.

Come to my soul, O Holy Flame! Burn away my wickedness, consume it utterly!

JOHN HENRY JOWETT

Pray About It: After Solomon prayed, the fire came. The fire that cleanses more than any disinfectant. The fire that consumes everything in its way that can be destroyed. The fire that purifies silver.

Our prayer closets should be like kilns, where we, the clay, allow the heat of God's presence to make us clean, purified pots, ready for His use.

Allow that heat to work today as you pray. Watch for the flame in your midst. Let all sin go.

> Thou Christ of burning cleansing flame,
>   send the fire.
> Thy blood bought gift today we claim,
>   send the fire.
> Look down and see this waiting host,
>   give us the promised Holy Ghost.
> We want another Pentecost,
> To make our weak hearts strong and brave,
>   send the fire.
> To live a dying world to save, send the fire.
> Oh, see us on Thine altar lay our lives, our all,
>   this very day
> To crown the offering, now we pray, send the fire.

WILLIAM BOOTH

November 18

His mother said to the servants, "Do whatever he tells you."

JOHN 2:5

Jesus, His mother, and His disciples were bidden to the wedding. In all likelihood the family was closely related to, or very friendly toward, the family of Jesus. At least, we notice that the host and hostess had acquainted the mother of Jesus with the embarrassing situation which had arisen when the wine had given out. Whereupon the mother of Jesus reveals herself as a tried and true woman of prayer.

In the first place, she goes to the right place with need which she has become acquainted. She goes to Jesus and tells Him everything.

In the next place, notice what she says to Jesus. Just these few simple words, "They have no wine." Note here what prayer is. To pray is to tell Jesus what we lack. Intercession is to tell Jesus what we see that others lack.

She also knew that she did not have to influence Him or persuade Him to give these friends a helping hand. No one is so willing to help as He is!

OLE HALLESBY

Pray About It: Prayer is amazingly simple when we remember Mary's words to Jesus, "They have no wine." That was all that was necessary—just verbalizing the need. Jesus took care of the rest.

Today, as you pray, just tell Him the need. You don't have to tell Him how to change your situation. He knows.

Take Mary as an example in prayer. Be simple.

It is in the personal presence of the Saviour, in intercourse with Him, that faith rises to grasp what at first appeared too high.

ANDREW MURRAY

November 19

The LORD does not look at the things man looks at. Man looks at the outward appearance, but the LORD looks at the heart.

1 SAMUEL 16:7

Perhaps these lines may be read by some believers who by reason of age and sickness are no longer able to work actively in the Lord's vineyard. Possibly in days gone by, you were a teacher, you were a preacher, a Sunday-school teacher, a tract-distributor: but now you are bed-ridden.

Yes, but you are still here on earth! Who knows but what God is leaving you here a few more days to engage in the ministry of prayer—and perhaps accomplish more by this than by all your past active service. If you are tempted to disparage others such a ministry, remember your Saviour. He prayed, prayed for others, prayed for sinners, even in His last hours.

ARTHUR PINK

Pray About It: No one is left on earth without a work they can do. For the invalid, that work is intercessory prayer, which is, interestingly, the highest work of all. Don't let seeming catastrophes, illness, or weakness rob you of your usefulness. God needs pray-ers. For this reason He has put you in a place on the front lines of His work.

Use your sickness to glorify God. Be a stalwart prayer warrior. Dwight Moody insisted that his success was due to the prayers of an obscure invalid woman who interceded for him.

If you're healthy, remember the sick today. Pray for them, call them, and give God thanks for your own good health.

Lord, let me not live to be useless.

JOHN WESLEY

Tend thy sick ones, O Lord Jesus Christ; rest thy weary ones; bless thy dying ones; soothe thy suffering ones; shield thy joyous ones; and all for thy Love's sake.

AUGUSTINE

November 20

Whom having not seen, ye love; in whom, though now ye see him not, yet believing, ye rejoice with joy unspeakable and full of glory.

1 PETER 1:8 KJV

Some people seem born with a sullen and feverish temper, and it is very difficult for them to brighten into smiles and songs. But whatever our natural disposition may be, if we belong to Christ it is our bounden duty to cultivate a thankful heart. A melancholy person has a bad effect upon others. It is miserable to have to work with or under a confirmed pessimist. Nothing is right, nothing pleases, there is no word of praise or encouragement.

Once at Aden I saw a gang of Lascars transshipping the mails. They were carrying the bags cheerily because their leader kept them singing as they did their work. If, instead of finding fault with people we would watch for things for which we could commend and thank them, we should probably find a miraculous change in their attitude.

F. B. MEYER

Pray About It: In God's presence, our mourning is turned to joy. We may enter our prayer closets in a melancholy mood, but we shouldn't leave without a full measure of joy. And our assignment for the rest of the day is to allow that joy to rub off on others.

Today, pray for His joy unspeakable. And then find ways to infect others with an encouraging word.

If I am asked how we are to get rid of discouragements, I can only say, as I have had to say of so many other wrong spiritual habits, we must give them up. It is never worthwhile to argue against discouragement. There is only one argument that can meet it, and that is the argument of God. When David was in the midst of what were perhaps the most discouraging moments of his life, when he had found his city burned, and his wives stolen, and he and the men with him had wept until they had no more power to weep; and when his men, exasperated at their misfortunes, spake of stoning him, then we are told, "But David encouraged himself in the Lord his God"; and the result was a magnificent victory, in which all that they had lost was more than restored to them. This always will be, and always must be the result of a courageous faith, because faith lays hold of the omnipotence of God.

HANNAH WHITALL SMITH

November 21

He breathed on them, and saith unto them, "Receive ye the Holy Ghost."

JOHN 20:22 KJV

The Church is "the body of Christ," an organism, possessed of His life. Our risen Lord, now a "life-giving Spirit," "breathed on them and saith unto them, 'Receive ye the Holy Ghost.'"

This is the basic fact of all Christian living. The Church's life, corporate as well as individual, in its beginning and in its continuing, is the very breath of the risen, glorified Son of God.

One of the ceaseless activities of the body is its breathing. It is essential to self-preservation. We do it involuntarily. Such is the function of prayer; hence its primal importance. It is the Church's part, practically, in the sustaining of her life.

But it is a law of the body that the more actively and vigorously it exercises the more deeply and freely it must breathe. Under exertion the body demands a quickened breathing, an ampler supply of air, to meet its necessities.

NORMAN B. HARRISON

Pray About It: How long could you hold your breath and still live? Not long. The life of the body depends on breathing air. So too the life of the church is dependent on the breath of prayer. Many churches are stagnant because they're holding their breath. How is your church? Is it a praying church? If so, it will also be a healthy, growing church. If not, can you suggest to the pastor, or start yourself, a small group that gathers regularly for prayer?

Give your church some fresh air and it will live.

Prayer is to the spiritual life what the beating of the pulse and the drawing of breath are to the life of the body.

JOHN HENRY NEWMAN

November 22

[Abraham] is our father in the sight of God, in whom he believed—the God who gives life to the dead and calls things that are not as though they were.

ROMANS 4:17

When we believe for a blessing, we must take the attitude of faith, and begin to act and pray as if we had our blessing. We must treat God as if He had given us our request. We must lean our weight over upon Him for the thing that we have claimed, and just take it for granted that He gives it, and is going to continue to give it. That is the attitude of trust.

A. B. SIMPSON

Pray About It: Is there something for which you're praying that God would have you simply begin to accept by faith? Can you begin to live as if you have that for which you're praying? Do so, but don't broadcast it to others. Simply live the answer to your prayers. Put your weight on Him as you do. This is trust.

Praying with a believing heart is more important than anything else that has to do with prayer.

MADAME GUYON

November 23

Continue in prayer.

COLOSSIANS 4:2 KJV

The great fault of the children of God is they do not continue in prayer; they do not go on praying; they do not persevere. If they desire anything for God's glory, they should pray until they get it.

Oh, how good, and kind, and gracious, and condescending is the One with Whom we have to do! He has given me, unworthy as I am, immeasurably above all I had asked or thought!

GEORGE MUELLER

Pray About It: The operative word today is "continue." Some of our requests turn into much more intensive prayer projects than we first imagined. It seemed so easy for God to simply grant our request and life would go on. But no, God has more in mind for this situation. When God wants to answer in a big way, He sometimes makes us stay on our knees longer. It makes the joy of answered prayer all the sweeter.

Prayer is to be incessant, without intermission, with no check in desire, in spirit or in act, the spirit and the life always in the attitude of prayer. The knees may not always be bended, the lips may not always be vocal with words of prayer, but the spirit is always in the act and intercourse of prayer.

E. M. BOUNDS

November 24

Jesus looked at them and said, "With man this is impossible, but with God all things are possible."

MATTHEW 19:26

I have found that there are three stages in every great work of God: first, it is impossible, then it is difficult, then it is done.

J. HUDSON TAYLOR

Pray About It: Every Christian should read *Hudson Taylor's Spiritual Secret*. The story of his hard missionary life and the answers to prayer will encourage the reader. One way he put the above statement to the test was in his motto: "To move man, through God, by prayer alone." To trust God to move in the heart of another, without his speaking a word to them, was his practice. It seemed impossible at times. But God didn't fail.

What stage is your situation today? Impossible? Difficult? Or done? Stay with it until it is the latter.

Remember this: All the resources of the Godhead are at our disposal.

JONATHAN GOFORTH

November 25

I consider everything a loss compared to the surpassing greatness of knowing Christ Jesus my Lord, for whose sake I have lost all things.

PHILIPPIANS 3:8

For true power in prayer, hold nothing back. Be surrendered to Christ. Go all out for Him. Forsake all to follow the Savior. The type of devotion that crowns Christ Lord of all is the kind that He loves to honor.

WILLIAM MACDONALD

Pray About It: When we hold back from God, we short-circuit our prayers. Sometimes we live our Christian life only partially surrendered to Him. We will give Him just so much—ten percent of our money, an hour or two on Sunday, a prayer every day, and a nod to Him every so often as if we'd just encountered an acquaintance on the street. Such surrender isn't surrender at all. Give up all to Him. Become totally dependent on God. By giving, you get. By keeping, you lose.

One of the greatest miracles the Lord can perform in our behalf is to cripple all our human efforts and make us totally dependent on Him.

DAVID WILKERSON

November 26

Tell it to your children,
and let your children tell it to their children,
and their children to the next generation.

JOEL 1:3

Give me a hundred men who love God with all
their hearts, and fear nothing but sin, and I will
move the world.

JOHN WESLEY

Pray About It: How is it with your family? John
Wesley was one of twenty children born to Susanna
Wesley. Even with such a large family and no modern
conveniences, she still set aside time every day to pray
for her children.

God honored her faithfulness by raising up John
and his brother Charles who both helped change the
world for Christ. As Susanna prayed for her children,
she had no way of knowing what God would do. She
simply kept at it, day after day, year after year.

Do you have children, grandchildren, nephews,
nieces, or other children in your family for whom
you can consistently pray? Be sure of one thing: If
we don't have Christian prayer warriors raising up the
next generation of believers through their prayers, history will once again be changed—but this time, not
for Christ, but for the advancement of evil.

Today, pray for the next generation. Pray specifically for those children whom you know and can regularly follow—thus knowing how to pray for them.

O God, I thank Thee because, when I have been for some time interrupted in my work and my thoughts of Thee have been diverted, I have found how pleasing it is to my mind to feel the motions of Thy Spirit quickening me and exciting me to return.

SUSANNA WESLEY

November 27

But as for me and my household, we will serve the LORD.

JOSHUA 24:15

A house without family worship has neither foundation nor covering.

J. M. MASON

Pray About It: Solitary prayer is important. Corporate church prayer is necessary, and having a prayer partner is desirable. However, for many Christians the most crucial time of prayer may be that of family worship. At regular times, the entire family should gather together for a brief reading of Scripture, discussion of family matters, and prayer for each other. Christianity in a family is both caught and taught. Your children must see that prayer is important to you as their parent and also the foundation for the family.

If you have no children, meet regularly for prayer with your spouse. If you're single, you can pray *for* families with a prayer partner. As the family goes, so goes the church of God.

Let family worship be short, savory, simple, plain, tender, heavenly.

RICHARD CECIL

November 28

In thy presence is fulness of joy; at thy right hand there are pleasures for evermore.

PSALM 16:11 KJV

Why is it that prayer in the name of Christ brings such fullness of joy? In part, because we get what we ask. But that is not the only reason, nor the greatest. It makes God real. When we ask something definite of God, and He gives it, how real God becomes! He is right there! It is blessed to have a God who is real, and not merely an idea.

I remember how once I was taken suddenly and seriously sick all alone in my study. I dropped upon my knees and cried to God for help. Instantly all pain left me—I was perfectly well. It seemed as if God stood right there, and had put out His hand and touched me. The joy of healing was not so great as the joy of meeting God.

There is no greater joy on earth or in heaven, than communion with God, and prayer in the name of Jesus brings us into communion with Him. The Psalmist was surely not speaking only of future blessedness, but also of present blessedness when he said, "in Thy presence is fullness of joy." O the unutterable joy of those moments when in our prayers we really press into the presence of God!

Does someone say, "I have never known any such joy as that in prayer"?

Do you take enough leisure for prayer to actually get into God's presence? Do you really give yourself up to prayer in the time which you do take?

R. A. TORREY

Pray About It: Every second we spend in prayer should be a rewarded second. First, there is the reward of God Himself. Second, the joy that His company brings. Third is the answer to our prayers. For Torrey, he experienced a dramatic physical healing. But note, he records that the joy of being healed wasn't as great as the joy of meeting with God. Never look to the joy of miracles. Look to the One who makes miracles.

When once touched with this divine magnet of prayer, for ever after the soul feels a divine attraction, and continually turns to its center: God. And if diverted therefrom by temptation, yet when that obstruction is removed, like as a needle touched by a lodestone when your finger is taken away, turns to its rest, its center, its God, its All, again.

GEORGE WHITEFIELD

November 29

Then Jesus told his disciples a parable to show them
that they should always pray and not give up.

LUKE 18:1

"Staying power" in prayer is a rare quality. Our
Lord realized this, and so gave at least two parables
to encourage us to persevere, [that of the man who
troubles his neighbor at midnight for bread because
of an unexpected visitor (Luke 11:5–8) and the
widow who besought the judge to avenge her of her
enemies (Luke 18:1–8)].

There is no realm of the Christian life in which
we weary so quickly as in prayer.

ARTHUR WALLIS

Pray About It: Why is it that we tire more quickly
of prayer than almost anything else? We can read the
Bible, talk about Christ, sit through a church service,
listen to Christian radio, watch Christian TV end-
lessly. But prayer . . . well, that's a different story. We
pray quickly and then we leave. But staying power is
what gets the job done.

If we would stay we would find refreshment. Our
problem is that we give up before the refreshments
arrive.

Stay awhile with God today.

Some people become tired at the end of ten minutes
or half an hour of prayer. What will they do when
they have to spend Eternity in the presence of God?

We must begin the habit here and become used to being with God.

SADHU SUNDAR SINGH

November 30

Do not worry about tomorrow, for tomorrow will worry about itself. Each day has enough trouble of its own.

MATTHEW 6:34

Let us think only of the present and not permit our minds to wander with idle curiosity into the future. The future is not yet ours — perhaps it never will be. We expose ourselves to temptation in trying to anticipate God, and to prepare ourselves for things which He may not destine for us. If such things should come to pass, He will give us light and strength according to the need.

Why should we desire to meet difficulties prematurely, when we have neither the strength nor light as yet provided for them?

Let us give heed to the present whose duties are pressing. It is faithfulness to the present which prepares us for faithfulness in the future.

FRANÇOIS FÉNELON

Pray About It: Often our prayers have too much to do with our future. Jesus taught us to pray that God would "give us this day our daily bread." The manna was always gathered just for the day ahead, not for tomorrow.

The future shouldn't be ignored, of course, but the best way to prepare for the uncertainty ahead is to live properly in the present.

Often Satan tempts us with doubts about our future: what will happen to our health? What if there's a recession and our income decreases? What if, what if, what if? These two words are the preface that Satan uses to instill fear in the believer.

Pray for your needs today and walk confidently into tomorrow.

> What [God] forbids is, that care which, sad experience shows, wastes the blood and drinks up the spirits; which anticipates all the misery it fears, and comes to torment us before the time. He forbids only that care which poisons the blessings of today, by fear of what may be tomorrow; which cannot enjoy the present plenty, through apprehensions of future want. This care is not only a sore disease, a grievous sickness of soul, but also an heinous offense against God, a sin of the deepest dye. It is a high affront to the gracious Governor and wise Disposer of all things; necessarily implying, that the great Judge does not do right; that he does not order all things well. It plainly implies, that he is wanting, either in wisdom, if he does not know what things we stand in need of; or in goodness, if he does not provide those things for all who put their trust in him. Beware, therefore, that you take not thought in this sense: Be ye anxiously careful for nothing.
>
> JOHN WESLEY

December 1

Taste and see that the LORD is good;
blessed is the man who takes refuge in him.

PSALM 34:8

Take time. Give God time to reveal Himself
to you. Give yourself time to be silent and quiet
before Him, waiting to receive through the Spirit
the assurance of His presence with you, His power
working in you.

Take time to read His Words as in His presence; that from it you may know what He asks
of you and what He promises you. Let the Word
create around you, create within you, a holy heavenly light in which your soul will be refreshed and
strengthened for the work of daily life.

ANDREW MURRAY

Pray About It: In many areas of our life, time seems
to be the enemy. We have so many possibilities for
use of our time — possibilities that our ancestors
never dreamed of. But in our pursuit of God, time
can be our friend. God will not be the kind of friend
with whom you can hold a casual acquaintance, and
perhaps exchange greetings only at Christmas. God
wants the kind of relationship that only time can buy.

Time with God may not be a recent invention,
but it's as modern and up-to-date as the newest com-
puter technology. But we must *take* the time to be
with Him. Savor the minutes in prayer as you would
the taste of a good meal. Taste and see that the Lord
is good.

When we rob God of time for quiet, we are robbing Him of ourselves. It is only in the quiet that we can really know Him and know ourselves, and be sure that we give ourselves back to Him. Oh, for God's sake, do not risk keeping the windows of heaven closed by robbing God of time.

GORDON GUINESS

December 2

There remains, then, a Sabbath-rest for the people of God; for anyone who enters God's rest also rests from his own work, just as God did from his.

HEBREWS 4:9–10

Praying for others can only flow from a heart at rest about itself, and knowing in itself the value of the desires which it expresses for another. I could not be truly happy praying otherwise.

J. BUTLER STONEY

Pray About It: Is your heart restless? So often our prayers can become the chattering of an insecure religious pretender. True prayer comes from a heart at rest, sure of itself and even more sure of the object of its prayer.

Happiness in prayer comes from certainty. A restless heart is an uncertain heart. Today, anchor your prayers in God. Quiet your heart and be still before your Father.

O God, make us children of quietness and heirs of peace.

CLEMENT OF ALEXANDRIA

December 3

For this reason, since the day we heard about you, we have not stopped praying for you and asking God to fill you with the knowledge of his will through all spiritual wisdom and understanding. And we pray this in order that you may live a life worthy of the Lord and may please him in every way: bearing fruit in every good work, growing in the knowledge of God, being strengthened with all power according to his glorious might so that you may have great endurance and patience, and joyfully giving thanks to the Father, who has qualified you to share in the inheritance of the saints in the kingdom of light.

COLOSSIANS 1:9–12

Fletcher of Madeley, a great teacher of a century and a half ago, used to lecture to the young theological students. He was one of the fellow-workers with Wesley and a man of most saintly character. When he had lectured on one of the great topics of the Word of God, such as the Fullness of God's Holy Spirit or on the power and blessing that He meant His people to have, he would close the lecture and say, "That is the theory; now will those who want the practice come along up to my room?" And again and again they closed their books and went away to his room, where the hour's theory would be followed by one or two hours of prayer.

HUBERT BROOKE

Pray About It: The men and the women who have spoken to you in the readings from this book would be disappointed if they learned that their words became only theory to their readers. To grasp their true message requires practicing what these godly Christians have preached.

In the future, you'll read other books on prayer or hear sermons teaching you how to pray. Whenever you hear or read about prayer, don't tuck the thought away as a nice inspiration. Always, always, put into practice what you've learned. Or you will lose it.

Prayer is the acid test of devotion.

SAMUEL CHADWICK

December 4

So [the unbeliever] will fall down and worship God, exclaiming, "God is really among you!"

1 CORINTHIANS 14:25

Every new Pentecost has had its preparatory period of prayer. . . . God has compelled His saints to seek Him at the throne of grace, so that every new advance might be so plainly due to His power that even the unbeliever would have to confess, "God is really among you!"

ARTHUR T. PIERSON

Pray About It: Watch and see. Will God move in a mighty way again before Christ returns? The only way to tell is to note whether the church is praying. Only through the prayers of the Christians does each new Pentecost come. Only when we see unbelievers remark about the move of God will we know that it has come.

> Revival is the heathen saying, "The Lord hath done great things for them."
>
> JAMES A. STEWART

December 5

> These were all commended for their faith, yet none of them received what had been promised.
>
> HEBREWS 11:39

[Throughout *Magnificent Prayer,* one of the names you've seen frequently is that of Oswald Chambers. Of all the prominent Christians I've read about, Chambers alone has the unique situation of being used by God far more after his death than when he was alive. He died suddenly at the age of forty-three in Egypt where he was ministering to British troops. Later, his best writings were edited into books, the most notable of which has been the classic daily devotional, *My Utmost for His Highest.* The following entries from Chambers's journal give us a peek at the man who would die before he saw what God would do with him.]

Portrush, Dec. 5, 1908. The great power and groan of the mighty sea seems to awaken that longing loneliness of the prophet about me for God. I am hungry with a vast desire for Him. As I go about for Him other lives seem to me to get clearer and clearer, but I find I dare not look to anyone to understand mine.

This is not pride, but the *call* is on me, intolerably strong at times. I am full of joy always, but a tremendous sorrow seems to be interwoven with it all. I seem to hear Him, but still I am sense and ark to His meaning. I wish He would take me into His counsel or let me live on the lower level. I am just sensitive enough to His Spirit to know that we are on the eve of new things, not the revival that every one seems to be talking about, that does not appeal to me. Nor is it the Second Coming, I know He is coming again, and coming again soon. But there is something He wants me to see and know, and I seem stupid. I can feel intuitively the Spirit of God striving with me.

Jan. 8, 1909. It came so clearly to me that in all ventures for God I had to go in faith, and now I do the same. It will be a great and joyful thing to see how God will open up the way. I never see my way, I know God Who guides so I fear nothing. I have never far-seeing plans, only confident trust.

OSWALD CHAMBERS

Pray About It: There is much to be said for planning ahead under God's direction. But sometimes God directs otherwise. A young Oswald Chambers had a call on his life. Yet it was an indistinct call that drove him to repeatedly ask God to let him know what that call was to mean.

And then in the January entry in his journal, Oswald says that in all ventures for God, he had to go in faith. He anticipated only that God would open up a way in response to his prayers.

Perhaps the reason that God didn't share His plan with Oswald or give him far-seeing plans was that Oswald would die soon. And yet, incredibly, God's plan for the young missionary was *extremely* far-reaching. Nearly a century later, Christians around the world are daily reading the best-selling devotional book of all time, compiled after his death by his wife, Biddy. That book is *My Utmost for His Highest* and it was the posthumous answer to Oswald's prayer. God has used Oswald Chambers far, far more after his death in ways he could never have imagined.

It was good that Oswald Chambers came to a place of trust that God would answer his prayers and use him. It is good when we do the same.

> One life may be of incalculable use to God: and *yours* may be that life.
>
> Oswald Chambers

December 6

> Ask and it will be given to you; seek and you will find; knock and the door will be opened to you. For everyone who asks receives; he who seeks finds; and to him who knocks, the door will be opened.
>
> Luke 11:9–10

Prevailing prayer is often offered in the present day, when Christians have been wrought up to such a pitch of importunity and such a holy boldness that afterwards when they looked back upon it, they were frightened and amazed at themselves, to think they should have dared to exercise such importunity with God. And yet these prayers have prevailed, and obtained the blessing. And many of these persons, with whom I am acquainted, are among the holiest persons I know in the world.

CHARLES G. FINNEY

Pray About It: The boldness that God honors comes from having been with God—having prayed often and prevailed. When we know our God as the One who answered prayers, God Himself reaches down and fills us with the boldness that comes only from His Holy Spirit. We pray with confidence and see results. Then we look back and wonder at our courage in coming to God with such insistence.

Expect that God will give you boldness as you pray. That's the fruit of prevailing prayer.

He who prays without boldness cannot hope that his prayer will be granted.

FRANÇOIS FÉNELON

December 7

Then Jesus answering . . .

LUKE 7:22 KJV

John was perplexed and sent from his prison to ask Jesus if he were indeed the promised Messiah. Jesus patiently answered the messengers. He always answers. Many of our prayers to Him are mixed with doubt; many of them are filled with complaints and fears and murmurings. Still He never grows impatient with us. He never shuts His door upon us. It must grieve and pain Him to have us doubt Him.

After all the sacrifices Jesus has made on our behalf and the blessings His love has bestowed upon us, when some shadow falls upon our heart we wonder whether Christ loves us or not, whether or not He has forgiven us, whether or not He will take care of us in the future. We are half the time perplexed about something—full of worries; and these doubts, fears, and anxieties get into our prayers. They take the joy out of our worship and the faith out of our supplications, and they give a sad tone to our devotions.

Does Jesus never get tired of such prayers? No, He listens, and hears all the disturbances made by the murmurings. His heart must be pained by them too; but He answers us nevertheless. He is very patient with us—He never condemns; He remembers how frail we are, and He sends the sweetest answers that His love can give. It is wonderful indeed how rich and gentle our Savior is.

J. R. MILLER

Pray About It: The compassionate Jesus Christ is always available for our prayers. Let's not misjudge Him by assuming He's reluctant to be with us. Nor should we insult Him by any doubting as evidenced by worry or sadness. Who could possibly remain downcast in the presence of Him who is our joy?

Bring all your prayers before Him today, even the murmurings and complaints. He will hear them, though He grieves at our small faith.

> Whever your hope seems to fail you and your joy begins to sink, the shortest method is to take to your knees.
>
> Charles Haddon Spurgeon

December 8

Kenaniah the head Levite was in charge of the singing; that was his responsibility because he was skillful at it.

1 Chronicles 15:22

I would sit alone, as I have done on many a day and night, praying God to give me the thoughts and the feelings wherewith to compose my hymn. . . . It may seem a little old-fashioned, always to begin one's work with prayer: but I never undertake a hymn without first asking the good Lord to be my inspiration in the work that I am about to do. . . .

Often I take in my mind some tune already known . . . this, however, does not imply that the tune will ultimately be chosen as the companion of the works: for it has probably already its own true and lawful mate, with which it is to be happy and useful. Sometimes a tune is furnished me for which to write the words. "Blessed Assurance" was made in this manner. . . .

After a particular hymn is done, I let it lie for a few days in the writing-desk of my mind, so to speak, until I have leisure to prune it, to read it through with the eyes of my memory, and in other ways mould it into as presentable shape as possible. I often cut, trim, and change it. . . .

I have no trouble in sorting and arranging my literary and lyric wares within the apartments of my mind. If I were given a little while in which to do it, I could take down from its shelves, hundreds if not thousands of hymns, that I have written during the sixty years in which I have been praising my Redeemer through this medium of song.

FANNY CROSBY

Pray About It: Fanny Crosby was one of the great hymn writers of the church. When only six weeks old she was blinded through her doctor's error. Never bitter with her lot, Fanny committed her life and her creativity to Christ. Through prayer, God spoke to her the words that are still being sung a century after her death. Today, as you read the following words of Fanny Crosby, listen to God's faithfulness to her personally between the lines.

He hears our prayers just as He heard hers. Turn your abilities over to God and He will create through you. He doeth all things well.

All the way my Savior leads me;
    What have I to ask beside?
    Can I doubt His faithful mercies
    Who through life has been my guide?
    Heavenly peace, divinest comfort,
    Ere by faith in Him to dwell;
    For I know whatever fall me,
    Jesus doeth all things well.

December 9

If a man shuts his ears to the cry of the poor,
    he too will cry out and not be answered.

PROVERBS 21:13

Whoever stoppeth his ears at the cry of the poor
cannot pray so that God will hear.

If we will not listen to the poor when they cry
unto us in their need, God will not listen unto us
when we cry unto Him in our need. The world's
maxim is, "The Lord helps those who help themselves." The truth is, The Lord helps those who
help others.

R. A. TORREY

Pray About It: There are very few reasons given in
Scripture why God will not hear prayers. Not listening to and responding to the cries of the poor is one
of those reasons.

Along with habitual praying, learn to be a habitual
giver to the poor. God hears our cries better when we
hear the cry of the poor with open ear.

Today, consider the poor as the holiday season approaches. Look for ways to put feet to your prayers.

A holy man will strive to be like our Lord Jesus Christ. He will not only live the life of faith in Him, and draw from Him all his daily peace and strength, but he will also labor to have the mind that was in Him . . . who thought more of godly poor men than of kings.

J. C. RYLE

December 10

And He took [the children] up in His arms, laid His hands on them, and blessed them.

MARK 10:16

Children's prayers are heard. Let us enlist them for our work. The great man of God Philip Melanchthon did not despise them. Cast down and disheartened once, we read, that taking an evening walk he heard the voices of children at prayer, and he at once brightened up, and exclaimed to some friends, "Brethren, take courage; the children are praying for us."

H. C. TRUMBULL

Pray About It: Teach the children with whom you're in contact to pray. It will open them to God and to great blessing. Spiritual knowledge can prosper a child more than any academic education.

Take their prayers seriously. Teach them to pray for others and to obey God. For your own benefit, covet their prayers and ask them to remember your needs as they pray.

O my Father, open the eyes of my heart to understand what it is to be a child of God: to live always as a child through always believing in Jesus, Thine only Son.

ANDREW MURRAY

December 11

They will make war against the Lamb, but the Lamb will overcome them because he is Lord of lords and King of kings—and with him will be his called, chosen and faithful followers.

REVELATION 17:14

Prayer is life passionately wanting, wishing, desiring God's triumph. Prayer is life striving and toiling everywhere and always for that ultimate victory.

GEORGE CAMPBELL MORGAN

Pray About It: All prayer is about triumph. That is, it's about God's triumphant will being done on earth. A Christian instinctively desires God's triumph, passionately wants to experience God as King. This is how prayer begins for the Christian—an all-consuming desire for life to play itself out with God front and center and crowned Lord of all.

Today, lean into the will of God with your wishing, desiring, and praying. Yearn for God's ultimate victory to be manifest.

Many of us have thought that one good battle with Satan and all will be over. But no such thing. We have security and the certainty of victory, but no promise of cessation from conflict.

JOHN NELSON DARBY

December 12

Dear friend, I pray that you may enjoy good health and that all may go well with you, even as your soul is getting along well.

3 JOHN 2

The secret of praying is praying in secret. Books on prayer are good, but not enough. As books on cooking are good but hopeless unless there is food to work on, so with prayer. One can read a library of prayer books and not be one whit more powerful in prayer. We must learn to pray, and we must pray to learn to pray.

While sitting in a chair reading the finest book in the world on physical health, one may waste away. So one may read about prayer, marvel at the endurance of Moses, or stagger at the weeping, groaning Jeremiah, and yet not be able to stammer the ABC's of intercessory prayer. As the bullet unspent bags no game, so the prayer-heart unburdened gathers no spoil.

LEONARD RAVENHILL

Pray About It: It would be a great tragedy if this book turned into just an interesting collection of sayings about prayer. By now, if you've been blessed by this book, your prayer life should be stronger. You should have seen some wonderful answers. And you should be enjoying sweeter friendship with God than before.

And as the year draws close to its end, my prayer for you is that next year might find your prayer life even richer and more rewarding as you continue to labor for God through prayer.

> When we read anything and understand it somewhat, we think that this is enough. No: we must give time, that it may make an impression and wield its own influence upon us. Read every portion the first time with consideration, to understand the good that is in it, and then see if you receive benefit from the thoughts that are there expressed.
>
> Read it the second time to see if it is really in accordance with God's word . . . ponder them in order to come under the full force of what God has said on the point. . . .
>
> Read it then the third time to find out the corresponding places, not in the Bible, but in your own life, in order to know if your life has been in harmony with the New Life, and to direct your life for the future entirely according to God's word.
>
> ANDREW MURRAY

December 13

The sacrifices of God are a broken spirit;
   a broken and contrite heart,
   O God, you will not despise.

PSALM 51:17

A hard heart cannot pray. A broken heart is made up of prayer.

JOHN MASON

Pray About It: Many pray-ers are drawn to prayer because of their broken hearts. Or if they begin with a hard heart, they will either stop praying or allow their hearts to be broken for God. We normally associate something "broken" as a loss, but in God's eyes, a broken heart, or spirit, is a very good thing.

Come to Him and have your heart broken for the things of God. Possibly no one thing will give your prayers a sharper focus than that of having a broken heart before God.

It is wonderful what God can do with a broken heart, if He gets all the pieces.

SAMUEL CHADWICK

December 14

I urge, then, first of all, that requests, prayers, intercession and thanksgiving be made for everyone — for kings and all those in authority, that we may live peaceful and quiet lives in all godliness and holiness. This is good, and pleases God our Savior, who wants all men to be saved and to come to a knowledge of the truth.

1 TIMOTHY 2:1–4

Scripture calls us to pray for many things: for all saints; for all men; for kings and all rulers; for all who are in adversity; for the sending forth of laborers; for those who labor in the gospel; for all converts; for believers who have fallen into sin; for one another in our immediate circles.

ANDREW MURRAY

Pray About It: As you pray through your prayer list, remember that God has one too. Some of the items Murray cites above are on God's prayer list for you. Be sure to incorporate them into your list.

The sad neglect of intercessory prayer really points to a lack of the divine life, since if that were mightily within us we should inevitably feel its throb and pulse [in urging us to pray for others].

F. B. MEYER

December 15

Praise ye the LORD. Praise, O ye servants of the LORD, praise the name of the LORD.
Blessed be the name of the LORD from this time forth and for evermore.
From the rising of the sun unto the going down of the same the LORD's name *is* to be praised.

PSALM 113:1–3 KJV

Receive every day as a resurrection from death, as a new enjoyment of life. Meet every rising sun with such sentiments of God's goodness, as if you had seen it; and all things, new created on your account: and under the sense of so great a blessing, let your joyful heart praise and magnify so good and glorious a Creator.

WILLIAM LAW

Pray About It: Each new day we live to breathe and enjoy life, we also live to pray once more. As is the sum of our days on this earth, so are the days of our prayers.

Thank God today for another day of the joy of being alive. Enjoy life today. Reflect on Him and all He's done through the years for you. And to think that there's more to come! Another year will soon be here to live, to work, to play, and to pray.

Praise Him!

Praise God from whom all blessings flow!
Praise Him all creatures here below!
Praise Him above, ye heavenly host!
Praise Father, Son, and Holy Ghost!

THOMAS KEN

December 16

And he repaired the altar of the LORD that was broken down.

1 KINGS 18:30 KJV

We read that Elijah began the demonstration of the
true God by repairing the altar of the Lord that was
broken down. Never was there a revival that did not
so begin. And if today God answers from heaven
we must begin to repair His broken altars: altars
of consecration where once we gave ourselves to
God and promised to do His will alone; where we
offered Him our talents and time and possessions,
ourselves; but with the years we have kept back part
of the price and lied unto God until it is a wonder
we do not drop dead like Ananias and Sapphira;
altars of dedication where we gave our children to
God, but later chose our way for them and denied
God; family altars where once we gathered to read
the Word and commit our way unto the Lord,
but now abandon with the silly excuse that since
times have changed, it is no longer practical; altars
of praise and testimony where once the redeemed
of the Lord said so, but sin and worldliness and
neglect have closed our lips and stolen our song;
altars of service where once we lived only, always,
for the King, but have now deserted because we live
for self and none beside, just as if Jesus had never
lived, just as if He had never died.

Here is our task, to repair these broken altars,
and all our pious dodges and clever substitutes to
avoid repentance will never avail. Stained-glass win-

dows and robed choirs and anthems and banquets and dramas and eloquence in the pulpit and elegance in the pew have never fooled God. He demands truth in the inward parts, and heaven will keep silent and no fire will ever fall until we approach Him with rebuilt altars in the name of the Lord.

VANCE HAVNER

Pray About It: What are the broken altars in your life? Is it your family? Your health? Your calling from God? Your spiritual life?

No matter what it is, the altars can be repaired. God will help. All He requires is truth in the inward parts.

Today, let God have those broken altars of family, health, or whatever has been neglected these last years. Surrender them all. God will heal and will be with you as the altars are repaired.

Revival is restoring the years the locusts have eaten.

JAMES A. STEWART

December 17

Yet he did not waver through unbelief regarding the promise of God, but was strengthened in his faith and gave glory to God, being fully persuaded that God had power to do what he had promised.

ROMANS 4:20–21

Let faith look to God more than the thing promised. The cure of a feeble faith is alone to be found in the invigoration of our whole spiritual life by intercourse with God. Learn to believe in God, to take hold of God, to let God take possession of thy life, and it will be easy to take hold of the promise. He that knows and trusts God finds it easy to trust the promise too.

ANDREW MURRAY

Pray About It: As you pray today, look beyond the answer to the Answerer. We all begin with feeble faith, but it's through spending time with God that we become invigorated.

Take hold of God today, take possession of your life. The promises of God will fall in place and never fail.

Let it once be fixed that a Christian's one ambition is to fit into God's plan for Him, and He has a North star ever in sight to guide him or her steadily over any sea, however shoreless it seems. The Christian has a compass that points true in the thickest fog and fiercest storm, and regardless of magnetic rocks.

S. D. GORDON

You also, like living stones, are being built into a spiritual house to be a holy priesthood, offering spiritual sacrifices acceptable to God through Jesus Christ.

1 PETER 2:5

Like the Aaronic priest under the law, the New Testament priest is born to his position. He is constituted a priest unto God as a part of the salvation that is in Jesus Christ. His position and his privileges, therefore, begin with his new birth into the nature and family of God.

It is most important to emphasize the truth that every believer is a priest unto God, though he may never intelligently exercise his glorious privilege. The full realization of this position, so far as it affects prayer, is one of the greatest needs among believers today. It is more than a belief in the general efficacy of prayer. It is to be able to say, "I believe God will do his greatest works solely in answer to my prayer."

LEWIS SPERRY CHAFER

Pray About It: The priesthood of the believer is a topic that isn't often discussed today, yet it's of crucial importance to the Christian pray-er. Under the Old Testament, God's priests were born to their calling by virtue of their lineage. But under the New Testament, all believers are constituted as priests and as such can intercede with assurance for others. God hears His priests. And like the priests of old, we were born to this calling as we were born into the family of God. It's in our lineage.

In the commonest actions of life wear the vestments of your sacred calling, and act as a royal priesthood serving the Most High. Glorify your Creator and Redeemer.

CHARLES HADDON SPURGEON

December 19

Brothers, if someone is caught in a sin, you who are spiritual should restore him gently. But watch yourself, or you also may be tempted.

GALATIANS 6:1

Intercessory prayer for one who is sinning prevails, God says so. The will of the man prayed for does not come into question at all, he is connected with God by prayer, and prayer on the basis of the Redemption sets the connection working and God gives life.

OSWALD CHAMBERS

Pray About It: Today, think of those you know who are caught in the web of sin. Intercede for them as if their life depended on it—it often does. God can do for them what you cannot. Keep them high on your prayer list and continue to pray until God intervenes.

> I have been benefited by praying for others. For by making an errand to God for them, I have gotten something for myself.
>
> SAMUEL RUTHERFORD

December 20

As the deer pants for streams of water,
 so my soul pants for you, O God.

PSALM 42:1

It is not necessary for a man to shout and scream in order to prove he's in earnest, yet on the other hand cold and formal askings must not expect to meet with any great response. God grants our requests only for Christ's sake, nevertheless unless we pray to Him with warmth and reality, with intensity of spirit and vehemency of entreaty, we shall not obtain the blessing desired.

A. W. PINK

Pray About It: When we pray from the heart, the result will be an honest outpouring of our deepest needs. The worst thing we can do is cry artificial tears and plead with false fervor. God knows the truth. Don't try to muster up excited emotions. God will have nothing to do with falsity.

Develop an inner stillness and confidence in God. And above all, be brutally honest with God. Approach Him with "warmth and reality."

God can take all you can give.

Be yourself exactly before God and present your problems, the things you have come to your wits' end about. Ask what you will, and Jesus Christ says your prayers will be answered.

OSWALD CHAMBERS

December 21

Here I am! I stand at the door and knock. If anyone hears my voice and opens the door, I will come in and eat with him, and he with me.

REVELATION 3:20

Prayer is not a monologue, but dialogue; God's voice in response to mine in its most essential part. Listening to God's voice is the secret of the assurance that He will listen to mine.

ANDREW MURRAY

Pray About It: Our prayers are frequently monologues with no chance for God to get a word in edgewise. And yet what God says to us in prayer is vastly more important than what we say to Him. Jesus Christ stands at the door and knocks for one reason alone—He desires fellowship with you.

Today, spend time listening and you'll actually find that you have less to pray for. He will give you answers before you ask.

Prayer is a dialogue between two people who love each other.

ROSALIND RINKER

December 22

My prayer is not for them alone. I pray also for those who will believe in me through their message.

JOHN 17:20

If I could hear Christ praying for me in the next room, I would not fear a million enemies. Yet distance makes no difference. He is praying for me.

ROBERT MURRAY McCHEYNE

Pray About It: Because we do not see Him or hear Him, we are prone to forget that Christ is ever-interceding for us. Not only is He praying for us *now*, but on that day 2,000 years ago, He prayed for us before we were born — we are those who believe in Him because of His disciples' message. Time means nothing to God. Distance means nothing. He is there in your place of prayer, as always.

Today, listen carefully to hear Christ as He mentions your name to the Father.

Praying on our behalf is the most important part of the present ministry of our risen Lord.

R. A. TORREY

December 23

The thief comes only to steal and kill and destroy;
I have come that they may have life, and have it to
the full.

JOHN 10:10

Brethren, we must fight for the prayer time, we
must have time to pray. If we wait until we have
some leisure moments to pray, we will never have
the chance to pray. We should set apart some definite time for prayer. "Those who have no set time
for prayer," warns Andrew Murray, "do not pray."
For this reason, we need to watch that we may get
time to pray. We must also use prayer to protect
this prayer time from being snatched away through
the wiles of the devil.

WATCHMAN NEE

Pray About It: For nearly one year now, we have
been reading about prayer and then praying. But is
it any easier now to take time to pray? I hope so. But
I know that the enemy will always make the case for
less prayer. His excuses fit our natural minds. If you
still have trouble finding time, know that you're not
alone. We all struggle for time to pray. But we must
do it because of the joy and the strength it yields.

Prayer must have priority. British author and histo-
rian Thomas Carlyle was brought up on a farm subject
to seasonal flooding. A watchman was sent to warn
the farmers when the water was rising so they could
prepare for the onrushing flood. On one occasion,

the watchman came to warn the Carlyles during their family worship time. Carlyle's father refused to hear a word until prayer was ended, and convinced the young messenger to kneel with the family as they prayed. When their worship was finished, *then* they arose and prepared for the flood. "Prayer first" was their motto.

As next year approaches, make that your commitment also. Determine now to be on the watch for the enemy not to make inroads into your time of prayer. Determine now to stand firm and not allow him to subvert this, the greatest weapon against him we can muster.

Stand firm!

> Only give Him time to hold converse with you and to work in you, and your heart shall overflow with the blessedness of God.
>
> ANDREW MURRAY

December 24

> They also will answer, "Lord, when did we see you hungry or thirsty or a stranger or needing clothes or sick or in prison, and did not help you?"
>
> He will reply, "I tell you the truth, whatever you did not do for one of the least of these, you did not do for me."
>
> MATTHEW 25:44–45

Doubtless some of the most acceptable and effective prayers that God has ever heard have ascended to Him from prison-cells. Prayer transforms a prison-cell into a portal of heaven.

R. A. TORREY

Pray About It: Christmas is a lonely time for prisoners. Tonight many men and women are separated from their families. Children and fathers are torn asunder by mistakes, sins, crimes committed. But when a man or woman is in prison, they often have time to think about their lives. As a result many make strong decisions for Christ. In so doing, Christmas no doubt becomes all the more lonely for them. Jesus said when we visited prisoners, we visited Him. Today, think about your brothers and sisters in prison who love Jesus. Pray for them and do what you can to help. Check with your local churches to see who is offering prison ministries. If God leads, join them in their work. It will open a whole new field of prayer for you. Support these ministries with your money and your prayers.

Tonight will be a lonely night for many. Remember them.

Remember too that you were once a prisoner — and are now set free. Think about that as you read the following story from Prison Fellowship founder, Charles Colson.

Several years ago a Brazilian prison was turned over to two Christian laymen. Their plan was to run it on Christian principles. The prison has only two full-time staff. The rest of the work is done by inmates. Every prisoner is assigned another inmate to whom he is accountable. In addition, every prisoner is assigned a volunteer family from the outside who works with him during his term and after his release from prison. Every prisoner joins the chapel program or else takes a course in character development.

When I visited the prison I found the inmates smiling—particularly the murderer who held the keys and opened the gates to let me in. Wherever I walked, I saw men at peace. I saw clean living areas. I saw people working industriously. The walls were decorated with biblical sayings from Psalms and Proverbs. The prison has an astonishing record. The recidivism rate is 4 percent, compared to 75 percent in the rest of Brazil and the U.S. How is that possible? I saw it with my own eyes. When my inmate guide escorted me to the notorious punishment cell once used for torture, he told me that today it houses only a single inmate. We walked down a long cell block, a long corridor of steel doors, and came to the end and he peeked in. He paused. "Yes, he's in there," he said. Then he turned to me and asked, "Are you sure you want to go in, Mr. Colson?"

"Of course," I replied impatiently. "I've been in punishment cells in 600 prisons all over the world." Slowly the inmate swung open the door and I saw the prisoner in the punishment cell. I walked in and turned to the right and there on the wall, beautifully carved by the inmates, was a crucifix. The prisoner Jesus was hanging on the cross. "He," said the inmate, "is doing the time for all the rest of us."

CHARLES COLSON

December 25

While they were there, the time came for the baby to be born, and she gave birth to her firstborn, a son. She wrapped him in cloths and placed him in a manger, because there was no room for them in the inn.

LUKE 2:6–7

We remember thy love, O Jesus, as it was manifest to us in thy holy life, from the manger of Bethlehem to the garden of Gethsemane. We track thee from the cradle to the grave—for every word and deed of thine was love—and we rejoice in thy love, which death did not exhaust; thy love which shone resplendent in thy resurrection. We remember that burning fire of love which will never let thee hold thy peace until thy chosen ones be all safely housed.

CHARLES HADDON SPURGEON

Pray About It: Today, think about what prayer owes to Christmas. How would prayer be different if Christ hadn't been born in that Bethlehem stable?

Today as you sing, "O Come Let Us Adore Him," listen to the words more closely. And truly adore Him.

Lord, through Your Holy Spirit, help me to understand so much of the victory and joy of Your coming to earth that I enjoy Christmas more than ever before.

CORRIE TEN BOOM

O come let us adore Him
O come let us adore Him
O come let us adore Him
    Christ the Lord

For He alone is worthy
For He alone is worthy
For He alone is worthy
    Christ the Lord

I'll give Him all the glory
I'll give Him all the glory
I'll give Him all the glory
    Christ the Lord

December 26

But I am a man of prayer.

PSALM 109:4

Prayer has been known to recall the souls of the departed from the very path of death, to transform the weak, to restore the sick, to purge the possessed, to open prison-bars, to loose the bonds of the innocent. Likewise it washes away faults, repels temptations, extinguishes persecutions, consoles the fainthearted, cheers the high-spirited, escorts travelers, appeases waves, makes robbers stand aghast, nourishes the poor, governs the rich, upraises the fallen, arrests the falling, confirms the standing.

TERTULLIAN

Pray About It: Tertullian was an early Christian. He tells us what he has seen prayer do. Now, two thousand years later, prayer still works, still does all those same things. Prayer is endless.

> Let me burn out for God! After all, whatever God may appoint, prayer is the great thing. Oh that I might be a man of prayer!
>
> HENRY MARTYN

December 27

A man with leprosy came and knelt before him and said, "Lord, if you are willing, you can make me clean."

Jesus reached out his hand and touched the man. "I am willing," he said. "Be clean!"

MATTHEW 8:2–3

In prayer you align yourselves to the purpose and power of God and He is able to do things through you that He couldn't do otherwise. For this is an open universe, where some things are left open, contingent upon our doing them. If we do not do them, they will never be done. For God has left certain things open to prayer — things which will never be done except as we pray.

E. Stanley Jones

Pray About It: God is sovereign. But in His sovereignty He calls us to work with Him. It's in that way that we must do our part so that He can do His. The leper asked Jesus to heal him, if He was willing. And Jesus, ever the compassionate healer, answered, "I am willing. Be clean!"

We ask according to His will and He concurs and the deed is done.

This year we've seen how prayer is used to accomplish God's will. Maybe these past twelve months have been preparation for all that is to be done by God through your prayers next year.

There *is* work to be done — and you're invited to be a part. Can anything be more exciting than an invitation from God?

> God wills a great deal of blessing to His people which never comes to them. He wills it most earnestly, but they do not will it, and it cannot come to them.

Andrew Murray

December 28

But grow in the grace and knowledge of our Lord and Savior Jesus Christ. To him be glory both now and forever! Amen.

2 PETER 3:18

It was a saying of George Mueller that faith grows with use. . . . Put it to work by reverent and faithful praying, and it will grow and become stronger day by day. Dare today to trust God for something small and ordinary and next week or next year you may be able to trust Him for answers bordering on the miraculous.

Everyone has some faith, said Mueller; the difference among us is one of degree only, and the man of small faith may be simply the one who has not dared to exercise the little faith he has.

A. W. TOZER

Pray About It: Has your faith grown this year? Has God given you problems and people to pray for which have strengthened your faith—even if you may not have seen the answer you wanted yet?

Next year you may be given even greater prayer assignments from God. Settle the issue today as to how you will respond, and how you will handle the joys, sorrows, and problems that await you next year.

> Faith tested is faith strengthened. It is to have learned your weaknesses, but to also have learned the faithfulness of God and His tender care even in sending the difficulties that we might be there with him.
>
> JOHN NELSON DARBY

December 29

Behold, what manner of love the Father hath bestowed upon us, that we should be called the sons of God.

1 JOHN 3:1 KJV

No matter what prayer has secured, attained or achieved for us, boundless possibilities still lie before us. It may be doubted whether we have yet touched more than the fringe of the garment of a prayer-hearing God. We come timid and trembling when we ought to come boldly and confidently. We ask but little, where we should only honor God by making large demands.

ARTHUR T. PIERSON

Pray About It: When Dr. Pierson was an old man, he preached one last time at Highbury and said these words, "I tell you as a dying man that no man has ever obtained all he might have obtained from God."

God has more to give us next year. There are more promises to claim, more ground to gain, more hope to be had. It can truthfully be said that God has more to give us next year than we can possibly obtain.

But let's give it a try anyway.

Prayer is the root, the fountain, the mother of a thousand blessings.

JOHN CHRYSOSTOM

December 30

To the only God our Savior be glory, majesty, power and authority, through Jesus Christ our Lord, before all ages, now and forevermore! Amen.

JUDE 25

It has often been said that prayer is the greatest force in the universe. This is no exaggeration. It will bear constant repetition. In this atomic age when forces are being released that stagger the thought and imagination of man, it is well to remember that prayer transcends all other forces.

F. J. HUEGEL

Pray About It: If one concept has been repeated more than any other during the past year, it's that *prayer works*. Prayer is a force against which no other force can prevail. And as Huegel says, "It will bear constant repetition." We are so prone to forget. For that reason, several themes regarding prayer have been repeated during this past year—we need to be reminded about them again and again, or else we forget to apply them.

Today, ask God to keep reminding you about prayer in the months ahead. Now's no time to stop learning.

The only power that God will yield to is that of prayer.

LEONARD RAVENHILL

December 31

I will remember the deeds of the LORD;
    yes, I will remember your miracles of long ago.

PSALM 77:11

So much for the past. It is gone, it is done, and it will remain what we have made it. All there was of God's Spirit in it, either in our failures or successes, will be abundantly blessed to His glory and others' good, as well as our own.

Seeing, then, that God's part is the good part which shall never be taken away from us, let us determine by His grace, that that part of all our work in its planning and in its execution shall have more and more prominence till God-likeness, which is our privilege, shall likewise be our exalted condition. Then, with prayer to sweeten labor, we shall rest content to leave results with our Father in Heaven.

ANNIE ARMSTRONG

Pray About It: The year is ending and with it all the joys and sorrows must be tucked away as part of our history with God. We can look back with thanksgiving and forward with confidence. His coming is that much closer, whether by rapture or by death.

On that day, all our questions will be answered and we shall see the end of our prayers.

Every turn in life brings me back to this: *more prayer.*

ELIZABETH PRENTISS

As the year ends, and thus your trip through *Magnificent Prayer*, it's my hope that your prayer life has been revolutionized forever. If you'd care to write me, I can be reached in care of the publisher.

Blessings to you,
Nick Harrison
c/o Zondervan
5300 Patterson Ave. SE
Grand Rapids, MI 49530

Reading List for Pray-ers

Although many of these classic books on prayer are still in print many decades after they were written, a few may be out of print. Your local Christian bookstore can order a copy of the titles still in print. For out of print books, try your local used bookstore or any one of the excellent used book search engines on the Internet.

This list is by no means exhaustive. I've had to omit many fine books on prayer lest I overwhelm you. May you be blessed as you continue to study the wonderful subject of prayer—just don't let your reading about prayer replace your *time* of prayer.

E. M. Bounds: This man was perhaps the best author on Christian prayer—ever. His books are still in print readily available at most Christian bookstores. Perhaps the best known of his books is *Power Through Prayer*.

Oswald Chambers: Every Christian should spend at least one year of his or her life going through the daily devotional *My Utmost for His Highest*. His book on prayer, *If Thou Wilt Ask*, is still in print and very useful.

Rosalind Goforth: *How I Know God Answers Prayer* is a wonderful book by this pioneer missionary to China.

S. D. Gordon: *Quiet Talks on Prayer* is one of a series of "Quiet Talks" books by this fine author.

Norman Grubb: This author's stirring biography *Rees Howells, Intercessor* is one of the great prayer stories of all time.

Madame Guyon: Any of her books are useful, but most notably for pray-ers is *Experiencing the Depths of Jesus Christ*.

O. Hallesby: His book *Prayer*, published by Augsburg, is a classic.

W. J. Harney: One of the most faith-building books on prayer I've read is this author's *Praying Clear Through*.

F. J. Huegel: This author's classic book *Bone of His Bone* portrays the believer's union with Christ beautifully.

Patrick Johnstone: For the serious intercessor, get the latest edition of *Operation World*, published by Zondervan.

Brother Lawrence: Many editions of his *Practice of the Presence of God* are available. This classic will no doubt never be out of print.

George Mueller: Many books have been written by or about Mueller. Try to read his autobiography.

Andrew Murray: Murray has written many books on prayer. Any are recommended. No doubt you won't be able to stop at just one.

Watchman Nee: No writer has influenced me more deeply than Watchman Nee. On the subject of prayer, I recommend *The Prayer Ministry of the Church* and *Let Us Pray*.

Jessie Penn-Lewis: *Communion with God* and *Prayer and Evangelism* are among this author's many excellent books.

John Piper: *The Pleasures of God* is my favorite of Piper's books.

Leonard Ravenhill: *Revival Praying* is highly recommended.

A. E. Richardson (An Unknown Christian): *The Kneeling Christian* is a fine book on prayer by this author, who is billed on the cover as "An Unknown Christian."

Rosalind Rinker: Miss Rinker's books on conversational prayer revolutionized the lives of many Christians only a few decades ago. Her titles include *Prayer: Conversing with God*, *Communicating Love Through Prayer*, and *Conversational Prayer*.

J. Hudson Taylor: Every Christian should read *Hudson Taylor's Spiritual Secret* at least once in their life—it's a classic.

R. A. Torrey: This author wrote many fine books, but on prayer, the one I recommend is *How to Pray*.

Arthur Wallis: Two books by this author are highly recommended: *Pray in the Spirit* and *God's Chosen Fast*.

Alexander Whyte: *Lord, Teach Us to Pray* is this author's work on prayer. Highly recommended.

Author Index

I applaud the men and women who have written and spoken so articulately on prayer. I wish I had the space to tell more of their interesting stories—particularly their experiences in prayer. Although the brief notes below will simply identify the author, my hope is that you may feel so drawn to some authors that you'll want to know more. A lot of information can be found on the Internet and in biographies and autobiographies of these prayer warriors.

Anselm of Canterbury (1033–1109) was born in northwest Italy, served as the abbot of Bec, Normandy, and as the Archbishop of Canterbury, and is regarded as the greatest church scholar between Augustine and Aquinas.

Annie Armstrong (1850–1938) was born in Baltimore, Maryland, and after her conversion at age nineteen, became an indefatigable worker on behalf of Baptist missions. She led in framing the constitution of the Women's Missionary Union for which she served for many years.

William Arthur (1819–1901) was born and raised in an Irish Presbyterian household in County Antrim, Ireland. For most of his adult life he served as a Wesleyan missionary and clergyman. He was also the author of many best-selling books on the Christian life.

Augustine of Hippo (354–430) was one of the most influential Christian writers of all time. The son of a pagan father and a Christian mother, Augustine lived a rebellious life in his youth, fathering a son by his mistress of thirteen years. After searching for truth through philosophy, he found Christ and wrote such compelling treatises as his *Confessions* and *City of God*, both of which are still widely read.

Basil the Great (330–79) came from a decidedly Christian family. His brother was Gregory of Nyssa. Basil was a hard worker in the church at Caesarea as a teacher, defender of the faith, and worker of charity.

J. Sidlow Baxter (1903–99) pastored in England and Scotland and has ministered in chruches, Bible conferences, and missionary centers around the world. He is the author of more than twenty books on the Christian life.

Richard Baxter (1615–91) was one of England's most renowned preachers. His book, *The Saint's Everlasting Rest*, was among the most widely read books of the seventeentn century.

Henry Ward Beecher (1813–87) served as the pastor of the Plymouth Congregational Church in Brooklyn, New York, for forty years. He was active in social causes such as the anti-slavery movement and women's suffrage. He was the brother of author Harriet Beecher Stowe (*Uncle Tom's Cabin*).

Bernard of Clairvaux (1090–1153) was one of the great Christian teachers of medieval Christianity. His motto, "To know Jesus and Jesus crucified" is still quoted as the essence of Christianity. His hymns include "Jesus, the Very Thought of Thee" and "O Sacred Head Now Wounded."

E. H. Bickersteth (1786–1850) was a British Evangelical clergyman. Though trained in law, he surrendered his practice for the ministry. He was a prolific writer and hymnologist.

Paul Billheimer (1897–1984) and his wife began their ministry in a tent in Anderson, Indiana in 1936. From that small beginning came a Bible Institute, a Christian high school, and a Christian television station. He authored several best selling books including *Destined for the Throne* and *Don't Waste Your Sorrows*.

Hugh Black (1868–1953) was a Scottish-American preacher, best remembered for his classic book *Friendship*.

Andrew Bonar (1810–92) was a Scottish minister and writer widely remembered for his work on the *Memoirs* of his friend Robert Murray McCheyne and his editing of Samuel Rutherford's *Letters*. Andrew Bonar was the brother of Horatius Bonar.

Horatius Bonar (1808–89) was a popular Scottish minister, author, and hymn writer. His hymns include "I Heard the Voice of Jesus Say." Horatius was the brother of Andrew Bonar.

Catherine Booth (1829–90) is considered the "Mother of the Salvation Army," which she and her husband, William Booth, founded. Mrs. Booth preached often to the masses and labored to improve the position of women in Great Britain.

William Booth (1829–1912) was an English evangelist and founder of the Salvation Army. His work continues today, nearly a century after his death.

F. W. Boreham (1871–1959) served as a pastor in New Zealand, Tasmania, and Australia. In his later ministry, he became one of the twentieth century's most well-known religious writers, authoring more than fifty books. In recent years his books have been reprinted and well received by a new generation of readers.

E(dward) M(cKendree) Bounds (1835–1913) was a minister in the American Methodist Episcopal Church, primarily in the Southern United States. He served as a captain in the Confederate Army. Today he's best known for his many books on prayer, notably *Power Through Prayer*.

David Brainerd (1718–47) was a young missionary to Native Americans near Stockbridge, Massachusetts. His diary, published posthumously by Jonathan Edwards, father of Edwards's fiancée, has inspired many to enter the mission field.

Samuel Logan Brengle (1860–1936) was an early Salvation Army officer. Upon returning to the United States from his training in England, he suffered the persecution common to many early Salvationists, including a brick to the head, which nearly ended his life. During his convalescence he started to write, resulting in several books with total sales of more than a million copies.

Hubert Brooke was a nineteenth-century author and clergyman.

Phillips Brooks (1835–93) was an American Episcopal minister active in the abolitionist movement. He served as bishop of Massachusetts in 1891 and preached extensively throughout the state until his death in 1893. Brooks also wrote the words to the popular Christmas carol "O Little Town of Bethlehem."

Thomas Brooks (1608–80) was an ardent nonconformist preacher in seventeenth-century England. He ministered through the Great Plague and Great Fire in London. Brooks authored more than a dozen books, mostly devotional in nature.

John Bunyan (1628–88), known as "the Tinker of Bedford," was an English nonconformist preacher and author of more than sixty books, including the classic best-seller *Pilgrim's Progress*.

George Buttrick (1892–1980) was an English-born Congregational preacher who served almost thirty years as pastor of Madison Avenue Presbyterian Church in New York City. He was also the author of books on the Christian life, including *Prayer*.

Mildred Cable (1877–1952) was a British Christian, trained as a chemist. She served for more than twenty years as a missionary with the China Inland Mission. In 1923, Miss Cable and a colleague ventured out to evangelize the polyglot people of central Asia. They crossed the Gobi Desert of Mongolia at least five times. For the next fifteen years they worked among the Gobi oases, "gossiping the gospel." Miss Cable later returned to England due to worsening political conditions in China. In England she wrote extensively about her work and labored for the British and Foreign Mission Society.

John Calvin (1509–64) was a French Protestant Reformer, trained in law, whose teachings have had a profound impact on Christian history.

William Carey (1761–1834) is considered the "father of modern missions." Truly a visionary, Carey, born near Northampton, England, hoped to take the gospel to the entire world. His courageous efforts inspired many missionaries to follow his example.

Thomas Carlyle (1795–1881) was an intellectual literary figure in nineteenth-century England.

Amy Carmichael (1867–1951) was a missionary to India and founder of Dohnavur Fellowship, a ministry devoted to saving neglected children. A prolific writer, many of Miss Carmichael's books are still widely circulated.

Captain E. G. Carre (1871–1951) was a member of the Merchant Service Officers' Christian Association and an early biographer of John "Praying" Hyde.

George Washington Carver (1864–1943) was an agricultural chemist whose many accomplishments include discovering more than three hundred uses for the peanut. He also helped develop a cure for infantile paralysis and was asked by both Henry Ford and Thomas Edison to join them in their respective works. Carver's laboratory was named "God's Little Workshop" because he never took scientific texts as his source but rather simply asked God how he should perform his experiments.

Catherine of Sienna (1347–1380) was an Italian mystic and member of the Dominican order of nuns. She devoted much of her ministry to the sick and plague-stricken poor, and to the conversion of sinners.

Richard Cecil (1748–1810) was an eighteenth-century clergyman and biographer of John Newton.

Samuel Chadwick (1860–1932) was a nineteenth-century preacher and writer. He served as the president of the National Council of Free Churches.

Lewis Sperry Chafer (1871–1952) was a popular preacher and writer in the early twentieth century. Chafer was also founder and president of Dallas Theological Seminary.

Oswald Chambers (1874–1917) was a Scottish missionary converted under the ministry of Charles Spurgeon. His popular public ministry was cut short at the age of forty-three when he was suddenly taken sick and died while ministering to British troops in Egypt. His wife later compiled many of his writings into what has become the classic devotional *My Utmost for His Highest*.

John Chrysostom (c. 347–407) was an early church father and Christian philosopher.

Adam Clarke (1762–1832) was a Wesleyan preacher, theologian, and commentator. The latter talent is best exemplified by his eight-volume commentary on the Bible, still in use by many Bible teachers.

Clement of Alexandria (c.155–c.220) was born in Athens of pagan parents but converted to Christianity through his study of philosophy. Clement wrote widely, mostly during his tenure as a teacher in Alexandria.

Charles Colson (1931– –) served as an aide for President Richard Nixon and was sentenced to prison as a result of his involvement in the Watergate scandal. While in prison, Colson was converted to Christ and later founded Prison Fellowship, a ministry to those behind bars. Since then he has written several best-selling and award-winning books, including *Born Again*, *The Body*, and *Who Speaks for God?*

Lettie B. Cowman (1870–1960), along with her husband, Charles, was a missionary, but is largely remembered for her work in compiling the popular devotional book *Streams in the Desert*.

Charles E. Cowman (1868–1924) was a missionary to Japan and China and founder and president of the Oriental Missionary Society. His widow, Lettie, compiled the popular *Streams in the Desert* daily devotional.

Fanny Crosby (1820–1915) was one of the church's best-known hymn writers. Blinded through a doctor's negligence at six weeks, she nonetheless took this accident as God's will. Her most popular hymns include "Blessed Assurance," "Sweet Hour of Prayer" and "To God Be the Glory."

Cyprian of Carthage (200–58) was a well educated and cultured man when in midlife he became a Christian. He then gave up his position to take vows of poverty and chastity. Cyprian was martyred for his faith in 258.

John Nelson Darby (1800–82) was a prolific writer, teacher, and leader among the Plymouth Brethren. His influence on subjects such as the deeper life and Bible prophecy have influenced millions of believers.

Jean-Pierre De Caussade (1675–1751) was a Jesuit ascetic writer, author of *Abandonment to Divine Providence*.

Francis De Sales (1567–1622) was the Catholic Bishop of Geneva and the author of the classic *Introduction to the Devout Life*.

A(mzi) C(larence) Dixon (1854–1925) was a Baptist pastor who served several congregations during his ministry, including Moody Memorial Church in Chicago.

Timothy Dwight (1752–1817) was an American Congregational clergyman, a grandson of Jonathan Edwards and served as the eighth president of Yale University. His grandson became the twelfth president of Yale.

Jonathan Edwards (1703–58) was one of America's most influential Colonial preachers, often remembered for his sermon "Sinners in the Hands of an Angry God" (1741).

John Eliot (1604–90) was a Cambridge-educated Englishman who emigrated to America to evangelize the Indians of Massachusetts. Due to his tireless efforts on behalf of the Native Americans he loved, he was dubbed "The Apostle to the Indians."

Joseph Eliot (1638–94) was the clergyman son of John Eliot, "Apostle to the Indians." He and his brother, John, helped their father prepare *The Indian Grammar Begun* and helped translate the Bible into the Algonquin language.

Philip James (Jim) Elliot (1927–56) was a missionary to the Auca Indians of eastern Ecuador. He and his four fellow missionaries were murdered by the Aucas — an event that garnered much attention among Christians worldwide. Subsequently many Aucas came to Christ. Jim Elliot's story has been told by his widow,

Elisabeth, in books such as *Through Gates of Splendor* and *Shadow of the Almighty*.

François Fénelon (1651–1715) was a French churchman and author, and served as Archbishop of Cambrai from 1695–1715.

Charles G. Finney (1792–1875) was trained as a lawyer but after his dramatic conversion to Christ became one of the most influential and popular revivalists of the nineteenth century. He authored many books and served as president of Oberlin College for fifteen years.

Jonathon Goforth (1859–1963) was a Canadian missionary to China with his wife, Roslind. After his missionary service, Goforth was in great demand as a conference and missionary speaker.

Rosalind Goforth (1864–1942) and her husband, Jonathan, were missionaries for many years to China, where they suffered many trials, including the death of five of their eleven children. The couple narrowly escaped death during the Boxer Rebellion.

A(doniram) J(udson) Gordon (1836–95) was a popular Boston minister and founder of the Gordon College and Divinity School.

S(amuel) D(ickey) Gordon (1859–1936) was a writer and missionary lecturer whose popular books include *Quiet Talks on Power* and *Quiet Talks on Prayer*.

Andrew Gray (1634–56) was a seventeenth-century Scots Christian, from the Reformed/Puritan tradition. His message was that of growth by grace. He was greatly used of God in his short life of twenty-two years.

Gregory the Great (540–604) was educated for government service, but after the death of his father, Gregory entered a monastery as a simple monk. He later became a pope in the Catholic church. He was noted for his ministry to the poor.

W. H. Griffith Thomas (1861–1924) was a noted Bible teacher, preacher, lecturer, and writer of devotional commentaries.

Norman Grubb (1895—1993) for many years was a popular writer and teacher on the deeper Christian life. His best known work is the biography, *Rees Howells, Intercessor*.

Gordon Guinness (1902—80) was a clergyman in the Church of England and a Canon of Winchester Cathedral..

Madame Jeanne Guyon (1648–1717) was a controversial advocate of Christian mysticism and abandonment to God. Her views brought her both supporters and enemies, ultimately result-ing in her confinement to a convent. Among her supporters was François Fénelon.

Newman Hall (1816–1902) was a British clergyman and the author of *Come to Jesus* (1863) in addition to several popular hymns.

Ole Hallesby (1879–1961) was a Norwegian clergyman and author. His best-known books include *Prayer* (1948) and *Why I Am a Christian* (1951).

Mordecai Ham (1878–1959) was an evangelist under whose ministry Billy Graham was converted to Christ. During his first year of ministry more than 33,000 conversions were recorded.

W. J. Harney was an evangelist and the author of the clas-sic book *Praying Clear Through*, published in the early twentieth century.

Norman B. Harrison was a pastor, Bible teacher, evangelist, and author of several books on the deeper life in the early twen-tieth century.

Frances Ridley Havergal (1836–79) was a popular English poet and hymn writer, most fondly remembered for such songs as "Take My Life and Let It Be" and "Like a River Glorious." She also authored the popular book *Kept for the Master's Use*.

Vance Havner (1901–86) was a popular preacher and confer-ence speaker. He wrote more than thirty books, many of which are still much sought after.

Matthew Henry (1662–1714) was an English Presbyterian minister best remembered for his exhaustive commentary on the Bible.

George Herbert (1593–1633) was an English clergyman, poet, and hymn writer. His life was so Christlike that he was known as "Holy George Herbert."

Dean Hole (Samuel Reynolds) (1819–1904) was a British clergyman, dean of Rochester in the latter part of the nineteenth century, and chaplain to the Archbishop of Canterbury. He was also an avid rose enthusiast and was the first president of the (Royal) National Rose Society.

Evan Hopkins (1837–1918) was a thirty-five-year-old vicar from Richmond in Surrey, England, when he encountered Bible teacher Pearsall Smith, husband of Hannah Whitall Smith. He would forever refer to that May 1 meeting as his "May Day experience." His ministry changed as he appropriated the truths of God's grace he'd heard. Later he was to be widely used in the Keswick movement as a popular Bible teacher.

F. J. Huegel served as a chaplain in World War I and a missionary in Mexico for more than twenty-five years. His writings on the deeper life include the classic *Bone of His Bone.*

John ("Praying") Hyde (1865 – 1912) was a Presbyterian missionary to the remote villages of India for twenty years. He was a tireless preacher and prayer—at times Hyde was known to spend upward of forty hours on his knees in prayer.

Ignatius of Antioch (died c. 107) was one of the early church fathers. Bishop of Antioch in Syria, he was martyred c. 107.

Arthur F. Winnington Ingram (1858 – 1946) served as the Lord Bishop of London during the early years of the twentieth century.

H(enry) A(llan) Ironside (1876 – 1951) was a popular Brethren preacher and author of many books, including his Bible commentaries, which are still popular with many Christians today.

Isaac the Syrian (died c.700), also known as Isaac of Nineveh, was a Syrian bishop, theologian, and mystical writer who influenced both Eastern and Western Christians.

Helen Hunt Jackson (1830 – 85) was an American writer and advocate for the American Indian. Her novel *Ramona* was a popular best-seller of the nineteenth century.

John of the Cross (1542 – 91) was a Spanish Roman Catholic clergyman and poet. He was a contemporary of Teresa of Ávila.

Patrick Johnstone (1938   ) has invested most of his life with missions, beginning in the early 1960s when he served as a missionary in Africa. His prayer manual, *Operation World,* has been translated into six languages and is widely distributed to Christians to encourage "prayer for the unreached."

E. Stanley Jones (1884 – 1973) became a Christian at age seventeen. Educated in law, he became a missionary to India, where he established Christian ashrams, centers for meditation and worship. He authored twenty-nine books and was twice nominated for the Nobel Peace Prize.

Lewis Ellis Jones (1865 – 1936) was a classmate of evangelist Billy Sunday at Moody Bible Institute. He later served with the YMCA. Today he's remembered for his popular hymn "There's Power in the Blood."

John Henry Jowett (1863–1923) was a popular English Congregationalist preacher who, for several years, pastored New York City's Fifth Avenue Presbyterian Church, before succeeding G. Campbell Morgan as pastor of Westminster Chapel in London.

Adoniram Judson (1788–1850) was a pioneer American missionary to Burma.

Julian of Norwich (c.1342–c.1413) was an English mystic who lived a solitary life of contemplation and prayer. Her reputation rests mainly on her book *The Sixteen Revelations of Divine Love*.

Thomas à Kempis (1380–1471) was a Catholic priest and the author of the classic *Imitation of Christ*.

Thomas Ken (1637–1711) was an English bishop and hymn writer.

Alexei Khomiakov (1804–60) was a Russian philosopher.

G. H. Knight was an English clergyman and author of *In the Secret of His Presence* and *The Master's Questions to His Disciples*.

John Knox (1514–72) was a Scottish churchman and reformer, largely regarded for his powerful impact on the development of the Scottish church.

William Law (1686–1761) was an English writer whose major work, *A Serious Call to a Devout and Holy Life*, continues to inspire Christians worldwide.

Brother Lawrence (1605–91) served as a "lay brother" for an order of the Discalced Carmelites. His duty in the order as a cook lasted for thirty years, during which time he wrote short spiritual notes that were published after his death. Today those notes comprise his book *The Practice of the Presence of God*, which has achieved classic status down through the centuries.

Eric Liddell (1902–45) won the 400-meter dash in the 1924 Olympics. The story of his refusal to race on Sunday during those games was depicted in the Academy Award-winning film *Chariots of Fire*. He went on to serve as a Christian missionary in war-torn China, where he died in a Japanese concentration camp near the end of World War II.

Abraham Lincoln (1809–65) was the sixteenth president of the United States.

Herbert Lockyer (1886–1984) was a twentieth-century author of many books on the Christian life.

Henry Wadsworth Longfellow (1807–82) was an American poet, best remembered for "Evangeline," "Hiawatha," and "The Courtship of Miles Standish."

Martin Luther (1483–1546) was a German priest whose belief that Christians were saved by faith alone ushered in the Reformation of the sixteenth century.

J. H. M. was an unidentified Brethren writer of the nineteenth century.

William MacDonald (1917––) is a Bible teacher and author living in northern California.

David MacIntyre was a Scottish clergyman and author of the classic book, *The Hidden Life of Prayer*.

C(harles) H(enry) Mackintosh (1820–96) was one of the early and most prolific Brethren writers and is still widely read today.

Robert Murray McCheyne (1813–43) was a Scottish minister who, though he died at the age of thirty, is still remembered for his *Memoirs* which were compiled by Andrew Bonar.

James McConkey (1859–1937) wrote widely on the deeper life in the early part of the twentieth century.

Alexander MacLaren (1826–1910) was a British Baptist clergyman who served forty-five years as pastor of Union Chapel, Manchester.

Henry Martyn (1781–1812) was an English missionary to Persia. He shunned the traditional methods of mission work and adopted Persian dress and customs so that he might more effectively reach the people.

John Mason (1646–94) was rector of Water-Stratford in Buckinghamshire and a poet and hymn writer.

J.M. Mason was a nineteenth-century American Presbyterian pastor and teacher.

George Matheson (1842–1906) was a blind Scottish pastor widely beloved for his beautiful sermons. He also wrote the hymn "O Love That Wilt Not Let Me Go" during a time he described as "the most severe mental suffering." Written in only five minutes, Matheson claimed the hymn was "dictated to me by some inward voice."

F(rederick) B(rotherton) Meyer (1847–1929) was the author of more than seventy books and a popular London preacher who fought the forces of immorality in early twentieth-century Britain.

J(ames) R(ussell) Miller (1840–1912) was a Presbyterian pastor (serving congregations in Illinois and Pennsylvania) and a prolific writer at the turn of the nineteenth century.

Michael Molinos (1628–96) was a Spanish believer in Christ. He came from a noble family and, through his popular writings, soon had many followers. His controversial views were at variance with the church authorities and he was put on trial before the Inquisition. Eventually he died as result of his imprisonment.

Dwight Lyman Moody (1837–99) was one of the greatest evangelists of all time. The Moody Bible Institute in Chicago still trains students as a testament to Moody's work.

G(eorge) Campbell Morgan (1863–1945) was a respected pastor, Bible teacher, and writer of more than sixty books.

Hendley C. G. Moule (1841–1920) was a popular leader of the evangelical wing of the Church of England and a speaker at Keswick conventions.

George Mueller (1805–98) was active in the Plymouth Brethren movement but most widely known for his work in establishing orphanages, which were run totally on faith. He concluded his last worldwide mission tour at the age of eighty-seven.

Andrew Murray (1828–1917) was a South African clergyman who strongly influenced the missionary movement to South Africa. Today he is largely remembered for his many devotional books, still in print and still strong sellers.

Watchman Nee (1903–72) was a prominent Christian worker in China during the first half of the twentieth century. He spent his last years in a Communist prison. Though he only authored one book, *The Spiritual Man*, his many oral messages have been transcribed into books, some of which have already obtained classic status, such as *The Normal Christian Life; Sit, Walk, Stand.*

William Newell (1868–1956) was an evangelist, Bible teacher, and author of excellent commentaries of the books of Romans, Hebrews, and Revelation. He was invited by Dwight L. Moody to become the assistant superintendent of Moody Bible Institute under R. A. Torrey. He also wrote the popular hymn "At Calvary."

John Henry Newman (1801–90) was an English clergyman who fought against what he perceived as the liberalism of the church in his age.

Isaac Newton (1642–1727) was an English mathematician and physicist and member of the Church of England.

John Newton (1725–1807) was the master of a slave ship before his conversion to Christ, after which he became an Anglican clergyman and hymn writer, best remembered today for writing the hymn "Amazing Grace."

B. H. P. was an unidentified Brethren writer, probably from the nineteenth century.

Blaise Pascal (1623–62) was a French mathematician, scientist, and Christian apologist. His best-known work was published after his death as *Pensées* ("Thoughts").

John Paton (1824–1907) was a Presbyterian missionary to the New Hebrides and a powerful man of prayer.

Ruth Paxson (1875–1949) was graduate of the State University of Iowa. She became a missionary and gifted Bible teacher, author of several fine books on Christian growth, including *Life on the Highest Plane.*

Thomas Payne was the author of *The Greatest Force on Earth: The Power of Intensified Prayer.*

Edward Payson (1783–1827) was an American Congregationalist minister. In the twenty years he pastored the Congregational Church in Portland, Maine, he saw more than seven hundred conversions to Christ in the congregation. He was the father of Elizabeth Payson Prentiss.

William Penn (1644–1718) was a Quaker leader and the founder of Pennyslvania.

Jessie Penn-Lewis (1861–1927) was a forceful Christian worker in the early part of the twentieth century. She wrote widely and served as editor of *The Overcomer,* one of the early deeper-life magazines.

Arthur T(appan) Pierson (1837–1911) was the clergyman who succeeded Charles Haddon Spurgeon at the noted Metropolitan Baptist Church in London. He was also the biographer of George Mueller.

A(rthur) W. Pink (1886–1952) was an American pastor, Bible conference leader, and author of more than forty books.

John Piper (1946– –) has served as senior pastor at Bethlehem Baptist Church in Minneapolis. He is the author of *Desiring God* and *The Pleasures of God.*

Elizabeth Payson Prentiss (1818–78) was the daughter of Edward Payson and a popular writer in the nineteenth century. She was also a teacher and hymn writer. Perhaps her best-known hymn is "More Love to Thee, O Christ."

Leonard Ravenhill (1904–1994) has taught widely on revival and the Christian life. His books include *Revival Praying* and *Why Revival Tarries.*

Alan Redpath (1907–89) was born in England. After working as an accountant, he answered God's call to preach the gospel. He pastored several churches in England before serving as senior pastor of the Moody Memorial Church in Chicago, after which he returned to pastor the Charlotte Baptist Chapel in Edinburgh, Scotland. He also wrote several excellent books on the Christian life.

A(lbert) E(rnest) Richardson was the name of the anonymous author of "An Unknown Christian," and the author of several books including *The Kneeling Christian* and *How to Live the Victorious Christian Life*.

Samuel Ridout (1855–1930) was a Navy man before he committed his life to the Lord's work full-time. He pastored in Baltimore and preached and taught throughout the United States. He died in 1930 after authoring more than a dozen volumes of Bible exposition.

Rosalind Rinker is a prolific twentieth-century writer, missionary, and evangelical worker best known for her books on conversational prayer.

Evan Roberts (1878–1951) was the ninth of fourteen children of a Welsh miner. At the age of twelve, he too began work in the mines but later received a call from God to enter the ministry. Roberts is largely remembered for his leadership in the Welsh revival of 1904–6.

Samuel Rutherford (1600–61) was the son of a Scottish farmer. He became an influential minister and writer.

J(ohn) C(harles) Ryle (1816–1900) was a minister in Liverpool and a leader of the evangelical wing of the Church of England.

J. H. Sammis (1836–1919) was a Presbyterian minister and hymn writer.

J. Oswald Sanders (1902–92) was an English pastor, teacher, and author.

W(illiam) E(dwin) Sangster (1900–60) was a British minister in the Methodist church and the author of several books on the Christian life.

Rachel Joy Scott (1981–99) of Littleton, Colorado, was a Christian teenager killed in the 1999 Columbine High School tragedy.

A(lbert) B(enjamin) Simpson (1844–1919) was a Canadian pastor and founder of what became the Christian and Missionary Alliance denomination.

Sadhu Sundar Singh (1889–c. 1933) was an Indian mystic turned Christian missionary.

Mary Slessor (1848–1915) was a Scottish missionary to West Africa.

Hannah Whitall Smith (1832–1911) was a popular speaker at the Keswick deeper life conventions of the nineteenth century and the author of the classic *Christian's Secret of a Happy Life.*

Oswald J. Smith (1889–1986) was a Canadian pastor, evangelist, poet, lyricist, and author. He pastored several churches but is perhaps best known as the founding pastor of the People's Church in Toronto.

Charles Haddon Spurgeon (1834–92) was a British Baptist preacher and a prolific writer. Spurgeon has probably had more influence on modern preaching than any other orator in history.

Miles Stanford (1914–99) was the author of several important books on the believer's position in Christ, notably *The Green Letters.*

Charles Stanley (1932– –) has served as pastor of Atlanta, Georgia's 13,000-member First Baptist Church for many years. He's the author of numerous books on the Christian life.

James A. Stewart (1831–1905) was a Presbyterian missionary from Scotland to southeastern Africa.

J(ames) B(utler) Stoney (1814–97) was a prolific and popular writer for the Brethren movement of the nineteenth century.

C(harles) T(homas) Studd (1860–1931) was a visionary English missionary to China, India, and Africa.

William ("Billy") Ashley Sunday (1862–1935) was born in Iowa and, while working as a professional baseball player, converted at the famed Pacific Garden Mission in Chicago. He eventually became one of the foremost evangelists of the early twentieth century.

Henry Suso (1295–1366) was a German monk and mystic. His best-known work is *The Little Book of Eternal Wisdom.*

Dewitt Talmadge (1832–1902) was an American Presbyterian minister. His sermons were widely circulated through newspapers in the latter part of the nineteenth century.

J(ames) Hudson Taylor (1832–1905) was one of the most well-known missionaries in the history of the Christian Church. Founder of the China Inland Mission, Taylor is also noted for the classic book *Hudson Taylor's Spiritual Secret*, edited by Howard and Mary Taylor.

William M. Taylor (1829–95) was a Scottish Congregational minister, who ministered in his homeland and also the United States where he pastored in New York. He was the author of more than forty published works.

Corrie ten Boom (1892–1983) was a rescuer of Jews in her native Holland. Arrested with her family for their illegal activities, she endured the atrocities of a German prison camp and, after the war, traveled the world retelling her experiences of God's love in the midst of the horrors of war. Her book *The Hiding Place* continues in wide circulation.

Teresa of Ávila (1515–82) was a Spanish mystic and founder of a reformed Carmelite order. Her books, which include *Autobiography* and *Interior Castle*, are still widely read.

Tertullian (c.160–225) was trained to be a lawyer but in his late thirties became a Christian and, eventually, a respected teacher in the church at Carthage.

Major Ian Thomas (1913– –) is the Founder and International Director of Capernwray Missionary Fellowship of Torchbearers. His best-known book is *The Saving Life of Christ*.

R(euben) A(rcher) Torrey (1856–1928) was a Congregationalist minister and colleague of Dwight L. Moody. He was instrumental in the work of both Moody Bible Institute in Chicago and Biola University in southern California. He also wrote several classic books on the Christian life, including *The Person and Work of the Holy Spirit*.

A(iden) W(ilson) Tozer (1897–1963) was a popular Christian and Missionary Alliance pastor and speaker. His best-known books are *The Knowledge of the Holy* and *The Pursuit of God*.

Lilias Trotter (1853–1928) was a pioneering missionary to Algeria, an artist, and a writer on the Christian life.

Charles G(allaudet) Trumbull (1872–1941) was an editor, journalist (staff writer for the *Toronto Globe*), and author of several books on the Christian life.

H. C. Trumbull (1830–1903) was a Congregational clergyman and editor.

Arthur Wallis (1923–88) is the author of *The Radical Christian, God's Chosen Fast,* and *Pray in the Spirit.*

Thomas Watson (c. 1620–86) was a Puritan preacher and pastor of St. Stephen's Church in London. When his health began to fail, he retired to Barnston in Essex, where he died suddenly while praying in secret.

John Wesley (1703–91) was an English evangelist and cofounder of Methodism.

Susanna Wesley (1669–1742) was an active prayer warrior and mother of two of the most highly regarded Christian leaders of all time—John and Charles Wesley.

George Whitefield (1714–70) was one of the most highly regarded evangelists of the eighteenth century and is the leading figure in the revival known as the Great Awakening.

Alexander Whyte (1836–1921) was a powerful orator and Scottish minister. It was said of him, "He failed in no activity, but his pulpit was his throne."

H. A. Maxwell Whyte (1908–88) was the author of 18 books, including *The Power of the Blood*.

David Wilkerson (1931– –) moved to the inner-city of New York City to preach to the young men and women of the inner-city gangs. From that experience came the Christian classic book *The Cross and the Switchblade*. Pastor Wilkerson currently preaches at Times Square in New York City. He's the author of many books on the Christian life.

Count Nicholaus Ludwig von Zinzendorf (1700–60) was an Austrian noble born in Germany, who devoted his life to Christ at age six. He is best known for his part in the formation of what became the Moravian Church.

Permissions

I'd like to thank the following publishers and individuals who granted me permission to use their copyrighted material in *Magnificent Prayer*. I've made every reasonable effort to contact the copyright holders of all the readings in this book that are not in the public domain. I offer apologies to any legitimate copyright holder I was unable to trace and I encourage anyone holding an unacknowledged copyright for any of these authors to contact me in care of the publisher so that proper arrangements can be made.

Abingdon

George Buttrick, *Prayer,* copyright © 1942 Abingdon-Cokesbury. • Eric Liddell, *Disciplines of the Christian Life,* Copyright ©1985 by the estate of Florence Liddell Hall. Reprinted by permission.

Fleming H. Revell, a Division of Baker Book House

Vance Havner, *By the Still Waters.* Copyright © 1934, Fleming H. Revell, a division of Baker Book House. • Alan Redpath, *The Making of a Man of God.* Copyright © 1962, Fleming H. Revell, a division of Baker Book House. • Corrie Ten Boom, *Each New Day.* Copyright © 1972, Fleming H. Revell, a division of Baker Book House. • Corrie Ten Boom, *The End Battle.* Copyright © 1970, Fleming H. Revell, a division of Baker Book House. Used by Permission.

J. Sidlow Baxter

Special thanks to Mrs. J. Sidlow Baxter for permission to use a quote from her late husband's writings.

Bethany House Publishers

Paul Billheimer, *Destined for the Throne.* Copyright © 1975. • Leonard Ravenhill, *Revival Praying,* Copyright © 1962. Used by permission.

Chosen Books

Corrie Ten Boom with John and Elizabeth Sherrill, *The Hiding Place.* Chosen Books, Chappaqua, New York. • David Wilkerson with John and Elizabeth Sherrill. *The Cross and the Switchblade.* Chosen Books, Chappaqua, New York. Used by permission.